ALSO BY RICHARD GRANT

Crazy River: Exploration and Folly in East Africa

God's Middle Finger: Into the Lawless Heart of the Sierra Madre

American Nomads: Travels with Lost Conquistadors, Mountain Men, Cowboys, Indians, Hoboes, Truckers, and Bullriders

Dispatches from Pluto

*Lost and Found in the
Mississippi Delta*

Richard Grant

Simon & Schuster Paperbacks

New York   London   Toronto   Sydney   New Delhi

Simon & Schuster Paperbacks
An Imprint of Simon & Schuster, Inc.
1230 Avenue of the Americas
New York, NY 10020

First Simon & Schuster trade paperback edition October 2015

SIMON & SCHUSTER PAPERBACKS and colophon are
registered trademarks of Simon & Schuster, Inc.

For information about special discounts for bulk purchases,
please contact Simon & Schuster Special Sales at
1-866-506-1949 or business@simonandschuster.com

The Simon & Schuster Speakers Bureau can bring authors to your live event.
For more information or to book an event contact the
Simon & Schuster Speakers Bureau at 1-866-248-3049
or visit our website at www.simonspeakers.com.

Interior design by Ruth Lee-Mui

Manufactured in the United States of America

7   9   10   8   6

Library of Congress Cataloging-in-Publication Data is available.

ISBN 978-1-4767-0964-2
ISBN 978-1-4767-0965-9 (ebook)

For Johnny, who would have loved it here

Some people who come here even say they have tumbled back in time, but I do not think that is true. They have merely slipped sideways into a place they do not recognize, and may never understand.

—Rick Bragg, *New Delta Rising*

A strange and detached fragment thrown off by the whirling comet that is America.

—David Cohn, *Where I Was Born and Raised*

Nothing in this world is a matter of black and white, not even in Mississippi, where everything is a matter of black and white.

—Richard Rubin, *Confederacy of Silence*

Contents

Dispatches from Pluto

Prologue

I WAS LIVING in New York City when I decided to buy an old plantation house in the Mississippi Delta. It was out in the cotton fields and
cypress swamps of Holmes County, the poorest county in America's
poorest state. "There's No Place Like Holmes, Catch The Southern
Spirit," announced a weather-beaten sign on the county line. It was
illustrated with magnolia blossoms and perforated by shotgun blasts.
The nearest neighbors were three miles away across fields and woods.
The nearest supermarket was twenty-five miles away. It was well
stocked with pig knuckles, hog jowls, boiled peanuts, and hunting
magazines, but it was another twenty-five miles to find organic eggs,
strong cheese, or crusty bread.

A few close friends understood why I wanted to live there, as a
misfit Englishman with a US passport and a taste for remote places,
but most people were genuinely mystified, or doubtful about my
sanity. Why would anyone in his right mind choose to live in the

backwoods of Mississippi? No state has a more beautiful name—Miss and Sis are sipping on something sippy, and it's probably a sweet tea or an iced bourbon drink—but no state is more synonymous in the rest of the country with racism, ignorance, and cultural backwardness.

When I told them about my plans, many friends and acquaintances felt compelled to sing me the chorus of a 1964 Nina Simone song, "Everybody knows about Mississippi Goddam!" In bad imitation Southern drawls, they cracked wise about toothlessness, banjo music, men named Bubba, and the probability of getting myself raped in the woods one Saturday night. One white woman accused me of being racist for wanting to live in Mississippi, even though it's the blackest state in America and Holmes County is more than 80 percent African-American. "All Southerners are racists, and Mississippi is the worst of all," she opined. She had never set foot in the state, and never intended to, because she already knew everything she needed to know about Mississippi.

One of my hopes in writing this book is to dissolve these clumsy old stereotypes, and illustrate my conviction that Mississippi is the best-kept secret in America. Nowhere else is so poorly understood by outsiders, so unfairly maligned, so surreal and peculiar, so charming and maddening. Individually, collectively, and above all politically, Mississippians have a kind of genius for charging after phantoms and lost causes. Nowhere else in the world have I met so many fine, generous, honorable people, but if you look at the statistics, and read the news stories coming out of Mississippi, the state gives every appearance of being a redneck disaster zone.

As I was scrabbling around for a mortgage, and trying to persuade my liberal girlfriend to move there with me, Mississippi was found once again to be the poorest state in the Union, a position it has held consistently since the end of the Civil War. Once again, it was the fattest state, with more than a third of its adult population classified as obese. It was number one in the nation for teenage pregnancy, illiteracy, failure to graduate high school, religious devotion, political conservatism, and sexually transmitted diseases. The Republican-dominated legislature, caricatured by *Saturday Night Live* as "thirty hissing possums in a barn," was trying to close down the state's last abortion clinic, and a fifty-two-year-old Delta man had just been arrested in a police sting operation while having carnal relations with a show hog.

"Do y'all even know what a show hog looks like when they get through with all the shampooing and blow-drying and beauty treatments?" said my friend Martha Foose the cookbook writer. She was calling from her house in the Delta town of Greenwood, less than a mile from the unnatural crime scene. "It's a beauty pageant for swine, and they get those hogs dolled *up*. They shave their underparts, and curl their eyelashes, and buff their little trotters, and I guess it's just more than some guys can stand. I call it 'dating down the food chain,' and frankly, it's a wonder it doesn't happen more often."

I first met Martha a few years ago in Oxford, Mississippi, the elegant, cultured, slightly dissolute university town in the northern hills of the state, where William Faulkner lived most of his life. I had stumbled across Oxford while interviewing elderly blues singers in the mid-1990s, fallen under its charms, and visited regularly ever since. Martha was there promoting her first cookbook, *Screen Doors and Sweet Tea*, a collection of recipes and stories drawn from her upbringing in the Mississippi Delta, and influenced by her training at a top cooking school in Paris. The book went on to win a James Beard Award for American Cooking. At the reading, she served high-octane bourbon cocktails, told some outlandish tales, and then we all decamped to the mayor's house for more drinks and an impromptu dance party. At that time, the mayor of Oxford was the owner of the local bookstore, Square Books, and he and his wife kept their doors open to visiting writers and anyone else in the mood for fun.

At the party Martha kept imploring me to visit her beloved home ground in the Delta, a part of the state I didn't know at all. She described it as a separate place from the rest of Mississippi, with its own unique history and culture, although nowhere on earth was more deeply Southern. She offered to take me on a grand tour of the Delta, and said I could stay for as long as I liked at her family's farm, in a remote and mysterious sounding place called Pluto.

"GPS doesn't work there, it just spins round and around, and that's the way we like it," she drawled in my ear as the mayor cranked up the music. "They took away our zip code, because we ran out of people and the postmistress drank too much. And it's so beautiful there, uh! You'll never want to leave."

Other people cautioned me about the Delta. "Things get weird as shit down there," said my friend Doug Roberts, and this made me pay attention, because Doug's standards of weirdness and normalcy are fairly skewed to begin with. A law school graduate who couldn't face being a lawyer, he sometimes appears at social functions wearing a penis gourd from Papua New Guinea and a coyote pelt on his head.

"The Delta is our Haiti," he said. "It's the third world right in the middle of America. Crime is bad, corruption is bad. It's seventy percent black and the poverty is hard-core. Whole towns are basically caving in and rotting away. And you've got a bunch of rich white farmers living the good life right in the middle of it, and trying to pretend like everything's normal. It's the South, we're great at denying reality, but the strain of it makes us weird sometimes, and you see a lot of that in the Delta. Lots of eccentrics, boozers, nutballs."

The mayor's wife described the Delta as, "beautiful, tragic, and totally batshit crazy." Then she resumed go-go dancing with Martha to Booker T. and the MG's until the mayor boogalooed headlong into the stereo and sent the needle skittering across the old record.

IT TOOK A couple of years, but I finally freed up the time and money for Martha's grand Delta tour. I drove down from New York City, where my girlfriend was on edge and my dog was depressed, all of us crammed into a tiny Manhattan apartment we couldn't afford. Our plan had been to live in New York for a year, because life is short, and our best friends were there, but four months had emptied out our bank accounts in a way that scarcely seemed possible. Lying awake in bed at night, I had the persistent illusion that the city's molars were gnawing on my skull, while its fingers rifled through my pockets for yet more money.

Neither of us wanted to go back to Tucson, Arizona, where Mariah had lived all her life, and I had kept an address for twenty years. But it was becoming clear that we didn't belong in New York. Mariah missed her garden and the presence of nature. Our dog Savanna lay on the floor of the apartment all day without moving, head resting on her paws, eyes open and mournful, a picture of canine despondency. A burly energetic German shepherd mix, she had grown up in a sunny Arizona backyard. Now she was cooped up in a four-hundred-and-twenty-five-square-foot apartment and getting increasingly aggressive at the dog park.

I knew the feeling. I was starting to experience violent revenge fantasies against strangers who cut in line. If one more person told me smugly what they weren't eating now, I was going to scream. As I was settling a billing dispute at a parking garage, trying to exit and get on the road to Mississippi, the driver behind me started honking his horn. I walked over to him in a coiled rage and pounded my fist on the roof of his car. New York was still a marvel, a wonder, an endless fascination, but as I left the city behind, I breathed a deep sigh of relief, and then realized how long it had been since I breathed deeply. Like most New Yorkers, I was in the habit of grabbing my oxygen in shallow snatches from the grimy air.

Driving south, I left the grimy dregs of winter behind and crossed over into spring. Redbuds were blooming. Wildflowers lined the two-lane highways as I came down through Tennessee and passed a big blue highway sign saying, "Welcome to Mississippi, Birthplace of America's Music." The music was the first thing I knew of Mississippi. As a teenager in London, working back through American popular music, I found my way to Jimmie Rodgers, the pioneer of country western, from Meridian, Mississippi; Elvis Presley from Tupelo; Ike Turner from Clarksdale; and above all, the Delta blues and the electrified version that Muddy Waters, Howlin' Wolf, and other Mississippians developed in Chicago. Around the same time, I discovered the novels of William Faulkner, which deepened the mystery of Mississippi in my young mind.

Now I drove through the hills around Oxford, which Faulkner had immortalized in a dozen books and renamed Yoknapatawpha County, and I kept driving west until the hills came to an end. Now the road swung me down on to the vast alluvial plain of the Delta, a place unlike anywhere I had seen before.

The sky yawned open and the horizons leapt out. The light turned golden and radiant, pouring down on shimmering fields of cotton and corn and soybeans. The land was as flat as the ocean, and as I drove across it, I came across primordial interruptions in the empire of modern agriculture: remnant swamps of cypress and tupelo gum, stretches of thick jungly woods. It was also a landscape of ruins. Abandoned barns and shacks were being swallowed whole by lush and monstrous growths of Virginia creeper and trumpet vines. Weeds fractured the forecourt of an old gas station with the pumps standing there like tombstones and a loose dog trotting past with his ribs showing.

I drove past rivers, creeks, and bayous, all brimful with the same muddy brown water, kept back from the croplands by an elaborate system of levees, pumps, sluice gates, and drainage ditches. The true delta of the Mississippi River, the place where it reaches the sea, is down in coastal Louisiana. The place known as the Mississippi Delta is the shared ancestral floodplain of the Mississippi and Yazoo Rivers, a place that still wants to go underwater every spring. Two hundred miles long and seventy miles across at its widest point, it begins just south of Memphis and ends at Vicksburg.

In 1865, at the end of the Civil War, nine-tenths of the Delta was still virgin wilderness. It was the last real frontier in the lower forty-eight states, a forbidding swamp forest full of immense trees and impenetrable canebrakes, teeming with wolves, bears, panthers, alligators, snakes, and disease-carrying insects. Then, by a staggering quantity of effort, most of it exerted by mules and newly freed slaves, the ancient forests were cleared to get at the rich alluvial soil. The swamps were drained, and levees built up to keep the rivers from flooding. Great fortunes were made and lost and made again on the new Delta cotton plantations. It was a fickle, demanding crop that promised to make you rich—if the weather cooperated, and the levee held back the high water, and the dreaded boll weevil didn't infest the fields, and overproduction didn't sink the price.

Lebanese, Jewish, and Chinese merchants arrived. Italian peasants were imported as farm labor, but didn't take to it. Black sharecroppers did most of the work and lived in dire poverty, as the white planters established a flamboyant quasi-aristocracy that was heavily dependent on credit at the bank. The ravages of malaria continued into the 1940s, and during bad outbreaks, a Delta planter might propose marriage to his belle by saying, "Miss Lucy, may I have the honor of buying your coffin?"

I MET UP with Martha in Greenwood, once the bustling, thriving, self-proclaimed Cotton Capital of the World. Now, like all Delta towns, it was in decline and losing population. We stayed up late drinking bourbon, and she told me about the wonderfully eccentric places she was going to take me. The next morning she showed up with a sausage-and-biscuit sandwich made by her husband Donald, a baker, and announced that my long-awaited Delta tour was canceled. "I'm too hungover," she said. "We'll go to Pluto instead. And don't give me any lip or I'll dump you in Tchula."

It was a heartbreakingly gorgeous spring day. We drove south on Highway 49 with red-tailed hawks wheeling overhead, wildflowers everywhere, the light slanting down through the clouds in ladders. Big hopping vultures were eating a road-killed dog by a road sign pointing to a town called Egypt. A few miles down the road, more vultures, another dead dog. Then a road-killed armadillo. Then a road-killed coyote. Mississippi calls itself the Magnolia State, and the Hospitality State. It could also claim the Loose Dog State, the Road-kill State, and the Dreamland of Highway Vultures.

In the cratered little town of Tchula, black men were standing around in a derelict gas station, drinking 40-ounce beers and smoking cigarettes. Behind them was a big red hand-painted sign that said NO LOITERING. People wandered in and out of the road without much regard for traffic. An unaccompanied infant toddled along through the roadside grit. There were swaybacked trailers, and listing shacks with sheets of plastic on the roof to keep the rain out, among neat little houses with well-kept lawns. Hard-eyed young men cruised up and down in flashy new cars and trucks. In a mile we passed seven or eight churches. Drugs, religion, and welfare appeared to be the cornerstones of the local economy.

South of Tchula, in the tiny hamlet of Mileston, Martha turned off the highway onto a dirt track. She drove past a small scruffy shack to an even smaller, scruffier shack. "This is Miss Pat's," she said. "Her real name is Willie Ruth. She used to have a sign saying "Pat's Kitchen," but it was making too much business, so she took it down. She does a plate lunch with fried chicken, three vegetables, cornbread, sweet tea and dessert, all for six bucks. I ate here every day when I was pregnant."

Miss Pat was a slow-moving, unflappable black woman with a bad knee and a kerchief tied around her head. Her customers were tractor drivers, farm hands, railroad workers, home health nurses with elaborate hairdos, picking up lunches to go. They spoke with a deep, thick, slurred accent, almost a dialect. It omitted so many consonants that I could barely understand it, and Martha had to quietly translate when it came time for me to order. I thought back to Indian reservations in South Dakota, the street gangs I had written about in South Central Los Angeles, poor whites in rural Appalachia. In none of those places did I feel like such an outsider, or have such trouble with basic communication. It added to the mounting impression that I had entered another country.

The air was heavy and still, with a metallic drone of insects, a languorous melancholy, an undercurrent of racial tension beneath a guarded surface politeness. There were cats everywhere, prowling after discarded chicken bones. A man sat on a table, staring into the middle distance, unmoving and inscrutable. We took our lunches to go, and drove along the shore of an oxbow lake. Cypress trees festooned with Spanish moss grew out in the water. Great blue herons and egrets flapped away. Turtles plopped off logs. A few miles more and we reached a small cluster of big houses with lawns and flower gardens and enormous shade trees full of mockingbirds.

"Welcome to Pluto, my favorite place on earth," said Martha, parking behind a two-story gabled house that had belonged to her grandmother. We sat in the deep green shade of a magnificent oak tree, eating Miss Pat's crunchy succulent fried chicken, drinking wine, watching cloud formations drift across the sky, and the changing light on the fields and catfish ponds. I took off my shoes and lay back in the grass, feeling relaxed for the first time in months. "Martha, this is just . . ."

"Isn't it, though? The Delta is such a mess, but it puts a spell on you. I've lived in Paris, LA, Vermont, Minneapolis, and here I am, back home at last."

"Why is it called Pluto?"

"Pluto was the Lord of the Underworld, that's the story I always heard. All this was just a big, mean, hellish swamp."

Later that afternoon, Martha said she might as well give me a tour of Pluto. She drove along a dirt road on top of a levee, passing her cousin's catfish ponds, and entered some sun-dappled woods hung with long tendrils of vine. Eight or nine deer ran across the road. We emerged a few minutes later in open fields, and drove up to a stately old house standing by itself in a grove of huge trees. It had a seven-columned front porch looking out over manicured lawns and ponds and flower gardens.

"What a beautiful house," I said.

"It's for sale," said Martha. "A 1910 plantation house with four bedrooms, three bathrooms, on six acres of land, I think. It's my daddy's house."

"How much?" I said, expecting to hear a figure somewhere in advance of $400,000.

"He's asking $160,000, I think, but you could probably pick it up for $130,000," said Martha.

"What kind of shape is it in?"

"It's in great shape. Daddy's been fixing it up for twenty years."

In all my restless nomadic adult life, I had never seen a house I wanted to own, or even live in for an extended period of time. Mortgages had always scared me. I'd never aspired to own property, because it meant getting trapped in one place. In twenty-two years, I had changed my address eighteen times. I was a wanderer, a drifter, forever passing through, taking notes, and moving on. That's what I told myself as Martha opened the front door and took me inside.

The rooms were large with wooden floors and a sturdy old-fashioned elegance. There was a six-sided dining room with glass-fronted cabinets, a farmhouse kitchen, a study with a built-in gun rack, open fireplaces in most of the rooms. Behind the house were extensive vegetable gardens, fruit trees, muscadine grapevines, a fenced-in dog run that was eight times larger than our New York apartment. There was a two-acre horse pasture with a barn, and nestled into a stand of bamboo was a small, compact studio that looked ideal for writing.

"Is it safe here?" I asked.

"You need a dog and a gun," said Martha. "You might get a crackhead looking for something to steal, or a meth-head coming through to poach deer or party on the lake. An alligator might show up when the water's high. That's the Yazoo River down through those trees, and that'd be your property line."

That night, while the frogs and insects worked up a sawing rhythmic music, and we sat drinking bourbon under the stars, I couldn't stop thinking about that old house down the levee. I pictured myself reading William Faulkner on the front porch, writing in the studio, Mariah working happily in the garden. We'd be able to grow our own vegetables, and harvest figs, pears, apples, persimmons, muscadines, and pecans. Maybe I could start hunting deer and putting meat on the table, if I could overcome my aversion to killing animals.

Martha and her cousins would be just down the road. We'd wake up listening to birdsong instead of traffic roar and jackhammers. We'd never hear a police siren. I'd been toying with the idea of living in Mississippi, and writing about it, for a long time. I liked the food, the music, the warmth of the culture, the easy conviviality and drawling repartee. Most of all, I liked the storytelling. It was an integral part of life here, an art form respected at all levels of society, and the stories themselves got so wild and improbable. They burned with a strange fever, and made a mockery of the usual standards of cause and effect. They were a window into a place and a culture where contradictions hung in the air like swamp gas, and eccentricity was as natural as rain.

Lyndon Johnson said, "There's America, there's the South, then there's Mississippi." To which Martha Foose added, "And then there's the Delta. You have no idea what you're getting into down here, and that's what makes it so perfect. I'll work on Daddy. You get back up there and work on Mariah. We're going to be neighbors, and you're going to write a book about the whole thing."

Chapter 1

First Landing

HOW TO PERSUADE Mariah to move from downtown Manhattan
to an isolated old farmhouse in the poorest county in Mississippi? It
would mean giving up most of the things she enjoyed: gourmet food,
interesting wines, yoga classes, art and photography exhibitions, her
friends, shopping for clothes. Sixteen years younger than me, she was
liberal, progressive, politically correct in her speech, and I was pro-
posing to take her to the most right-wing state in the Bible Belt.

On the other hand, she loved gardening, trees, birds, the open
sky, and the city had not been treating her kindly during my absence.
She was trying to find part-time work in New York City's library system, while taking an online master's degree in library science, and
she had now submitted more than twenty applications without getting a single response. In financial desperation, she had started apply-
ing for barista jobs. She had years of experience in the coffee trade,
but again, she got no calls back, no emails, just a growing feeling of

rejection every day. She tightened her budget once again, and cooked cheap meals for herself in a narrow slot of basement hallway pretending to be our kitchen. She was lectured to by the anxiety-ridden allergy-plagued landlady upstairs, and woken up six mornings a week by immense thumping and crashing sounds from the construction site next door.

I returned from Mississippi with photographs of a seven-columned porch bathed in honeyed light, flower gardens and vegetable beds, the misty apricot dawn filtering through the fairytale trees. I talked excitedly of 4,500 square feet and six acres, and calculated that the monthly mortgage payment for all this space would be less than a quarter of what we were paying for our light-starved underground shoebox. "I know this is coming out of nowhere, I know it sounds crazy, but you've got to at least see this place," I said.

"I'm not against it," she said. "It looks amazing. But how would we support ourselves? And I don't want to be stuck out there by myself when you're off traveling. It doesn't sound safe."

I promised to give up my incessant traveling if we moved there, write about Mississippi instead, and support her until she graduated. I spun out a vision of self-sufficient homesteading and adventure, surrounded by birds and wildlife and drenched in natural beauty. Assuming we could get an Internet connection, she could continue to take her classes online, and then find a job in the Delta. There was a lovely old library about twenty miles from the house where Martha had some inside connections and could surely swing something.

Mariah agreed to go and see the house. We went down to Pluto, and along that levee road, and I walked her up on to the front porch, and she fell instantly in love with the place. She looked happier than I had seen her in months. Martha's father, Mike Foose, a country doctor with a trimmed white beard and horn-rimmed glasses, came out to meet us with his second wife, Beth, an Episcopalian preacher and passionate gardener. Mariah spent a couple of hours talking plants and growing cycles with Beth, while I asked Mike about the heating and cooling, the well and the septic system, the fireplace chimneys, the likelihood of a robbery or home invasion, which he said was extremely small.

They took us on a tour of the area, showing us a watery wildlife refuge packed with birds, alligators, turtles, big rodents called nutria whose mating cries sounded like babies in distress. They pointed out good places nearer the house to hunt, fish, camp, and canoe, walked us through some cathedral-like woods, and cooked us a stout breakfast of delicious venison sausages with eggs and bacon. "The deer are so plentiful around here, and they taste so good, that we hardly ever eat beef anymore," said Mike.

"If it all works out, this would be a good place for me to learn to hunt," I said.

"It would be my honor to teach you," he said.

It all sounded too good to be true, like something that happened in story books, not twenty-first century America.

•

WE WENT BACK to New York eager to take the plunge, and I started meeting with mortgage specialists in fabric-lined office cubicles. One after another, they assured me that my erratic freelance income wouldn't be a problem, since I was able to make a good down payment, and they congratulated me on getting so much property for so little money, even if it did mean moving to Mississippi. Then they sent my data to head office, and one after another, my applications came back rejected. The American mortgage industry had recently been on a wild reckless binge that had wrecked global prosperity. Now, under tighter regulations, it was acting sober, penitent, and averse to low-level risks like me.

Mike and Beth Foose very much wanted us to have the house. They saw us as kindred spirits who would keep the vegetable gardens organic, respect the wildlife, appreciate the built-in bookshelves, and be good neighbors for Martha and her relatives down the road in Pluto. So Mike did something extraordinary. He offered to lend me the money himself, by taking out a mortgage on my behalf, and assuming the risk if I defaulted. To work out the details, and see if there might be a better solution, he asked me to come down to Mississippi again, and meet with his banker Butch Gary in Yazoo City.

I drove there from Martha's house on a hot June morning, passing bizarre natural sculpture gardens created by the invasive kudzu vine. It can grow twelve inches a day under optimal conditions, and not many places in this world can out-fecund the Mississippi Delta in early summer. The vines had swallowed up entire trees, telephone poles, and other structures that were no longer identifiable. It had turned them into fuzzy green shapes, mostly phallic, but also resembling children's drawings of giraffes, dinosaurs, two-headed sheep, sailboats, and nuclear explosions.

Yazoo City, a gently decaying, once prosperous town of 11,000 people, straddles the divide between the hills and the alluvial flatland. Souvenir T-shirts describe it as, "Half Hills, Half Delta, All Crazy." Butch Gary's bank was on the tallest hill, a brick building with a hint of Greek Revival in its architecture. Clutching my tax returns and financial papers, sweating into my ironed shirt, I walked toward its white columned entrance, feeling like I'd fallen through a trapdoor into someone else's life. I was forty-nine years old, a drifter tired of drifting, a person I didn't recognize.

"Okay, now let me get this straight," said Butch Gary, a small trim figure with immaculate hair, shrewd eyes, and a soft, husky drawl. "You're a writer from London, England. You were living in Arizona, and traveling a lot in Mexico and Africa. Now you're in New York

City. And you're wanting to buy Mike Foose's house out in the country over there in Holmes County? I'll be honest with you. I'm more accustomed to giving equipment loans to cotton farmers. So I need to understand your thought process here. Why are you doing this?"

I explained my reasons as best I could: beautiful house, peace and quiet, a good place to write, my enduring affection for Mississippi. Butch started talking about all the great writers the state has produced: William Faulkner, Eudora Welty, Tennessee Williams, Willie Morris from right here in Yazoo City, Shelby Foote and Walker Percy from Greenville, Richard Ford from Jackson, Donna Tartt, John Grisham. To his list, I added Richard Wright, Barry Hannah, Larry Brown, Lewis Nordan, Alice Walker, Rick Bass, and there are many more. Outsiders often see it as a paradox, that such a poor, conservative, religious state should also have such a rich literary tradition, but it makes sense to Mississippians. Not only are they great tellers and admirers of colorful stories, with a rich supply of material. There's also an intangible, mysterious quality to life here that Mississippi writers have felt compelled to tackle, a kind of magical realism that comes out of the state's long insularity, the urge to mythologize its history of defeat and oppression, the deep influence of the Old Testament and faith-based thinking, and perhaps the drama of the natural landscape.

"I love to read books and I think it'd be just great to have a writer, and a world traveler, and a guy from London, England, living here in our community," said Butch Gary. "So I'll tell you what I'll do. I'll loan you the money right out of my bank on one condition."

"What's the condition?" I said, not quite believing my ears.

"Y'all have to come over for dinner with me and my wife, and tell us some stories about these places you've been. We don't get out of Yazoo County as much as we should, but we're real interested in what's going on in the rest of the world."

We shook hands on the deal, and that's how I got my mortgage.

"That never happens," said Mariah, when I told her about it later. "Maybe it used to in 1952, or 1975, but not anymore. Bankers don't give mortgages to writers because they like to read books. And people selling houses don't offer to loan the money to the buyer. What is going on here? Why is everyone being so incredibly kind and helpful? I've been in New York too long. I can't help being suspicious."

BUTCH GARY AND Mike Foose rounded up a lawyer, an insurance man, a house inspector, and a termite inspector. Everything went smoothly, and people who believe in such things said it was meant to be. At the end of June, I was back in Yazoo City, sitting at a big mahogany table in a lawyer's office, surrounded by drawling Mississippi gentlemen in white Oxford shirts. I had the sensation of hovering above myself, looking down, as my obedient hand signed about eighteen different legal documents.

It was late August before we were able to move into the house. Coming down through the Delta at the helm of a U-Haul truck, with our possessions in the back and Mariah flying out to meet me, I stopped on the edge of Money (pop. 35) to let the dog out. An old Ford Ranchero with one whitewall tire drew slowly to a halt beside me. I saw his left hand first, resting on the steering wheel and missing three fingers. Then the face came into view. He was a white man in his fifties or sixties with a hard-bitten look and a scraggly mustache. He did not hail me with the usual warm, welcoming Mississippi greeting. He turned his engine off, and gave me a long hard challenging stare.

"Sightseein'?" he said.

"No," I said. "I've bought a house down near Yazoo City. I'm moving in. How are you doing?"

He jerked his thumb toward a rickety old two-storey building covered in vines, preparing for its final collapse. "This is where that colored boy got hisself in trouble," he said. "You heard of Emmett Till?"

I said, "That was here?" I knew the story, but I'd forgotten that it happened in Money. Emmett "Bobo" Till, fourteen years old, full of spark and mischief, was down here from Chicago visiting relatives. His great-uncle warned him that white people were dangerous in Mississippi, and told him how he needed to act to be safe. Bobo didn't take the warnings seriously. He went into the Bryant Grocery, and wolf-whistled at the pretty young white woman working behind the counter, or so the story goes. It was an August day, hot like this one, in 1955.

Four nights later, the woman's husband and his half-brother came for Emmett Till. They dragged him out of his great-uncle's house and drove him away into the Delta night, thinking to teach him a lesson. "He was hopeless," one of the men said later, meaning he wouldn't submit or repent or beg for mercy. So they beat him, stripped him, gouged out one of his eyes, and shot him in the head. They dumped the body in the Tallahatchie River, and to stop it from floating, they tied a 70-pound cotton-gin fan around Till's neck with barbed wire.

"The boys went a little too far," said the man with the missing fingers. His tone was even, with an undercurrent of threat.

"They killed him, didn't they?" I said.

"Did they?" he said. "I don't know the story real well. But you couldn't act that way with another man's wife, white or colored. Not in them days."

Now the shaky old wisp of a building across the street, the Bryant Grocery, was a destination for tourists on the Mississippi Freedom Trail, a series of marker signs honoring the state's contribution to the civil rights movement. A plaque in front of the building tells the Emmett Till story in detail, which made me wonder if the man knew it better than he was letting on, or if he'd never bothered to read the plaque. Mainly I wondered at his choice of words. Colored boy? Got hisself into trouble? A little too far? He seemed to have no sympathy for the fourteen-year-old victim whatsoever.

It was different being in Mississippi as a resident and a property owner, rather than a visitor passing through. The history of racial violence and injustice was no longer their problem, but mine too, I now realized. I would be living in its aftermath, alongside the man with the missing fingers. And because everyone knows everyone in the Delta, I'd probably run into him again, or someone that knows him, and others that shared his opinions. This made me slower to judge, more willing to consider what he'd been taught as a child and heard from his peers as a young man. I couldn't just write him off, tick the box marked "racist," and move on.

Things have come a long way in Mississippi. That's the usual shorthand. Perhaps nowhere else in America has made more progress in its race relations, but then again, nowhere else had so far to go. Mississippi had the most lynchings, the worst Klan violence, the staunchest resistance to the civil rights movement. When the Emmett Till case was tried, the all-white jury found the two defendants not guilty in an hour and eight minutes. One juror said it would have been quicker if they hadn't taken a break to drink Coca-Colas. Those days are gone now, but inevitably, they bleed through and stain the present.

The man with the missing fingers said there wasn't much left of Money. The big farms didn't need workers anymore, white or colored, just plenty of capital and credit to buy the latest tractors and harvesting machines, and chemicals for the crop duster planes to spray on the bugs and weeds. They were getting a few tourists now with the Freedom Trail, but the last store had closed down, so there was no way to profit from these visitors. Money couldn't even sell them gasoline or a soda pop.

"Where are you from?" he said.

I told him and he nodded. "We get y'all. We had Germans yesterday. Go on, read the sign. Take a look around. Come on back."

He started up his engine and pulled slowly away. I read the sign and got back in the U-Haul. Ten miles down the road, I stopped off at Martha's house in Greenwood. I told her about my encounter, and she said, "Those people in Money are sick and tired of being judged for something that happened more than fifty years ago. But they don't want to be ignored and forgotten about either."

She was sitting in her backyard smoking cigarettes and drinking sweet iced tea, "the house wine of the Deep South," as it's sometimes called. A big noisy industrial fan kept the air circulating and thwarted the mosquitoes.

"There's a secret to living here," she said. "Compartmentalize, compartmentalize, and then compartmentalize some more. If someone tells you that the Muslims are plotting to destroy America, or Obama is the Antichrist, you just seal that away in its own separate compartment, and carry on till you find their good side. There's no sense in arguing with them. Folks around here are stubborn as they come."

I COLLECTED MARIAH from the airport, and neither of us was able to feel excited, or apprehensive, because the whole experience of moving into our new home felt so utterly unreal. It was impossible to believe that we lived here now. Turtles slid into the ponds as we pulled up in front. Butterflies and dragonflies flitted about. Thick woody vines snaked and coiled through the trees. The front porch was now screened in by banana plants that had grown twelve feet high in the two months since we were last here.

We walked up to the house holding hands, with Savanna on the leash, not wanting her to run off and get bitten by a snake, eaten by an alligator, ambushed by coyotes, or gored by a wild hog. The house was vast and bare and empty, with the rooms arranged on both sides of a long central hallway. If you ran up and down the hallway, we discovered, you could build up serious speed before you needed to slow down. We wandered through the eleven empty rooms, and kept losing each other, calling out each other's names.

Mike and Beth Foose had left us a bottle of champagne in the fridge, and eggs, bacon, bread, coffee, and milk for our first breakfast. Let no one underestimate Southern hospitality, or Mississippi generosity. They'd also cleaned the house, kept the lawns mowed, left all the appliances, a few nice pieces of antique furniture, a gas-powered lawnmower, a kayak, a barbecue grill, gardening tools, and a small starter library of books about the area. They had bought us a big black cast-iron skillet as a gift, because life in the South is unimaginable without one, and a beautiful illustrated hardback book about gardening. What they hadn't given us was any keys to the house, because no keys existed.

"You could get some made, I suppose, but you're really better off leaving the house unlocked," Mike had explained. "If someone comes out here to rob the place and they find a locked door, they're just going to smash it in, and then you've got the cost and hassle of getting it repaired."

My wandering life had not gathered much in the way of possessions, and Mariah had purged her belongings for the move to New York. To furnish eleven rooms, we had two beds, one armchair, one desk chair, two small tables, a credenza, two rugs, a few lamps and framed photographs, and one painting. When we got them unpacked and set up, they made the house look even emptier. Even our book collection, which numbered three or four hundred volumes, left yards of empty space on the built-in bookshelves.

We opened the champagne, found two wineglasses in our moving boxes, and went out on the porch at sunset. Almost immediately, Mariah got five mosquito bites, and we hustled back inside. The bites swelled and hardened. Then they turned into big throbbing lumps, and grew hot to the touch. She was having an allergic reaction, and I was trying to conceal a plummeting feeling of gloom and despair, because this could ruin everything.

The Mississippi Delta is notorious for its mosquitoes, and our new house was in a particularly bad place for them. On one side was a river flanked with low-lying swampy woods and flooded areas. On the other side was a stagnant oxbow lake and more swampy woods. Two large ponds were in front of the house. As the sun went down, mosquitoes by the thousands started crawling over the outside of the windows. They formed a gauzy cloud around the security light by the side of the house. Inside the house, Mariah killed twelve or fifteen in short order. I wrote "mosquito net" on the enormous list of things we needed.

We ate cold cuts for dinner, sitting on the kitchen floor and leaning against a wall. A wind came up, rattling the old sash windows, and we could hear thunder in the distance. Mariah's bites didn't swell any further, but they were still burning hot to the touch. She found a Benadryl. I dug out a bottle of bourbon. We wandered around the house, pleasantly tipsy, imagining how great it would look if we ever had the money to buy some furniture, rugs, and art to hang on the endless blank walls.

A lone set of headlights came along the long curve of the paved road, then turned down the unpaved road that comes past the house. I became suddenly aware of how incredibly isolated and vulnerable and unarmed we were. It was a pickup truck with throaty pipes and it went past the house and turned down the levee. Twenty minutes later, it came back, and we watched the tail lights disappear into the night. We told each other it was probably just kids out cruising, and wondered privately if it was ghoulish meth-head rednecks. "It's Mississippi," I said. "Everyone is going to assume we're armed to the teeth out here. But we do need to get some guns."

The wind blew harder. The sky erupted with thunder and lightning. The rain came down in sheets and ropes. I was setting up the stereo, enjoying the drama of the storm, when I heard an alarmed cry of "Honey!" The ceiling of the middle bedroom was leaking fat steady drops of rainwater. The plaster was sagging around the leak and looked like it was going to fall down. I went up into the attic with a flashlight. I found many wasps' nests and an abundance of rodent droppings, but not the source of the leak. What could I do about it anyway? As a lifelong renter, I'd never learned how to fix anything. That would have to change.

We put a bucket under the leak and went to bed. We made love and fell asleep, and woke up at the sound of a mouse or a rat inside the wall. It was chewing away, eating the damn house I'd just bought, and there was no way to get in there to stop it. Thumping the wall didn't work. I made a mental note to put "mousetraps" on the list. Then something bigger—a squirrel, a feral cat?—started running around in the attic.

Mariah found a way to sleep through this, but I spent most of the night grimly awake, drinking bourbon in our one armchair, and brooding over the enormous mistake of buying this huge, leaky old rodent-infested house, trapping myself in debt and never-ending chores and repairs, in a mosquito-ridden swamp in the middle of nowhere. What sort of idiot goes on a picnic and ends up buying a house?

Chapter 2

Serpents in the Garden

THE RAISED VEGETABLE beds behind the house, which had looked
so fluffy and ready to plant in June, were now four feet deep in a
choking tangle of weeds and vines, and crawling with weird-looking
beetles and other insects. This is the flipside of the famously fertile
Delta soil and climate. Cotton and vegetable crops grow prolifically
here, and so do noxious weeds and swarms of pestilential bugs. I
thought about how much time and sweat and muscle ache we could
save by spraying herbicides and insecticides, but Mariah wanted our
vegetable garden to be organic, and I suppose I did too.

The jungle that had occupied our vegetable garden was about
forty yards long and eight yards across. In some places, the vegetation was over my head. I put on gloves and my new green LaCrosse
rubber boots, a ubiquitous wardrobe item in these muddy zip codes.
I took one step in, and a snake shot out from under my feet. It looked
too thin and narrow-headed to be poisonous, but what did I know?

I was a fool here. We both were. We couldn't tell a soybean from a cotton seedling, a slough from a bayou, a harmless water snake from a cottonmouth water moccasin that could kill a child and put a man like me in hospital.

I knew enough to spray myself down with mosquito repellant, but that didn't stop a horsefly from delivering a painful bite to my neck. Gnats whined around my head as I tugged and hacked away. By ten in the morning, it was ninety-two degrees with 90 percent humidity, and my clothes were soaked through. Sweat was dripping off my nose and earlobes, and I was already thinking about cold beer. Grabbing the roots of a vine by a small mound of fluffy soil, I felt sharp stabbing pains around my wrists, and ripped off my gloves spitting out curses. So began my learning curve with fire ants. An hour later, the bites had swollen up and filled with pus. A week later, the pustules still itched like crazy.

Inside the house, the air conditioning system, well past its prime, was struggling to keep the temperature below eighty-two degrees. Mariah had found some mouse droppings in the pantry, pinned her hair up, and gone into a cleaning frenzy. We'd stacked some cans of tomatoes and beans on the pantry shelves, and now she was washing those cans in hot soapy water because they'd been *near* the tiny little mouse turds.

I said, "Seriously? You're going to wash up the cans, and then put them back in the pantry, where the mice are going to keep shitting until we trap the little fuckers. You're wasting your time."

"You want to live in shit!" she protested. "Have you looked at the window frames? They're covered in spider shit. The baseboards are covered in spider shit. There's mouse shit all over the pantry. I'm not living in shit. I don't want shit near my food. So I'm washing the cans of food that have been in the shitty pantry. Because that's what you do."

Her mosquito bites had cooled off, but they were still hard, itchy, asymmetrical lumps about the size of a kidney bean, and you can imagine how she felt about the one on her face. I stormed outside and went back to tugging and hacking, as she should be doing, instead of washing a dozen cans that were already clean, and scrubbing a damn baseboard that was never going to give us any food. Then my anger subsided, and I saw that I'd misarranged my priorities. Nothing was more important than my relationship. We'd been together for eight years, and it had been well worth it. What if we split up and I was stuck out here by myself with the bugs and the jungle and the bourbon?

I came back inside, full of calm conciliation. My best weapon— the loving hug—was unavailable because my clothes were sodden and filthy. "Look," I said. "I'm sorry. I didn't mean to get on your case. We'll take it one day at a time. We'll put in a few hours working on the house, a few hours on the garden, and then we'll relax and enjoy ourselves. Otherwise we're going to drown in chores and drive ourselves crazy out here."

"Okay," she said. "Just don't leave me to scrub all the shit by myself."

"It's a deal," I said, not realizing that this statement would turn out to be a lie.

There were so many other things to do. Clear the jungle and prepare the soil for the winter garden. Fix the lawnmower and mow the grass before it turned into a snake-harboring jungle. Trap the rodents. Paint the rooms, refinish the floors. Buy firearms and learn how to use them, for home defense, and for meat if I could get over my tender feelings about animals.

I needed to fell a tree so the firewood would have a chance to cure by winter, but first I needed to buy a chainsaw and learn how to fell a tree. I needed to crawl under the house and pull out the old, falling-down insulation, but I was afraid of under the house. It was dank and claustrophobic, strewn with cobwebs, itchy fiberglass, rat shit, desiccated carcasses of possums and armadillos, and it looked like a textbook perfect habitat for snakes and black widow spiders. At some point, I also needed to start making sense of human society in the Delta, which many wise and thoughtful Mississippians had assured me was an impossible task.

First things first. I called Mike Foose and told him about the leak in the roof. He sounded utterly mortified and promised to call a roofer right away. "Make sure he bills me for the work, and I'll pay for any damage it's caused," he said. "Oh, and there's going to be a black guy coming over with his mother to pick up a few things in boxes. She's Lucy Neal. He's William Neal, but everybody calls him Monk. Both of them are real fine people."

Before they got here, another black man rolled up in a farm truck, curious to meet the new people and wondering if we might have any yard work for him. His name was James Jefferson, and he drove a tractor in the fields around the house. I invited him on the front porch, but he said he preferred to stand in the shade of a big pecan tree by the levee. He was reluctant to look me in the eye, preferring to stare out across the cotton fields. Was it shyness in front of a stranger? Was he acting subservient toward me because I was white, and living in the big plantation house? I didn't know. I certainly hoped not.

We carried on talking for more than an hour, and slowly grew more comfortable with each other. I started to see him more as an individual, realizing how much I had seen him as a representative of his race and class and geographical background. He began by small degrees to turn his shoulders more squarely toward me, and look me directly in the eyes. "Farming is like life," he said. "You try to take everything into account, and do the best you can with what you have.

The rest is up to God, so they ain't no sense worrying your mind about it. Lord, I seen some changes though. When I was a boy, they was plowing mules here. Now we got GPS tractors that plow they-selves."

I asked him where he grew up, and he pointed to a spot about half a mile away. "I was born right there in a tenant house," he said, meaning a sharecropper's shack. "There was two hundred people living on this plantation, tenant houses all along the levee, and over by the lake. They had a commissary, a schoolhouse, a cotton gin right there, a mule barn right over there. People had hogs and chickens. It was a good life."

I said, "Really? That's not how they write about it in books. They say it was terrible poverty and prejudice and discrimination."

"Well, some of that is true, but it was the life we had, and we knew how to enjoy it," he said. "Everybody knew everybody, we were close, and the white folks around here, they treated us fair. Mr. Sonny owned the plantation and he treated us more than fair. Only thing I regret is not getting an education. I was too busy working in the fields."

All traces of the tightly knit community that had lived here were now gone, except for our new home. When the machines and chemicals took over in the 1980s, the tenant houses were burned down and ploughed under, along with the barns, commissary, cotton gin, and schoolhouse. If you look at the history of the Delta as a struggle between white capital and black labor, this was the final triumph of white capital. Except for a few tractor drivers like James Jefferson, black labor was no longer needed.

White planters divested themselves of their old paternalistic re-sponsibilities, and the uprooted, uneducated farm laborers, accus-tomed to being dependent on the white man, were left to their own devices in Tchula and dozens of other decaying, impoverished towns around the Delta. But that's only one way of looking at things, one facet of a deeper and more complicated relationship between whites and blacks in this place.

SOON AFTER JAMES Jefferson left, Lucy Neal and Monk arrived in a red pickup truck. She was a big woman who had been famously strong in her prime. Now she was elderly and wheeling an oxygen tank. She spoke in a deep rasping voice, and radiated kindness and calm patient goodwill. Her son Monk was a big man with a belly like Buddha and a face full of charm, personality, intelligence, and good humor. He had a stutter when he talked, and his eyes shone and sparkled when he smiled.

Lucy sat down in the kitchen and started naming off all the children she had raised, three of her own, and ten white children for Dr. Foose and his extended family. "I love 'em all just like my own," she rasped. "Each and every one of them chirrens is real special in my heart."

"That's right," said Monk. "She came up working for Dr. Foose grandmother, back when they ploughed a mule around here. When Dr. Foose got married and had kids, she started working for him."

"I raised Martha," said Lucy. "Ooh, she was lazy! I taught her how to cook. Now they say she cook real good."

Whenever the conversation reached a pause, one of them would say, "Mmm-hmmm," or "That's right," and every few seconds, the oxygen tank would make a sound like a brush on a cymbal. Lucy had helped raise two children for Bobby Thompson, or Bobby T as people called him. I hadn't met him yet, but I'd seen the Confederate flag flying from his carport opposite Martha's house. Presumably, he saw it as a symbol of his proud Southern heritage. Presumably, Lucy and Monk saw it as an endorsement of slavery and a symbol of racism.

I wanted to ask them about this, but it seemed too soon to pry into such a sensitive subject.

I had heard that black and white families in the Delta often become very close, because they've lived and worked together on the same land for generations. But it was an odd sort of closeness, because the races didn't socialize or worship together, and most whites didn't regard blacks as equals. In the feudal society of the Delta, whites were the lords of the manor, and blacks were the serfs.

There was still a social taboo in the Delta against blacks and whites eating together at the same table, but it hadn't been observed in this house. Lucy and Monk said they'd eaten dinner here many times with Mike and Beth, and her two daughters, who Lucy also helped to raise. Mike and Beth, from what I could gather, were trying to move race relations forward in their own small, personal way. But again, what did I know? I was as ignorant of Delta race relations as everything else here, but I too hoped to move them forward in my own small personal way, or at least maintain what progress had been made in this house. I told Monk and Lucy that they were welcome here any time, and we'd like to have them over for dinner once we had a table and some chairs. "I'd like that too," said Lucy, and she seemed to mean it.

THE FOLLOWING DAY, our nearest neighbors came over at sundown with a bottle of wine. Louie Thompson, a catfish farmer, was Mike Foose's first cousin. Tanned and weathered with a white-flecked beard, wearing shorts and an old Hawaiian shirt, he was quick to laugh, and the way he laughed made everything else funnier. There was also a hint of something steely in his blue eyes. He seemed trustworthy and honorable, an easy man to like and perhaps a bad man to cross.

His wife Cathy was a labor and delivery nurse who ran a hospital ward in Jackson. She enveloped us in hugs and Southern charm, and seemed absolutely delighted that we were going to be neighbors. Their youngest daughter Cadi was home for the summer after graduating college. She was strong, athletic, fresh-faced, and confident, wearing shorts and a tank top emblazoned with the logo of the Mississippi State University Bulldogs, her beloved college football team. Unlike her two older sisters, Cadi had a fearless tomboy streak. She liked hunting, and would go out into the swamps at night to grab bullfrogs with her bare hands. When alligators got into Louie's catfish ponds, Cadi would catch them alive with a fishing line and a roll of duct tape to keep their jaws shut.

Her face lit up when I said that we'd met Lucy and Monk. "Lucy helped raise me and my sisters," she said. "I adore that woman. She's amazing. She never forgets a birthday or a graduation. She's my black mama."

"Lucy is really a part of our family," said Cathy. "And Monk has turned into a fine young man. I'm so glad you got the chance to visit with them."

Cadi spotted an armadillo waddling past the pond, and grabbed a .22 rifle out of her Dad's pickup. "Those things'll tear up your yard," she said, and shot it in the side. The armadillo lay there twitching and flipping, and she put another round in its head. "That's so it won't suffer," she said. Then she grabbed it by the tail and pitched it into the bushes. "Mexicans eat them, but I sure wouldn't," she said, flashing a winning smile and striding back up on to the porch.

Mariah and I exchanged a glance. Neither of us had ever shot an animal before, or killed anything bigger than a scorpion. We were lovers of wildlife, birdwatchers, environmentalists. Was it really necessary to kill armadillos?

We drank a glass of wine on the front porch, and the Thompsons made some generalizations about black people that made us feel uncomfortable, although I had certainly heard worse from my father and his friends in London. They loved Lucy and Monk like family, and Cadi loved to go to black church, but there were a lot of worthless blacks on welfare who didn't want to work, and we should never stop in Tchula, even if we ran down a pedestrian, because the people there would surely rob us, and quite possibly rape Mariah by the side of the road.

Louie had given up using what he called the "local help" to work on his catfish farm. Instead, he employed Mexicans, and had gone to the trouble of hiring them legally. "Most catfish farmers around here have switched to Mexicans," he said. "They show up on time, they're happy to work, they're not looking to borrow money all the time, they don't show up for work drunk— well, hardly ever. I could never get anything done on a Monday with the local help, because someone would always need bailing out of jail, or be too hungover to work, and I got tired of it, man. I really did."

Cadi changed the subject by fetching an empty plastic jug and throwing it in the pond. In a calm, patient, sisterly way, she showed Mariah how to load, aim, and shoot two different rifles. Standing side by side, Cadi looked so tough and commanding, and Mariah looked so petite and feminine. I could see the Thompsons exchanging glances: this little city girl is not going to make it out here.

When Mariah started hitting the jug, Cadi said, "Alright! You and me are going deer hunting, girl!" Then it was my turn. My shooting was abysmal, mainly because my eyesight was in middle-aged decline and the gun sights were a blur. The Thompsons assured me that a telescopic sight would cure that problem, and then there was talk of calibers, grains, bullet trajectories, the pros and cons of different brands and models. This, we discovered in the weeks and months to come, was a staple Delta conversation. People here talk about firearms and hunting in the same way that urban liberals go on about nutrition and exercise.

Cathy's gun collection included an AK-47 that she'd bought for stress relief during the onset of menopause. "I don't know what women in New York do," she said. "Probably go see a therapist, or get on meds. I got my AK and a T-shirt that said, 'I'm Out of Estrogen and I Have a Gun.'"

"Did it help with the stress relief?" I asked.

"It did," said Louie with a grin. "But it was hard on the local frog population."

Then Cathy told a story about going frog hunting with Louie when she was heavily pregnant with Julia, their first child. "I was poppin' frogs just fine, like I always do, and then I missed one," she said. "Louie looked at me, and he said, 'Are you okay?' I said, 'Honey, you better take me to the hospital. I think my water is fixing to break.'"

Cathy grew up in modest circumstances in the hills, and she started hunting for the table as a young girl. Louie was from the Delta plantation gentry, and in the 1970s when they met, he was wearing cut-off jeans and driving a gold Cadillac. Cathy married him when she was seventeen, and after that, hunting was something she did for recreation.

"I might shoot a frog, or a dove, but I'll never shoot another deer," she said. "I hate to say it y'all, but I shot Bambi. She looked so big through the scope, and I shot her, and then Cadi went out there to get her, and the deer was so small that Cadi just picked her up and slung her over her shoulder. Cadi was only ten years old at the time. Oh, I felt so bad. I had killed a baby."

The way she said it, it flashed into my head that Cathy was probably against abortion, and that our warm, fun, welcoming neighbors were almost certainly Christian Republicans. Presumably, they had pegged us as liberal Democrats, but that didn't seem to have impeded their hospitality in the slightest. In a nation so angry and divided over politics, that was heartening to see, although there was a little voice in my head saying: What if we were black? What if we were Muslim? Would we get the same welcome? Again, I just didn't know.

The following night, Cathy cooked us a big Southern meal with chicken-fried deer meat, cornbread, green beans, butter beans, mashed potatoes, tomato gravy, and salad, with two desserts to follow. When she had us all assembled at the table, she said, "Louie, let's bless." He asked the heavenly father to bless the food on the table, and the company of new friends and neighbors, and Mariah and I bowed our heads and said, "Amen." Neither of us grew up in Christian families. The blessing was a new custom for us, and one that we came to appreciate, although we were more likely to feel thankful to the animal for giving us meat, the earth for growing the vegetables, and the sun for ripening the wine grapes.

In the days and weeks to come, we had more meals with the Thompsons, more sunset cocktails at their house or ours. In a gentle, easygoing, incredibly kind and generous way, they took us under their wing and helped us feel less overwhelmed by our circumstances. Louie brought over his backhoe and scraped the remaining weeds and vines out of our vegetable garden, saving us many hours of labor. His Mexican laborers came over and mowed our grass with his riding lawnmower. When I offered to pay for this service, Louie said, "Naw. We'll keep your grass cut for the rest of the year, as a Southern hospitality thing." Considering that we had two acres of grass that needed cutting once a week, this was no small gesture.

Cathy was concerned about our lack of furniture. She hunted through her storage areas, and produced a couch, two armchairs, two wing-back chairs, two beds for the spare rooms, a butcher's block kitchen table, and four kitchen chairs. "Y'all can have this stuff on permanent loan, for as long as you need it," she said. "And I noticed y'all just have the one vehicle. That's going to get inconvenient out here, so until you get a second vehicle, I want you to drive our Envoy whenever you need to. I'll show you where the keys are. Just think of it as your second car."

That floored us. Mariah said, "I thought Republicans were supposed to be stingy and mean-spirited. No liberal has ever given me the keys to their car, or a whole bunch of furniture."

Then John Newcomb, a wealthy farmer living in a big house four miles away, came over with a bottle of Glenlivet and a silver ice bucket as housewarming gifts. The ice bucket was engraved with the original name of our house: Gum Grove. He must have noticed all the wood-burning stoves in the house, because a few days later his "help," as the term went for laborers, arrived in one of John's Cadillac Escalade pickup trucks towing a cord of split oak wood on a trailer.

I helped them unload and stack it, and it made them extremely uncomfortable. They wouldn't look at me, and my attempts at conversation stalled out amid mumbles, awkwardness, and mutual incomprehension. I could barely understand a word of what they said, and my British accent was giving them equal difficulties. Plus, they seemed to think it strange, or perhaps wrong, that a white man in a plantation house wanted to stack wood with them and chat with them like equals.

At the end of those long, hot, itchy summer days, Mariah and I would crawl under the mosquito net with sweating tumblers of iced bourbon, and compare our welts and pustules. As the mosquitoes furred over the windowpanes, and the mice gnawed on the walls, and the coyotes howled, and the owls carried on three-way conversations, we sipped our drinks and puzzled over the mysteries of our new homeland. How could the races be so separate and yet so close? The Thompsons had real love and respect for many of the black people who had worked for them, but they didn't appear to have black friends who came over for dinner. They entrusted their daughters into the maternal care of a black woman, but they wouldn't allow them to have black boyfriends. Further complicating things, we couldn't help loving the Thompsons, while disagreeing with some of their views, and they seemed to love us back.

When I left on a magazine assignment, to boost our flagging finances, Cathy wouldn't hear about Mariah staying in our house by herself. Mariah had admitted that she'd probably get scared, especially if she heard a truck coming down the levee in the middle of the night. Cathy said, "That's not going to happen. I've made up the bed in the spare room, and we're not calling it that any more. It's Mariah's room now."

Martha came down to Pluto for a visit, took stock of the situation, and explained what was really happening. "You get it, right?" she said. "Land is family here. You can't just move to the Delta like you'd move to a new neighborhood or a new city. You can't separate the land from the families that have lived on it for generations. Y'all are about the only people in the Delta who aren't related to anyone else, except you kinda are now."

"How do you mean?" I said.

"Cathy has basically adopted Mariah as a fourth daughter. You're part of our family now. And we have a shadow family that's black. It goes deeper than Lucy and Monk. It used to be that the black people here named their children after the white landowners. Now it's happening the other way around. My son Joe is named after a black man called Joseph Newton. You'll have to ask my dad about him."

Chapter 3

Joseph Brake

I WAS NAKED in the hallway one morning, heading for the shower, when I heard a powerful engine getting louder and closer. Through the front door glass, I saw a small plane flying insanely low to the ground and aiming straight at me. I hopped behind a bookcase. I watched transfixed as the plane got ready to smash through the front door and fly down the hall. At the last possible moment, it reared up to clear the porch and the roof, and behind it a long misty spray settled on the GMO cornfield in front of the house.

The crop duster pilot, or ag pilot as they prefer to be called, banked around in a tight circle, skimming the treetops along the Yazoo River, and laid down another stripe of chemicals next to the last one. Again he looked all set to fly under the porch eaves. It was like a scene from a Hitchcock movie—isolated old farmhouse, small aggressive plane, bucolic location strafed by poison gas attack. Within a few moments, there was a foul taste on my tongue, and it stayed there for several hours.

The cotton field behind the house required even more spraying with herbicides, insecticides, fertilizers, and then defoliants to burn away the leaves of the cotton plants, and expose the fluffy white bolls for the harvesting machines. We had been warned about all this in advance, but nothing brought it home like that vile cloying acrid taste in your mouth, a taste that makes you want to spit out your saliva rather than swallow it.

In the midst of all this petroleum-fueled, poison-laced, genetically engineered state-of-the-art modern agriculture was our modest haven of lawns, ponds, trees, and gardens. The Delta is so drenched in farm chemicals that it's impossible to grow anything that could be certified organic, but Mike and Beth had raised fruits and vegetables here without using commercial insecticides and weed killers, and we were intending to do the same.

Rather than spray poison on the rapidly encroaching poison ivy, we put on rubber gloves and carefully pulled it out by hand. We boiled endless pans of water to pour on the fire ant mounds, rather than sprinkling them with an evil-smelling powder like our neighbors. When we got back to the vegetable beds, ten days after Louie's backhoe rode off into the sunset, they were carpeted with thousands of new weeds and vine sprigs, and I began to understand what the farmers were up against in their fields.

Mariah developed her love of gardening in Tucson, where the weeds were sparse, and the insects few. If you kept your soil well watered and fertilized, growing vegetables didn't take a lot of effort, and it had been one of her main sources of relaxation and pleasure. Here it was a grim battle against remorseless enemies, and she didn't have the time or energy to keep it up. She was busy now with the final semesters of her online master's degree, and increasingly frustrated with our rustic Internet connection.

So I ended up doing most of the weeding, and to keep my sanity,

I developed a way of tuning into the birdsong. There were always mockingbirds, cardinals, blue jays, red-winged blackbirds, various woodpeckers, finches, hummingbirds, and at least a dozen other species chirping, squawking, and twittering away around the house. I learned to distinguish the different songs, and lose myself in their rhythms and melodies as my fingers pulled weeds automatically.

But it was still endless drudgery, and I began to fantasize about dousing everything with weed killer. I also fantasized about jumping in the truck, leaving it all behind, and living like a nomad again. I'd signed away the freedom of the road now, but on the other hand, I was living in a place where no one could remember ever seeing a cop. If I wanted to, I was free to piss naked off my porch, shoot guns, take drugs, drive drunk, and make all the noise I wanted. I had a river on one side, a lake on the other, plenty of woods to roam, and the freedom to go wherever I pleased without worrying about rules, restrictions, fences, or laws. Our generous neighbors had given us access to a vast area of land, at least twelve thousand acres, that was not regulated or policed in any way.

When the long task of weeding was finished, we mixed in organic fertilizer and compost to prepare the soil for planting. In the supercharged soil, a new crop of weeds grew even faster than the last one. We grew disheartened and lost motivation. We pretended the vegetable beds didn't exist, and never talked about them. Eventually, we rallied, weeded again, and got some kale, cabbage, cauliflower, radishes, and other winter vegetables planted.

IN THE LULLS between crop dustings, it was easy to forget that the Delta was covered in toxins. Frogs and toads hopped all over the roads, and sang all night. Dragonflies refracted the sunlight through their art-deco wings, and the insects were so thick at night that they pitter-pattered on the truck windshield like raindrops. Raccoons and possums wandered up on the porch. Armadillos, as Cadi had warned, rooted up the flower beds and excavated many ugly ankle-twisting holes in the lawns. Snakes slithered away, disappeared under the house, swam through the ponds. One managed to climb up the back door frame and drape itself horizontally across the screen door. I saw it there as I was reaching for the handle, and leapt back involuntarily with my heart in my throat.

Another snake spent an hour eating a small green tree frog in a flower bed by the front porch. The frog was alive and emitting tiny screams at the beginning of this process. Everywhere life was teeming, fighting, killing, dying, rotting, breeding, gorging itself on the riches of the Delta's biomass. The coyotes looked huge compared to their scrawny Western cousins. So did the bobcats, raccoons, and hawks.

We soon learned to distinguish the cottonmouths. They were the fat, black, menacing snakes with viper heads. Instead of slithering away, they would coil up and flash open their mouths, which were bright white on the inside. "They mad when they wake up in the morning," said Albert Johnson, one of John Newcomb's tractor drivers. I left the other snakes alone, on the theory that they would keep the rodent population down, but the cottonmouths scared me, and I kept a garden hoe around the porch for severing their heads.

When we started letting Savanna off the leash, she immediately went charging into thickets, woodpiles, tall grass, ditch banks—all the places where she was most likely to run into a snake. It seemed only a matter of time before she'd come back with a grotesquely swollen head. The neighbors said most dogs would survive a cottonmouth bite, laying up in misery for a week or so, and that coyotes and alligators were a more serious danger.

In the woods along the Yazoo River, where immense old cypress trees stood with their knobby knees protruding from the swamp water, alligators floated motionless, or sunned themselves on logs, slipping into the water as you approached. I walked slowly and nervously in the woods, scanning the ground for snakes, trying not to brush against the thorny vines or poison ivy, wary of hornets, red wasps, yellow jackets, trying to take in the sheer quantity of visual information all around me. I often startled whitetail deer. I found it impossible to picture myself pointing a gun at one of these beautiful creatures and pulling the trigger, but Mariah and I had made the intellectual decision to start hunting them when deer season came around in November.

Neither of us had any desire to kill a deer. But we were short of money, we both loved eating meat, and the factory-farmed meat in the Delta supermarkets didn't taste nearly as good as the organic meat we were used to. Nor did we like supporting the cruelty of industrial meat production, or consuming all the hormones and antibiotics that were fed to the animals. We could drive an hour and fifteen minutes to Jackson, and buy good quality pork and beef there. Or we could walk ten minutes into the woods, shoot a deer, skin it, gut it, and see if we both still loved eating meat.

HUNTING HAD BEEN a lifelong passion for Mike Foose, and he had very definite ideas on how it should be done. He was an old-fashioned purist, firmly opposed to all the high-tech gear and gadgetry so popular with the modern American hunter.

"Hunting is a way to participate more deeply in the natural world than you could do otherwise," he said. "That is my unfashionable view, at any rate, and the more gear you have, the more you separate yourself from the natural world. And the more you stack the odds in your favor, the less skill and knowledge you need to have.

Sometimes I'll take only one bullet into the woods, because that's all a good hunter should need."

He advised me to get a Ruger .22 rifle with a telescopic scope, because Ruger still makes guns in the classic style he prefers. Once I could shoot accurately at targets, I should then upgrade to a more powerful deer rifle with the same type of design and scope. But before he would take me into the woods with a gun, there were many other things I needed to know and understand.

He met me at the house one morning, and we put on our rubber boots and sprayed ourselves down with bug juice. His white beard was immaculately trimmed as always, and his thin white hair was neatly combed across his sun-reddened scalp. His eyes were lively and bright behind his horn-rimmed glasses, and he walked with a jaunty stride for a man in his late sixties, snapping the fingers on his right hand. He spoke with a genteel Mississippi accent. The vowels were long with a Southern swerve, the diction precise, and there was an obvious pleasure taken in the sound of words and the music of language.

We went down the levee to a small cemetery, where the black families that had lived on the plantation still buried their dead under a big oak tree. The graves were freshly tended and decorated with wreaths of plastic flowers and white plastic canes. Mike owned a stretch of woods across the levee from the cemetery, and he called it Joseph Brake.

Before I could ask, he said, "Joseph was a black man who worked for my grandmother, and he was more of a father to me than my own daddy was. He taught me all about hunting and fishing and the woods. I revered that man while he was alive, and I revere his memory, so I named my woods after him. Some of what Joseph taught me is what I want to pass on to you."

Those words hung in the air for a moment.

"This is the same Joseph that Martha's son is named after?" I asked.

"That's right. Joseph Newton."

I had heard around Pluto that Mike's father was a bad drunk, that scenes of Tennessee Williams–style drama had taken place in the house, and that Joseph had found a way to step through the racial politics involved and look after Mike. I didn't know Mike well enough to delve into that yet, but it seemed typical of the Delta that an instructional nature walk in the woods should be so deeply shadowed by racial complexity and alcoholic family drama.

"What's a brake?" I asked.

"*Brake* is an old word still used around here, and it describes a low-lying piece of woods with a slough running through it."

"And a slough?" I said, pronouncing it *slew* as he had.

"It's a body of water that might dry up in the summer, and usually has cypress trees or tupelo gums growing in it."

There were many terms in the Delta to describe wet swampy places. A deadening was a drowned hardwood forest. A bayou, pronounced *bayo*, was a stagnant or slow-moving body of water connecting to a larger body of water. An oxbow was an old meander abandoned by a river that had changed course, and it often had cypress trees in it. A true swamp was bigger than any of these. And a true Deltan didn't use the word *flood*. When rivers overwhelmed the levees and inundated the land, that was "high water"—not a natural disaster, but something within the range of expectations.

Mike imparted this knowledge while walking briskly along the edge of the slough, unconcerned by a cottonmouth that flashed its fangs at him. He was intently focused on the trees, and started pointing out different leaf shapes and bark patterns. This was a water oak, a sycamore, a sweet gum, a sassafras. This was a hackberry, known colloquially as the scaly-bark tree. That was a button willow, and nobody knew why the cypress trees grew their knobby outlying knees. They were either to stabilize the tree in the wet muddy ground, or a way for the tree to get more oxygen. The scientists couldn't tell.

Then he turned my attention to the ground, showing me a muddy groove worn by otters sliding into the water, the handlike footprints of a raccoon, an armadillo's burrow, a willow stump gnawed off by a beaver. All this was important knowledge for a deer hunter, since his aim was to become part of these woods and conceal himself here. The deer had left plenty of useful information in their heart-shaped tracks on the muddy ground. A good tracker could tell how fast they had been moving, and how long ago, and it was easy to see which paths and trails the deer traveled regularly, although these would change at different times of year, and according to different water levels in the slough.

Mike showed me where the bucks had scraped their antlers against trees, scoring the bark, and where deer had made their day-beds, flattening down a circle in tall grass. He talked about the extraordinary keenness of their senses. A whitetail deer can hear an acorn fall into the leaf litter fifty yards away, and know what it is. They can see a hunter's eye blink at the same distance. And only bears have a more sensitive nose. "You really have to pay attention to the wind, because it'll carry your scent to them a quarter mile away," he said.

When Mike was a boy, roaming the woods with Joseph Newton, they mostly hunted squirrels. "There were hardly any deer back then," he said. "They'd been hunted out. Now they're everywhere. Folks aren't as hungry, I guess, and by and large they respect the game laws. But squirrel hunting, that'll really teach you the woods and how to be patient. Me and Joseph would be out all day, in any kind of weather. It was such a privilege to spend so much time with him."

I said to Mike that I was having trouble getting a handle on race relations around here. How was it that such close bonds sometimes formed between black and white in a place so notorious for racism and segregation? Did he agree that in the South whites didn't mind how close blacks got, so long as they didn't get too high socially and economically, and that in the North, it was the other way around?

"Oh boy," he said. "You know, I've been thinking about these things all my life, and I can't say that I've arrived at any clear answers yet. I wish you luck on that one, I really do."

I WENT DOWN to the hardware store in Yazoo City to buy myself a gun. As usual, men in camouflage and work clothes were standing around by the cash register, drawling away about the size of the things they had killed lately. The people that owned the store were sitting on a bench with their dog. I was already a regular customer, and the young teenage daughter rushed up to me. "Will you say banana like you say it?" she implored.

I obliged her, not for the first time, with an exaggerated, "Ba-*nahhh*-ner." She burst out into peals of laughter, and said, "Do it again!"

"You should put me in a cage out front," I said. "Put up a sign saying, 'Five dollars, listen to the Englishman talk.' We'll split the profits fifty-fifty."

"Nah," she said. "They won't go five bucks. Fifty cents maybe."

I was a novelty item in the Delta, where nearly everyone has deep family roots, and knows everyone else. People in stores would hear my accent, ask where I'm from, and start beckoning for their spouses, "Now how in the *hail* did you end up down here? Honey, get over here. This fella is from—weird-jew say you're from? That's right. London, Angland. Welcome to the Delta! We're proud to have you here."

The guns were over in the far corner of the store, past the barbecue grills and chainsaws, the hunting clothes, fishing lures, scented candles, lotions and picture frames for the ladies, and the display of doe estrus packaged in fake wine bottles. It made an amusing party gift and drew in the bucks just like doe estrus packaged any other way.

At the gun counter, a pleasant, efficient man named Jim fed my information into a computer, then punched his iPhone to talk to someone in Quantico, Virginia, who verified my information and confirmed that I had no felonies or history of mental illness. "So that's a pro-ceed?" said Jim, punching in a code. Then he swiped my credit card and that was that, no license required to own a gun in Mississippi. It took about five minutes to buy a semiautomatic* Ruger .22 rifle and two different boxes of bullets, "one for plinking, one for varmints," as Jim explained it.

Buying a gun was so much easier than getting a Mississippi driver's license. The nearest DMV was thirty-five miles away in Greenwood, next to a Shoney's restaurant with a burned-out *S* in its neon sign, so it read "honey's." The first time I went there, the electricity was out at the DMV, although not at the Shoney's. I walked into the small, shabby, gloomy building, stood around for a while, asked the staff what was happening, and met with shrugs, murmurs, "ain't no tellin'."

I came back a few days later. A large African-American state trooper sat at a desk behind a numbered-ticket dispenser, telling a woman that it was just as important to whup a dog as whup a child, even though it wasn't specified in the Bible. "But it's the same thing," he said. "Spare the rod, and that dog be acting just like that child you ain't whupped."

---

*The term semiautomatic is widely misunderstood by gun control advocates, so let me be clear. A semiautomatic weapon has a clip full of bullets. After shooting one round, the next one loads itself into the chamber automatically. It does not fire a burst of bullets like a fully automatic weapon. You have to pull the trigger every time.

I stepped up in front of him. "Take a number," he said. "Take a seat and fill out the form." The form was a blurry photocopy of a form that had already been photocopied many times over the decades. Instead of race or ethnicity, it asked for my color. As I watched the officer send people up to the window, I realized that the numbered tickets were just for show. He wasn't calling out the numbers, or keeping track of them. He just pointed to the person he thought was next in line.

When it was my turn, a bored-looking woman asked for proof of address. I gave her an electricity bill and a printout of my online bank statement, since I hadn't received my first paper statement in the mail yet. "Uh-uh," she said. "I can't use this. I need a real bank statement, or something else. Ain't you got no water bill?"

"No ma'am," I said, practicing my Southern honorifics. "Our water comes from a well."

"Well, I don't know then."

I waited two weeks for the paper bank statement to arrive, and went back up to Greenwood. I filled out another blurry form, took another meaningless number. The same police officer was there, talking about a dog he'd had to shoot. A different woman was working behind the counter. "US citizen?" she asked, pointing out where I had filled in "Kuala Lumpur, Malaysia," as my place of birth.

"Yes ma'am," I said.

"Where your naturalization papers?" she said.

"I don't have them with me. But I have my Arizona driver's license, my Social Security card, and my US passport."

"Uh-uh. I need your naturalization papers."

I came back the next day with my certificate of naturalization. The lights were flickering in the building. All the computers were down. I asked one of the technicians working on them if it was worth waiting. He got up from what he was doing, stared at me, shrugged, didn't say a word. Two days later, I went back to the DMV and got my Mississippi driver's license.

It was all so familiar from Latin America, Africa, and the Caribbean: the collapsing infrastructure, the intermittent electricity supply, the air of lassitude and disorganization, the ancient forms. It brought back memories of multiple trips to the visa office in Bujumbura, in the small African country of Burundi. I was also reminded of Britain in the 1970s, when nothing worked properly, the tea break was sacrosanct, and an obstructive time-wasting surliness prevailed at every interface between institutions and the public. But I'd never come across anything like it in America before.

Chapter 4

Wing Shooter

THE PLUTO DOVE hunt was the first gender-segregated social event of Mariah's life. She joined the ladies at Cathy Thompson's house and felt like she'd plunged into the deep end of Southern womanhood— the excited chorus of accents, the sporty outfits, a lot more makeup than she was used to, especially when paired with camo shorts. The ladies were welcoming, with a few exceptions, and highly organized. Mountains of food were already cooked, wrapped, and ready for transportation to the dove field. Coolers were stocked with ice, beer, Cokes, bottles of water. The women were now drinking Bloody Marys—"Bloodies," in Delta parlance—and avidly discussing *50 Shades of Grey*, which Mariah had not read.

I parked my small Toyota pickup among the big Fords and Chevys at the Pluto tractor shed. The men were standing outside in a rough circle, and the mood was outdoor masculine formal: squared shoulders, firm handshakes, curt greetings, no leaning or slouching.

I was the only man there without any camouflage clothing. Mike Foose hadn't arrived yet. Neither had William Thompson, Louie's older brother, who had invited me on the hunt and was loaning me a shotgun. I knew none of these other men, and listening to them drawl away about hunting doves, ducks, deer, wild hogs, gators, with some college football talk thrown in and a few laconic jabs at Obama, I too felt like I was drowning in the deep end of the Deep South.

I had never handled a shotgun before, and I had ambivalent feelings about killing innocent creatures. With my new .22 rifle, I had shot an armadillo, failed to kill it, failed to find it after it flipped over and skittered into a brush pile, and then lain awake half the night, knowing the poor wounded animal was probably dying in agony less than sixty yards from my bed. Two nights later, with fifty fresh holes dug in my yard, I shot another armadillo and killed it cleanly. The following night, I shot two more armadillos. One of them escaped wounded, and this time I didn't feel so bad.

Armadillos were an invasive, destructive, ungainly species that had waddled over here from Texas in the last thirty years or so. Mourning doves, on the other hand, were pretty little birds with soft cooing songs and acrobatic flight patterns. I was here because they were supposed to taste good, and because I wanted to get used to the idea of hunting for meat. Also, I'd heard that the Labor Day dove hunt is an important social ritual in the South and nowhere more so than in the Mississippi Delta—"the South's South," as some call it.

Charles Henry Shelton, wearing full camouflage and Oakley-style sunglasses, was the president of the local electric power company. He spoke with a particularly slow and precisely enunciated drawl, and there was something sad, strange, and charming about him. I told him I enjoyed the newsletter that the power company sent out every month, with recommended books to read about Mississippi, events listings, recipes, and gardening tips.

"Oh, we're going to send you something in the mail every month, I guarantee," he quipped. "We just want you to be comfortable in your home—comfortable at any price."

He asked if I'd ever dove hunted in England. "No, it's my first time shooting at any kind of bird," I said. "Where I come from, hunting is really for the upper crust. In America it's more open to everybody."

There was an awkward silence. Men repositioned their boots, and looked off to the side. Intending to compliment America's democratic spirit, I had just insulted these fine Southern gentlemen by insinuating they were less than upper crust. I often forgot how hierarchical the South is compared to the egalitarian West, mainly because I was so preoccupied by race. Finally, one man grinned with tobacco-stained teeth, and broke the silence. "Well shoot," he said. "This rightcheer is where folks like me get to hunt with the bigshots."

The dove hunt marked the end of summer, even though temperatures were still in the nineties, and the beginning of hunting and football season. It was also an occasion for landowners to show hospitality to friends, relatives, business partners, coworkers, and acquaintances who were not fortunate enough to own a large spread of prime Delta farmland, and set aside a few acres for dove hunting.

When we first arrived on Pluto, we marveled at the beauty of the sunflower fields behind the catfish ponds. Martha told us that no bride at a Pluto wedding ever looked prettier than when she had her picture taken in the sunflower field. We got the idea that the sunflowers were grown for aesthetic reasons, or maybe to sell the flowers. Then we discovered that the sunflowers were planted because their seeds attract doves for the hunters. When I told people in New York and London about this, they would invariably say, "Isn't the dove the bird of peace?" To which I could only reply, "Not in Mississippi."

Mike Foose arrived, and I was glad to see a familiar face, and note that he wasn't wearing any camo either. "Well, well," he said, shaking my hand. "Are you ready to try your hand at some wing shooting?" Then William Thompson pulled up in a big white truck. He was a successful banker in Jackson and in charge of Pluto plantation,* which had been in his family for four generations. He was more straight-laced than his brothers, but with the same fine generous spirit and quick sense of humor. He unzipped a gun case and produced a gorgeously engraved Browning shotgun, made in Belgium. He showed me how to load and shoot it, and gave me three boxes of shells, a bag for dead birds and empty shell casings, and a pair of earplugs. Then he got back in his truck, and we all convoyed out to the dove field and parked on a levee that bordered it.

The sunflowers were dead and wilted now, and lanes had been cut through them by a supercharged lawnmower known as a bush hog. Mike Foose had brought me a vital piece of dove-hunting equipment: an empty five-gallon bucket to sit on while waiting for the birds. "Wing shooting is fast, it's exciting, it's more instinctual in the way you aim and shoot," he said. "You swing your barrel in line with the bird's flight, and you lead a dove."

"What does that mean?" I said.

"Don't aim directly at them. They're too fast. Find the magical distance ahead of them and aim there."

We all spread out, concealed ourselves among the wilted stalks, and sat down on our buckets. Some of the hunters had the new cushioned, camo-patterned buckets that were being sold in the hunting stores, which were as numerous in the Delta as liquor stores or banks. We waited for about twenty minutes, sweating in the heat. Then two doves came whipping in, and a man across the field stood up and took a shot at them. He missed with both barrels. More doves appeared,

---

*The word *plantation*, with its connotations of slavery, was going out of style in the Delta. Landowners usually talked about their "farms" instead.

coming in twos and threes, diving and zigzagging, making a small twittering sound that I assumed was an alarm call, because all around me now was the percussive boom of shotguns.

I missed the first three doves that came my way, and hit the fourth. It fell to the ground still fluttering its wings in a wounded death panic. I swallowed my horror, and following Mike's example, I picked it up by the head and twirled it around to break its neck. Its feathers were so soft, its beauty so marred by blood and death.

I felt sad, upset, shaky, and proud all at the same time, and it occurred to me that these were boyhood emotions in Mississippi, where parents start their children hunting young. It's normal for boys, and increasingly for girls, to kill their first deer at the age of six or seven, and sometimes even younger. Most of these men were over the age of fifty now, and "fun" was the word they kept using to describe the feeling of shooting doves out of the sky.

The women appeared on four-wheelers, with hats and sun visors and cocktails in their hands, one with a baby on her knee. "Hey y'all," they called out. "How about a cold beer? We got Cokes and waters too." I took two bottles of water and guzzled them straight down. It was ninety-something in the shade, but there was no shade in the dove field. The sun was a tyrant who reigned cruel and unopposed in a vast blue sky.

The doves made such small, fast-moving unpredictable targets, a smudge of grey darting and veering, but I managed to bring down two more, and I started to feel the excitement of it, the quickening of the blood, the total absorption in what I was trying to do. When I missed six birds in a row, I grew frustrated. The doves could break and change direction with astonishing agility, especially when you led them too far, and the lead shot whistled through the air just in front of them. I sensed their fear and panic, and yet I kept on shooting at them, and killed two more.

They stopped flying in the late afternoon with the sun fat and malevolent, still beaming out shimmering waves of heat. The women had set up picnic tables in the shade of some trees on the levee, and the men headed over there, looking red-faced, sweaty, tired, and happy. One paused at his truck to change into a pair of après-hunt camo loafers.

The tables were loaded with liquor and wine, and platters of grilled marinated flank steak, served with rolls and horseradish, corn salad, potato salad made with olive oil so it wouldn't spoil in the heat, a salad of raw vegetables marinated in oil and vinegar. Three different cheeses had been cut into cubes, for snacking on with crackers, olives, grapes, slices of venison summer sausage, boiled peanuts, and watermelon wedges. Mariah had made mushrooms stuffed with sausage, garlic, Parmesan cheese, sage, and red pepper flakes, an unusual dish for the Mississippians but one they ate with relish. No one was gluten free, lactose intolerant, vegetarian, or vegan.

THE FACT THAT Mariah and I were living together, but not married, produced some socially awkward moments at the dove hunt party. One woman tried to put a brave face on it by saying, "I think it's so exciting that y'all are just dating."

When it came to courtship and marriage, the white Delta was still in the 1950s. The gentry sent their sons and daughters off to university with the expectation that they'd find someone suitable to marry, and soon after graduation, they would throw them the most lavish weddings they could possibly afford. So they felt bad for Mariah that I hadn't made an honest woman out of her. Or they thought that she had no morals. Or they worried that she would assume that's what they were thinking. "Basically I'm a harlot and you're a rogue," Mariah whispered in my ear.

In Tucson or New York or London, we were boyfriend and girl-friend, but down here those terms were usually applied to younger people in more casual relationships. To call Mariah my girlfriend ran the risk of belittling and insulting her. And the word *partner*, which I disliked because it made a romantic relationship sound like a law firm, hadn't made it down to the Delta. So when Charles Henry invited me to have dinner sometime, he said, "And do please bring your . . . friend."

William Thompson's son Michael arrived, taking a break from harvesting. He ran the day-to-day farming on Pluto, and Martha jokingly called him "the face of industrial chemical corporate agri-culture," because Michael had such a sweet face and kind disposition. I talked to him about farming, which he described as a high-stakes gambling operation. You put down a ton of money for the patented GMO seeds, which were priced by Monsanto to squeeze the Ameri-can farmer as much as possible without putting him out of business. The same seeds were sold for far less in other countries. Tractors now came with a suite of computer systems which increased your yield just enough to justify the astronomical price tag, and the ex-pense of fixing them when they went wrong, which they did with maddening frequency. Then came the expense of all the herbicides, pesticides, and defoliants, which Michael didn't like using, but his crops would be ruined without them. Like many people in the Delta, he pointed out that the chemicals weren't nearly as toxic as they used to be, and if they were as bad as some people said, everyone around here would be dead.

Then there were the crop prices, which rose and fell according to international events, the Chinese economy, and many other factors. Ninety percent of the cotton grown in Mississippi was shipped to China and turned into clothes, and many of those clothes were then shipped back to America. And finally there was the weather, which was always a gamble in this region of hurricanes, tornadoes, floods, and monster thunderstorms. A few years ago, he said, a combination of bad weather and low prices put them within a few days of losing everything, when the price of corn picked up unexpectedly and saved them.

"What does that feel like?" I asked.

"You feel sick in a way that you've never felt sick before. I kept saying to myself, 'What else would you like to do except farming?' And there wasn't anything. Luckily I'm still farming, but every year it's the same big-ass gamble."

His father William disagreed. "Sometimes in a bad year it looks real tough, but our family's been farming here for four generations. If it was that big of a gamble, we wouldn't still be here."

"I guess so, but we've come awful damn close a few times," said Michael.

The après-hunt party was winding down now. Women were packing up what was left of the food, and all up and down the levee came the sound of big American truck doors slamming shut, followed by tires crunching gravel. William Thompson showed us how to clean the doves I had shot. Mariah, who is dainty and squeamish about some things, had no problem snapping the wings off, and ripping out the breasts with her fingers. William added three ziplock bags full of cleaned dove breasts to the five birds I had shot. "I wantchawl to have these and build up your game freezer," he said. "They're good eating, but not if you overcook them."

The usual way of cooking dove breasts here is to wrap them in bacon and put them on the grill, or batter and fry them. In fact, this was the first rule of Delta cuisine: if it can't be battered and fried, cook it with fatty pig meat. Down at Clancy's in Yazoo City, the house special was a battered deep-fried hamburger. That horrified us, but we'd grown to love the battered deep-fried dill pickle slices, and what they call "Mexican okra," which are pickled jalapeno slices given the same treatment, and excellent with cold beer.

Our culinary habits and instincts, however, were shaped by the Italian tradition, so we rubbed salt, pepper, and olive oil on the dove breasts, grilled them over a wood fire until they were medium rare, and then hit them with a squirt of lemon juice. We put a simple salad next to them, and poured a glass of white wine.

Biting into it, the first meat I'd ever killed, was a profound and extremely tasty moment. Mariah, who was raised vegetarian and used to date vegans and raw foodists, looked at me across the table, her face suffused with pleasure and happiness. She said, "Honey, when are you going to buy a shotgun and get us some more of these?"

ON MONDAY MORNING I went to the bank in Yazoo City. I had just walked through the door when a young man in a suit rushed up to me with an excited smile on his face. Had I met him before? I didn't think so. "Nice shooting, sir!" he said. "Heard you got five of them with one box of shells." Then Howard the mortgage specialist came out of his office to shake my hand, and say, "Well congratulations, I hear you're a wing shooter now."

Butch Gary had also heard the news. "That's wonderful," he said. "You know, I love to dove hunt, and fine English shotguns are a weakness of mine. Normally I would have been right there next to where you were shooting, in a spot they call Butch's corner, but unfortunately I couldn't make it this year. What brings you into the bank?"

"Well, Butch, we made a gentleman's agreement, and it's high time that I honored my end of it. I'm free all week if you want to have dinner."

"Great!" he said. "Why don't you come over to our house on Friday, and please do bring your . . . Mariah."

Butch arranged for us to rendezvous with another dinner guest in Yazoo City, and then come out to his house together. "Sam Olden is his name, and he's a real unusual character for around here, or anywhere else I would think," he said. Since Sam was ninety-three years old, Butch was probably hoping that we could give him a ride, but that wasn't the way it worked out.

At 5:45 we knocked on the door of a freshly painted Victorian house in downtown Yazoo City and were greeted by the most alert and vigorous ninety-three-year-old that either of us had ever met, or imagined possible. He had a good head of white hair combed straight back, a slightly rakish smile, monogrammed French cuffs on a crisply ironed white shirt worn with khakis and loafers. He shook my hand and grasped me with surprising strength by the shoulder.

"It's so mah-vellous that you're here," he said in a refined Southern accent. "You know I spent three years in Nigeria in an almost entirely British milieu. I must say, I thoroughly enjoyed my immersion, and I believe it has affected my speech patterns even now. I still enunciate far more clearly than most people around here, and of course I adore Tennyson and Wordsworth and the other English poets of that era. And you Mariah, from Tucson, which is a charming town that I've been able to visit on several occasions. Do please come inside. I'll show you a few things in the house that you might find of interest. Unfortunately, my collection of pre-Incan Peruvian pottery is on loan to the Museum of Art in Jackson. Are you familiar with *huacos*?"

We confessed that we were not, and he gave us a short lecture on the history and iconography of these fascinating clay figures. Then he showed us an oil painting on the wall, depicting a robed figure. "This is Peruvian, but the Spanish influence is strong. You can see the honeyed sweetness of a Murillo, and the sweep of an El Greco." In the kitchen were some copper lamps that he had picked up in Algiers when he lived there in the early 1960s, and a Talavera tile plate to remind him of his years in Madrid. I notice a framed certificate recognizing Sam B. Olden as a former president of the Mississippi Historical Society.

With no difficulty whatsoever he climbed a steep set of stairs to an upstairs room where he housed the bulk of his books, and some other *objets* and mementoes, including a letter signed by Queen Isabella of Spain in 1501. "I bought it in New York," he said. "I assume that you, Richard, as a cultured man, at least read some Spanish."

He read out some of the letter in flawless lisping Castilian. It authorized payment for some straw mats for the Alhambra palace in Granada. He dropped *bon mots* in French, Italian, and German. In the course of his monologue, some obscure fact would occasionally slip his mind, and he would look to me, as a well-traveled man of the world, to come up with it, "From Zamboanga you fly out over the Sula Sea to those little islands in that section of the Pacific, and I can't for the life of me remember their name. . . . and what's the name of that port city outside Perth? . . . I assume you're familiar with the history of the Swedish crown in the latter part of the 1700s. . . . and Bagan, of course, is one of the architectural wonders of the world, although I forget exactly how many pagodas . . ."

He'd had the most marvelous time living in Brazzaville, in what is now the Central African Republic, and would never forget meeting Albert Schweitzer at his hospital on the Ogooué River, or placing Eleanor Roosevelt's injured foot on a stool in New York City, and perhaps nowhere in the world was closer to his heart than Vienna. "As Butch has probably told you, I was with the CIA for a number of years, and I was in Vienna right after the war. The most marvelous city! You know, to this day, on New Year's Eve, I open a bottle of good champagne and listen to the Viennese symphony until I start to weep."

"Butch said only that you were an unusual character for around here," I said.

"Well, I suppose that's true, but Yazoo City has always been my home, and I love it here, and I have so many friends here, and many of them are in fact the children and grandchildren of my original friends."

"We should probably be going to Butch's," said Mariah. "Can we give you a ride, Sam?"

"Oh no, no, no, absolutely not," he said. "We'll go in my car."

He drove flawlessly on the winding country roads that took us through the hills, and he talked with enormous energy and enthusiasm the entire way, "Now Butch's wife is Neetsie, which is short for Juanita, and I knew her grandmother very well indeed. She was a great beauty and for the life of me, I cannot look at Neetsie without seeing her. The resemblance is remarkable. Ah, now there is a banker's house if ever I saw one."

It was a large and imposing house on a knoll with a great sweep of lawn and gardens. Butch came out of his carport with an amiable smile, and then we met Neetsie, a small, slim, attractive blonde with a calm, gentle, slightly ethereal air and bright blue eyes. She had baked three different desserts, which sat on the kitchen table looking like they belonged on the cover of a magazine, and set out nuts, olives, cheeses to snack on before dinner.

We all drank wine except Sam, who drained a large Scotch on the rocks, and then another, while delivering an incisive analysis of current events in Eastern Europe and a brief history of the Greek-Turkish conflict. I had to ask the obvious question, "Sam, how do you account for your vigor and sharpness at the age of ninety-three?"

"I still have enormous enthusiasm and a great deal of curiosity about the world," he said. "I rise quite late, and at ten a.m. I eat breakfast—bacon, sausage, grits, eggs, and English muffins, every day—then I read the *New York Times* on my iPad. When *The Economist* drops into my mailbox, I fall on it like a hungry lion. I have a great many friends of all ages, and apparently I've been blessed with good genes."

Neetsie called us through for dinner, and as we ate our steaks and roasted sweet potatoes, I told some stories from Mexico and Africa, to keep up my end of the gentleman's agreement that had allowed me to buy the house. Then Sam took charge of the conversation and told us about his time with Albert Schweitzer, and Norman Vincent Peale, and how he met his dear friend Eudora Welty, the great Mississippi novelist.

"I was mad for archaeology as a young man, and a group of us had driven to the *altiplano* in Mexico to look at ruins. We were on a rather remote country road when we saw another car with Mississippi license plates. It was Eudora Welty, and she'd just run over a shepherd boy. He had sustained some injuries, none too serious. Eudora was quite upset, and understandably surprised to meet some fellow Mississippians there . . ."

He had also been great friends with Willie Morris, the Yazoo City writer, and by the time he started telling those stories, it was getting late, and the rest of us were feeling tired. Somewhat reluctantly, Sam Olden was persuaded that it was time to go. We said our farewells and thank yous, and then, after a slight fumble getting out of the driveway in the dark, Sam drove us back to Yazoo City and bid us good night on his doorstep.

"Next time we'll have some Moët et Chandon champagne, and you'll have to meet my dear friend John."

On the road home to Pluto, Mariah and I felt pummeled and shell-shocked by the force of Sam's intellect. How was it possible that his short-term memory and grasp of current affairs was so much better than ours? "He knew all those presidents and prime ministers in Central Asia and the Caucasus," I said. "All the rivers and mountain ranges."

"I've never met anyone with a mind like that in my life," said Mariah. "At any age, let alone ninety-three."

"He never married?"

"No. Neetsie said it was because he was a 'bachelor.'"

"I see. He's not what you expect to find in a small town in Mississippi."

"I don't know what to expect anymore. It seems like every time I leave the house, something weird or wonderful happens."

Chapter 5

The Oncologist's Hitmen

IT WAS MARTHA who got me hooked on the local Delta newspapers. Even before I bought the house, she was sending me stories by email and calling up to discuss them on the phone, "I mean, where else are you going to find an unlicensed mortuary on a residential street? That is really keeping it Delta. Screw the license, we've got a big-ass needle and a bunch of embalming fluid right here. We'll get your loved one fixed up in the front room."

Another time she called up, and without preamble or hello, she said, "'Big Hungry Woman Found Wandering in Woods.'" I started to picture a distraught woman stumbling heavily through the thickets and swamps. Then Martha said, "Big Hungry is a little community near here, but all the same, isn't that the greatest headline? Because I bet she did get hungry wandering around in those woods. And around here, I wouldn't be a bit surprised if she was a plus-size gal."

Martha kept me up to speed on the Greenwood show-hog rapist, or the "Love Hog," as some were calling him. He got seven years in the state penitentiary on twelve counts of what she called "dating down the food chain," and the state criminal statutes defined as "unnatural intercourse." Then there were the fraud and embezzlement stories, which came in a steady stream—school superintendents taking kickbacks and hiring their relatives for fictitious jobs, public officials accepting bribes from undercover agents and contractors, hospice owners defrauding Medicare, a court clerk pocketing cash fines. "It's the Delta way," said Martha. "We have a real broad definition of free enterprise down here, and no one ever thinks they're going to get caught."

Normally she laced her news reports with irony and gallows humor, but one morning Martha called me up genuinely distraught and half-hysterical, "Oh my god! You're not going to—they shot two freaking *hitmen* in Lee Abraham's office! I was just talking to him right after the pawn shop monkey got burned up, and they've arrested stabbed-his-self-in-the-legs Dr. Smith for murder, and the whole thing is just so freaking *crazy* I can't even!"

That was my incomprehensible introduction to the most sensational crime story to hit Greenwood in many years. As Mike Foose put it, "Even by the standards of around here, that is truly a weird one." It was attached with all kinds of improbable subplots and bizarre spin-offs, but in essence, the police concluded it was a botched murder-for-hire scheme involving two of Greenwood's wealthiest, most prominent citizens, one of whom was consumed with an insane hatred for the other.

To fully appreciate why the town was so riveted by the case, it's necessary to take a slow cruise along Grand Boulevard, where the social elite lives in genteel Southern mansions that recall a bygone era, when cotton was king and Greenwood was its capital. The lawns and flower gardens are manicured to perfection. The sidewalks are shaded by majestic oak trees. Big luxury vehicles are parked in the driveways and garages, and the only black people around are maids, cooks, nannies, and gardeners.

The grandest house on Grand Boulevard is an imposing red-brick pile with flags and bunting unfurled from its balconies, and white columns flanking the front entrance. It looks something like a museum or an embassy, but it's the home of Lee Abraham, a lawyer, business entrepreneur, and political figure who lives here by himself, with sheets of bulletproof steel installed around his bedroom walls, and at least a dozen loaded firearms within easy reach.

A big stout bulldog of a man with swelling chins and a comb-over, Lee Abraham wears business suits with alligator skin cowboy boots. Folksy, garrulous and charismatic, he talks with the most or-nate, molasses-dripping, vowel-bending Mississippi drawl you can possibly imagine. But he's full-blooded Lebanese.

During its cotton prosperity in the late nineteenth and early twentieth century, the Delta attracted and nourished thriving popu-lations of Chinese, Jewish, Italian, Syrian, and Lebanese immigrants, and over time, many of their descendants have taken on the attitudes and manners of the white gentry. To hear a Chinese or Syrian grocery owner defending the Confederacy in a broad Mississippi accent is one of the many strange delights to be found in the region.

Catty-corner across Grand Boulevard from Lee Abraham's house, and a few doors down, is a more restrained and secluded man-sion belonging to the doctor who allegedly tried to murder him. Dr. Arnold Smith, now resident in the state mental asylum, was a mul-timillionaire oncologist who sang in the Episcopalian church choir and advertised his services on local and national television. A tall white man with silver hair, glasses, and a slightly protruding mouth, Dr. Smith specialized in late-stage cancers; many of his patients had been told by other doctors there was no hope.

He used the full range of traditional oncology techniques, with an emphasis on radiation, and his own special immune-strengthening cancer-fighting compounds. His commercials were slickly produced and featured upbeat testimonials from happily cured patients, many of them African-American. "If Dr. Smith can't cure it, ain't nobody can," says one joyful patient in his late middle age. "I feel better now than I did when I was twenty-five."

Some people thought he was a quack, or a fraud, but even now, after all that's happened and been revealed, most people in Greenwood still describe Arnold Smith as a first-rate cancer doctor, and everyone seems to know someone who was cured by him, or at least put in remission for longer than expected. But this is not to say they thought Dr. Smith was sane. His eccentricities were legendary, and the town was well accustomed to his delusional ravings.

On the Internet, you can still see some of the videos that he made, exposing the plots and schemes of his enemies. In one, he explains to the camera, and an increasingly uncomfortable elderly upholsteress sitting next to him, that expert thieves have been stealing his antique chairs and other household furnishings, and substituting them with worthless copies that they've had specially made in China. An entire maple-wood bedroom suite was removed while his family was on vacation, he insists, and replaced with an inferior look-alike. The motive of the thieves, he says, was to gain access to his papers, and make him sound crazy when he spoke out in public about what they were doing. Once he was discredited, they would then move in to take control of his cancer business.

"If you detailed the nature of these individual substitutions or thefts to the average person, they would begin to wonder whether you were telling the truth, or whether you were somehow not totally balanced in the brain," he says. "But that's the object of the type of skill I was up against. These people were not amateurs."

After falling out with his medical partner, Ed Rafique, Smith denounced him as a secret Muslim and international drug trafficker, who was plotting to take over the entire cancer business in northern Mississippi. And he repeatedly made wild, ranting, baseless accusations against Lee Abraham, accusing him of running an empire of child sex slavery, based on mind-control techniques he had learned with the Delta Illuminati, an organization that exists only in Dr. Smith's mind.

In another part of the country, perhaps, this sort of behavior might have damaged his credibility as a doctor, or got him investigated and disbarred from practicing medicine, but that didn't happen here. Several complaints about his mental competency were filed with the Mississippi Board of Medical Licensure, but the subsequent inquiry didn't go anywhere.

The prevailing view in Greenwood was that Dr. Smith was a little nuts but harmless. As one well-to-do Greenwood lady told me, "We rather enjoy our eccentrics down here, and nurture them with great care and affection, so long as they're no danger to themselves or other people. People enjoyed telling stories about Dr. Smith, and we thought he was saving lives at the cancer center. It never occurred to us that he would try to kill anyone."

THE ROOTS OF Dr. Smith's hatred for Lee Abraham are easy enough to trace. Abraham represented Smith's ex-wife Sara in a nasty, protracted, expensive divorce in the mid-1990s. During the course of it she accused him of sexually molesting two of his young daughters—Smith has nine children from two marriages—but prosecutors didn't find enough evidence to proceed with charges.

Hating your ex-wife's divorce attorney is common enough, but in Dr. Smith's case, hatred curdled into lunacy. He became convinced that Lee Abraham, a devout Catholic, was a secret Muslim plotting to destroy America and a crime boss running drugs and underage prostitutes. Both accusations were equally unfounded and absurd, but in Dr. Smith's unraveling mind, evidence was building all the time in his video collection.

On the streets of South Greenwood, the crumbling, pockmarked ghetto across the river and the railroad tracks from Grand Boulevard, Dr. Smith was widely known to be an easy mark. He would pay cash to any enterprising hustler who would come up to the cancer center, stand in front of a video camera, and recount all the heinous things that Lee Abraham had paid them to do, or had done himself to their young female relatives. A series of young women collected money too, by claiming that Abraham had forced them into unspeakable acts. It didn't matter that these claims were untrue. You could make up any old lie about Lee Abraham, and so long it was lurid and nasty, Dr. Smith would believe it and give you two or three hundred dollars.

Two weeks before the bullets started flying, there began a series of events that look in hindsight like the culmination of a long, slow-burning madness. In a blood-drenched shirt and pants, Dr. Smith staggered out of his car and into the emergency room at the Greenwood Leflore Hospital, where doctors found stab wounds and bruises on his legs, and another stab wound in his stomach. After getting treated, Smith went over to the offices of the *Greenwood Commonwealth*, rather than contacting the police. He showed his wounds to the editor and a reporter, who photographed them and published them the next day, along with Dr. Smith's version of what happened.

He said he'd been lured into a trap by a man who claimed to have compromising photographs of Lee Abraham. They arranged to meet on River Road at 6:00 p.m. When Smith looked at the photographs, he saw nothing incriminating and said he wasn't interested. The man then demanded Smith's wallet and pulled out a hammer—or so Smith told the newspapermen.

"He starts trying to hit me, and I keep thinking that I'm going to take a sock at this guy's face and sock his nose in," Smith said. "But then the next thing I know he pulls out this big ole long knife."

Smith said that he tripped and fell on his back in the street. The only way he could defend himself was by kicking, which led to the knife and hammer wounds on his legs. He described his assailant as a tall black man about thirty years old with blue tattoos covering both forearms. The assailant's plan, he said, was to cut him into pieces and feed him to the fishes.

After hearing this story, the newspapermen asked if perhaps the wounds might have been self-inflicted. Dr. Smith laughed at that suggestion. "You think I hammered on my legs too?" he said. The journalists ended up believing him. The assistant district attorney, Tim Jones, who went on to prosecute Dr. Smith, also doubted that these wounds were self-inflicted. But there were many people in Greenwood, including Martha and most of her friends, who found it all too easy to visualize their town's most prominent oncologist injecting himself with a painkiller and then stabbing himself violently in the legs.

Dr. Smith described it as an attempted assassination, and he accused Lee Abraham of masterminding it. He told the journalists to look at the timing. Just a few days previously, Smith had asked the local medical association to create a committee on child sex slavery, and the state medical association to investigate lawyers for ties to organized crime. He had targeted Lee Abraham with these proposals, and now Lee had answered him by sending a knife-wielding assassin.

Then Dr. Smith laid out the whole conspiracy in a two-and-a-half-page letter that he sent by certified mail to Mississippi governor Phil Bryant, with copies to all the Republicans in the legislature. "I am certain beyond reasonable doubt the assassin was a post-hypnotic delusional victim of Lee Abraham's Illuminati drug manipulation," he wrote. He went on to present "evidence" of Abraham's child prostitution ring: "Several virginal black females age 9 to 15 tell me they climbed into Lee's black truck, innocently drank his cool aid, passed out, and awakened naked with wet sore bottoms, deflowered, and were then told they were 'working for Lee now.'"

Needless to say, no action was taken by the governor or state Republicans.

LEE ABRAHAM WAS certainly a powerful and controversial figure in Greenwood, although no one but Dr. Smith thought he was a Muslim crime boss. In addition to his downtown law practice, Abraham owns a property management company, construction, trucking, and salvage companies, various farms, and Honest Abe's Donuts. His brother Sam, who wears similar boots and speaks with the same accent, is the chancery clerk and county administrator. The mayor of Greenwood, Carolyn McAdams, is an old friend and ally. Jim Hood, the Democratic attorney general for the state of Mississippi, is a close friend and hunting partner.

By the time the stabbing incident took place on River Road, Lee Abraham was already hearing whispers from the street that Dr. Smith was plotting to kill him. A few days later, he received a suspicious phone call from someone he didn't know. Later he found out it was Keaira Byrd, a local hustler with a criminal record for burglary and an arrest for armed robbery. Byrd wanted to meet Abraham after hours and show him some damning evidence regarding Dr. Smith. Abraham mentioned the call to Jim Hood, and Hood dispatched three armed investigators from the attorney general's office. They met at Lee Abraham's house and then rode with him to his law office on Market Street, where Abraham had agreed to meet Byrd. It was a Saturday night just after 7:30 p.m.

What happened next is disputed and unclear. When Martha first called me, she had just seen the rushed-out Sunday edition of the *Greenwood Commonwealth*. The front page headline read, "1 Slain at Abraham Law Office, 2 More Men Wounded in Shooting." The story said that two black males, one wearing a ski mask, entered Lee Abraham's law office around 8:30 p.m. and a gunfight ensued. One of the attorney general's investigators was wounded, and Keaira Byrd, twenty-three, was shot several times and killed. His accomplice, Derrick Lacy, twenty-five, was also shot but survived.

Just before dawn on Sunday morning, a convoy of police cars came down Grand Boulevard with their lights flashing, and parked outside Dr. Smith's house. The officers arrested him for conspiracy to murder Lee Abraham, who was standing on his balcony watching it all happen. Dr. Smith went quietly into custody and was taken away to the county jail.

There were two key pieces of evidence against him. One was an interview with the wounded Derrick Lacy, conducted on the helipad at the Greenwood Leflore Hospital before he was flown to Jackson for medical treatment. Lacy told a detective that he'd overheard a conversation on speakerphone, in which Dr. Smith had agreed to pay Byrd $20,000 to murder Lee Abraham. He also said that Byrd forced him to participate in the attempted murder.

The most damning piece of evidence came during a search of Dr. Smith's cancer center. Along with fourteen guns, boxes of ammunition, a three-part paperback book series entitled *Shariah: Threat to America*, and video and voice recording equipment, detectives found a poorly lit twelve-minute video recording, shot by hidden camera in Dr. Smith's office. It's impossible to make out the faces, but the voices indicate that Dr. Smith is talking to Keaira Byrd, and the subject sounds a lot like murder for hire.

"You have to get the twenty thousand dollars to your house, and when it's done, I'll let you know," says Byrd.

Dr. Smith wants proof before he'll pay. "Too many times I've dealt with you and had deceptions," he says. "You've got a cell phone. Take a fucking picture with a hole between his eyes."

AS MORE INFORMATION was released, the more confusing the story became. Keaira Byrd was carrying a MAC-11 machine pistol, with a janky-looking homemade gun sling fashioned out of a bedsheet, but Derrick Lacy was unarmed. If Lacy was there as a second hitman, why didn't he have a weapon? Then it was reported that Lacy had been shot three times, maybe more. Even allowing for the fear and adrenaline in a close-quarters gunfight, to repeatedly shoot an unarmed man sounded like execution to many people in Greenwood's black community, and a rumor spread that Lacy had been shot seven times in the back.

Workmen were patching up the bullet holes in Lee Abraham's law office when a group of thirty-eight African-American protestors gathered outside the fine old neo-Classical courthouse across the street. They were waving placards, dancing, and chanting, "I Am Lacy, I Am Byrd! No justice, no peace!" The protest was led by a college student with a name you couldn't make up: Duchess Dallas. She told the *Commonwealth* that they were demanding "equal treatment" for Lacy and Byrd, although it's unclear what she meant by that.

Keaira Byrd had entered a law office wearing a ski mask and holding a machine pistol. He was on videotape agreeing to kill Lee Abraham for $20,000, and on his cell phone, as if more incriminating evidence were needed, police found photographs of the ski mask, the MAC-11, the loaded magazine, the bedsheet on his bed, and the same bedsheet converted into a gun sling.

This did not deter the protestors from seeing Byrd as a victim, and they called on the local NAACP to investigate his shooting as a race and civil rights issue. The African-American congressman for the area, Bennie Thompson, citing the numerous complaints his office had received, wrote to the US Department of Justice, US Attorney's office and the FBI, demanding a federal investigation. Duchess Dallas marched again with a bigger crowd.

White Greenwood found the protests, and the attempts to cast Keaira Byrd as the victim of racism, to be utterly risible. North of the tracks, the prevailing view was that Byrd was a dumb criminal whose greed and stupidity got him killed. As one blogger put it, "You could have carved a better hitman out of a bar of soap."

Dr. Smith was denied bail, and at his first court appearance, he accused the judge of destroying his medical practice and sentencing his patients to death. A sheriff's deputy had to drag him physically out of the courtroom. Facing the death penalty, and with vast financial resources at his disposal—one unconfirmed report said he had $22 million in the bank—Dr. Smith hired a team of expensive lawyers, a private investigator from New York named William Acosta, and a young aspiring politician from Greenwood named Jelani Barr, who was a frequent critic of the police department and a keen amateur theatricalist. The newspaper ran a photograph of him wearing a bunny suit for his role as Rabbit in a local production of *Winnie the Pooh*.

The Dr. Smith case, as people called it, then turned into a long, drawn-out legal saga that flared up in the headlines from time to time, delivering new bursts of craziness and fuel for the ever-churning rumor mill. The prosecutor tried to charge Dr. Smith for murder, holding him responsible for getting his hitman killed. The defense claimed that Lee Abraham had pressed the hot barrel of his pistol to the head of Keaira Byrd and executed him while saying the n-word. Abraham insisted that he never fired a shot.

Then Jelani Barr and the private investigator became convinced that Lee Abraham had set fire to one of his businesses for the insurance money. It was a donut shop filled with elephant skulls and mounted lions, across the highway from a historically black college in Itta Bena. Barr and the investigator attempted to serve a subpoena on Vonzell Self, the fire chief of Itta Bena, accusing him of a cover-up. An inglorious fistfight ensued and Barr was arrested, which he trumpeted as further evidence that the police were out to get him.

Dr. Smith continued to write wild screeds to the newspaper, and was finally hauled off to the state mental asylum at Whitfield, and found unfit to stand trial. But many of his patients were outraged that he wasn't allowed to continue treating them. His lawyers denied that a gunfight had taken place in the law office, characterizing what had happened as an "illegal sting operation." Among Dr. Smith's supporters, the sentiment grew that the whole thing was a frame-up by Lee Abraham and Jim Hood, designed to take out Dr. Smith because he knew too much about their dirty political dealings. And the African-American protestors saw it as one more black man gunned down by white cops.

For Mariah and me, the case was a steady reminder that we were living in a place where the normal rules of cause and effect didn't apply. We couldn't get past stage one: how on earth could such a madman be allowed to operate a medical practice? How could he be so popular with patients, to the extent that they were clamoring for his release from the nuthouse? In the Dr. Smith case, and many other stories in the local newspapers, reality seemed to have drifted away from its moorings, and taken on a warped fevered quality.

In addition to insults, members hurled shoes at each other in a school board meeting. A man was beaten in the Greenwood Waffle House after accusing another man's girlfriend of wearing "Christmas pants" in July. People seemed uniquely primed to believe in plots and conspiracies, miracles and demons. When the outgoing police chief in Greenwood stood up to deliver his farewell speech, he had this to say about the mayor: "Antichrist, Beelzebub, deceiver, destructor, liar, seven heads and ten horns, oh, Satan, the devil himself—that's the Carolyn McAdams I know."

IT WAS DIFFICULT for Lee Abraham to talk about the case, because he had a civil suit pending against Dr. Smith, but we would meet up from time to time in the windowless bunker of his office, with its stuffed alligator diorama and mounted hunting trophies on the walls, or at his bulletproof mansion, where he slept on one side of an extra-large king bed, with six or seven guns lined up on the other. He didn't like to appear in public places anymore, and when he had to, he would generally arm himself with three handguns.

Tough and ruthless in business, politics, or the law, he was also big-hearted and generous with a lively sense of humor. "The undertaker will let you down before I will," was one of his mottos. His sharp, canny intellect went hand-in-hand with a deep religiosity, and his eyes shone with wonder when he talked about the many blessings and miracles the Lord had brought into his life. To show his love and gratitude, and to have a place where he could worship without fear of assassins, he had built a private chapel on a spread of land that he owned behind Walmart. One evening he invited Mariah and me to come and see it.

We barreled out there at high speed on a dirt road. Lee was driving one of his beefy black trucks. Gravel and dust flared out from the wheels, and the Delta sun sank fat and orange toward the flat horizon. "It was just so amazing how all this fell into place," he said. "But that's how it goes when you're doing the Lord's work. The first thing was Greenwood Utilities putting in this road. It was a blessing come out of nowhere."

The chapel was on a small knoll overlooking an artificial lake. He punched the security code on the front door, and we stepped into a warm, restful, serene space with the light coming through stained glass windows. Rows of beautiful antique church pews were lined up facing the altar, and as Mariah ran her hand over the smooth carved wood, Lee Abraham told us how the Lord had provided them. They belonged to a woman in Wisconsin who didn't want to sell them, until she heard that he wanted to put them in a Catholic chapel, whereupon she refused to take money for them. With God's help, one of his semi trucks was able to brave a terrible blizzard in order to get them and bring them back to the Delta. For an added miracle, they fit in the chapel perfectly.

Over dinner that night at the private racquet club and Catholic retreat he was building nearby, he started talking about the gunfight in his law office, the terrible sound of it, and how close he had come to losing everything. "I felt the wind of the wings of the Angel of Death, I really did," he said. "That man was paid to put a bullet between my eyes, and take a picture of it as I lay there on the floor."

When the gun smoke had cleared, and the dead and wounded had been taken away, his sister Magdalene came to comfort him, and she offered him an explanation of what had just happened.

"She told me, 'Lee, what did you think the Devil would do to someone building a chapel to the Lord? Did you really think the Devil was going to stand by and let it happen?'"

He looked at me, and then he looked at Mariah, making sure we understood.

I said, "So the Devil was behind it?"

"That's right," said Lee Abraham. "And it's only by the grace of God that I'm alive today."

Chapter 6

Field Trip

I WAS STILL packing my suitcase when Savanna barked and Martha walked through the front door of her daddy's former house. Our long-awaited tour of the Delta was finally happening. She handed me an oat bran muffin, and said, "Here, this is the last roughage you're going to see for a while."

Hundreds of red-winged blackbirds were chattering and squawking in our pecan trees and bamboo grooves. "Y'all need to shoot some fireworks at those birds," said Martha. "Otherwise they'll shit all over everything and you'll get Darling's disease."

"What's that?" I said.

"Histoplasmosis."

"What's that?"

"The disease you get from bird shit. Cathy Jacobs got it and almost died."

"Cathy who?"

"Charlie Jacobs the dead saxophone player's older sister. Chesley Pearman thought he got it, but he got the imaginary version."

Maybe because she was a doctor's daughter, Martha loved to rattle off the scientific names of obscure diseases with dire outcomes. When she was telling stories, which was most of the time, she always assumed that you knew the people involved, or had at least heard of them. This was usually the case when she was talking to people from the Delta, where everyone knows everyone, and almost never the case when she was talking to me. But it seemed rude to keep interrupting her stories to ask who was who, or how could such a thing possibly be true, so most of the time I just listened to the music of her stories, and her pretty Southern accent, and let it all wash through my mind.

On the road to Eden and Yazoo City, with me driving and Martha making a vague effort to blow her cigarette smoke out of the passenger side window, she came up with a kind of verbal collage made out of disjointed story fragments, "Linda Jane was in Chuck's Cypress Room, and who should walk in but Xerxes Vancleave with his whole coven. She swears to this day that Chuck turned into a lion-like dog, came across the bar, and sniffed her all over. Now Junkie Crump Pearman's little brother is Chesley, and we call him Chelvis. He found a sign by the side of the road that said PREPARE TO MEET THY GOD, and he took it and wired it to the foot of his bed with baling wire. That Chelvis! Such a ladies' man!"

I said, "So the Delta was pretty druggy in its day?"

Martha said, "Duh."

We drove across a repeating flatscape of fields, woods, murky bodies of water, and old rusting cotton gins, with the telephone poles listing slightly by the side of the road. They were planted in muddy ploughed ground, and the wind had prevailed against their verticality. For Martha, it was a landscape of story triggers and family trees. Over there was Chat Phillips's place—Big Chat, as he was known, a friend of the family and all-around great guy. One of his sons was Little Chat, and if Delta naming patterns held true, one of his grandsons would probably be known as Baby Chat.

Martha had the *DeLorme Mississippi Atlas & Gazetteer* open on her lap, and she was examining the route ahead, "We're going to Midnight, Louise, and Belzoni, up through Hard Cash, Hushpuckena, Alligator, and Bobo," she said. "We'll swing over to Panther Burn and Nitta Yuma, and we can also go to Christmas, Stringtown, Egypt, and Africa, all right here in the Delta. There's Hot Coffee too. That's down by Laurel, Miss-sippi, where Parker Posey and that momma of hers are from."

There wasn't much left of Midnight, a town named after a card game. A cotton planter bet his entire plantation on a hand of poker and lost on the stroke of midnight. The winner renamed the plantation and the town. It was now mostly derelict, but there was a big handsome cotton gin still in operation, whirring and clanking away inside its rusting corrugated tin walls. I took a photograph of its beautifully weathered sign: MIDNIGHT GIN. "Don't be a culture vulture," said Martha. "Don't go back to New York and be putting that sign on the label of your small-batch artisanal gin."

Next stop Louise, pop. 196, another study in American ruin. A third of its residents had left in the last ten years. We passed three prostitutes soliciting in front of a tumbledown shack, and a small crumbling box of a building with a hand-painted sign that said JAIL. Most of Main Street was boarded up, but the Lee Hong Grocery was still open for business.

We stepped through its grimy portals and were greeted effusively by the white-haired owner Hoover Lee, and his wife Freeda. They were both full-blooded Chinese, and they spoke with Delta drawls nearly as deep and rich as Lee Abraham's. "My folks come from the South of China, that's how come I got this accent," said

Hoover, signaling the joke with a wink and a little hitch of his shoulder. They had the Delta's characteristic warmth and friendliness, and a kind of down-home splendor that you often saw, as if people had polished up their spirits so they shone a little more brightly. Martha asked if Hoover was still in politics, and he said no, he was retired now, having served as the mayor of Louise for twenty-four years. "I'm still trying to make a dollar out of this old grocery store, and still making my sauce," he said.

Hoover Lee had embodied his mixed cultural heritage in a marinade and basting sauce that was legendary in the Delta. Martha described it as a salty sweet blend of soy sauce, hoisin sauce, and Southern barbecue sauce. When I asked Hoover what was in it, he said, "If I tell you, I'll have to cut your tongue out."

He showed us his order list. He was packing up and sending out bottles and cases of Hoover Sauce to Delta émigrés living in Nashville, New Orleans, St. Louis, Chicago, New York, and elsewhere. "They can't live without they Hoover Sauce," he said. "Folks are always telling me I could be a millionaire if I marketed it, so how about you pay me half a million, and I give you the recipe, and we split the profits fifty-fifty?" Then came the wink, the shoulder hitch.

Freeda still looked at least faintly amused by her husband's antics, as she peered at him over the top of her glasses. Her Chinese parents had named her Free Day, because she was born on the Fourth of July, but it had soon contracted to Freeda. She told a story about going to Washington, DC, to meet President Nixon: "They had never heard Mississippi accents coming out of Chinese people before, and they made such a fuss about it. I was glad to get back home."

A ragged black man with bad teeth came through the door to buy beer and cigarettes, and Hoover greeted him warmly, asked about his family members, and introduced him to us. The man looked uncomfortable and left. "I've known him all his life," said Hoover. "There's not much work around here now, and plenty of people who don't want to work. That's just how it is. I get on with everybody."

He told us to get ourselves a couple of cold beers from the cooler, on the house. Martha doesn't drink beer, and it was too early for me, so we took Cokes instead. The aisles of the cramped little store were heaped up with boxes. Ancient novelty items were gathering dust on the high shelves. Hoover tried to sell us a bottle of Swamp Root tonic, and then discovered that its sell-by date was 1978. He gave me a vintage-looking Stage Plank candy bar instead. There was a plastic statue of James Brown by the cash register. Hoover pushed a button and it started moving jerkily and singing "I Feel Good." Then it quit. "Oh, come on, James!" implored Hoover, jabbing at the button.

We walked out of there with two half-gallons of Hoover sauce, fresh Cokes, the Stage Planks, and Hoover Lee's phone number on a scrap of paper. We'd been hoping to fill up the gas tank in Louise, but the gas station had closed down, and Hoover said we'd have to make it to Belzoni. "If y'all run out of gas trying to get there, just give me a call, and I'll bring you some," he said. "It'll cost you ninety-nine dollars, what do you think about that?"

Then the wink, the shoulder hitch, Freeda's smile at Hoover's little joke. "Don't worry," he said. "It won't cost you nothing. I'd be proud to help y'all out. How about a beer for the road? It's on me. Take a forty-ounce."

WE MADE IT into Belzoni, pronounced "Belzona." We filled the tank at a Double Quick gas station known for the quality of its fried chicken, and took a slow cruise through downtown, which had caught only a mild case of the Delta blight. Martha wondered how Belzoni got its name, and for once, I was able to tell her an odd story about the Delta that she didn't already know.

Before it was a town, it was a short, violent stretch of grog shops and gambling joints known as Greasy Row. It had no law, government, or official name. A wealthy cotton planter from Natchez called Alvarez Fisk bought land nearby and established a plantation. He named it Belzoni in honor of an Italian circus giant and rogue Egyptologist called Giovanni Battista Belzoni. Known as The Great Belzoni for his colossal physique, he liked to dress in turbans and robes, and he's still notorious among Egyptologists for his unscrupulous thefts and tomb raidings. Alvarez Fisk admired his bold swashbuckling style, and may have met him somewhere. In 1895, the fledgling town named itself after Fisk's plantation, and it has been Belzoni ever since.

More recently, it named itself the Catfish Capital of the World. In the 1970s and 1980s, catfish farming was booming all over the Delta, and Belzoni had more ponds and processing plants than anywhere else. The town put up brightly colored statues of catfish on the downtown sidewalks and street corners, and inaugurated a catfish festival, with a proud young woman crowned Catfish Queen every year.

The catfish industry was now in serious decline, due to rising feed costs, market saturation, and competition from cheap, imported Asian fish that didn't have to meet the same stringent quality controls. Louie Thompson, Martha's cousin and our neighbor, was going through tough times with his catfish hatchery on Pluto. "It's so unfair," said Martha. "Delta farm-raised catfish is a great product. Asian fish doesn't taste as good, and it really isn't surprising when you consider how much human shit is in their catfish ponds." She was referring to the Vietnamese practice of positioning the village latrine over the catfish pond.

Cruising around Belzoni, Martha pointed out a store advertising Sno-Cones, Fireworks and Gravestones. "I love a multipurpose business," said Martha. "Juanita's in Greenwood has a sign that says,

'Beauty Salon, Bail Bonding, Bridal Boutique.' We're all about multi-tasking here in the Delta."

Then she showed me an African-American bakery. "That's right," she said. "Even our wedding cakes are segregated down here. We make them differently, and decorate them differently."

"What's the difference?"

"Well, you know I hate to stereotype, but black folks like a cake that really shows out."

"What does that mean?" I said.

"Fifty pounds of powdered sugar, a champagne fountain, and a trellis."

I ADDED BAKERIES to a list I was keeping. There were black clothing stores (zoot suits, church crowns, extra-big extra-long white T-shirts), and white clothing stores (fishing shirts, party frocks, archery equipment). Blacks and whites took their cars to different mechanics and car washes. They shopped at different florists, who arranged flowers in different ways. There were black funeral homes and white funeral homes. They buried their dead separately. In Belzoni, some local African Americans had decided the Catfish Festival was racist, and so they started up a rival Buffalo Fish Festival—it was a fish white people didn't eat.

At the Yazoo County Fair, whites and blacks came on different days. Their children played in different parks, swam in different swimming pools. They worshiped in separate churches, and sixty years after *Brown vs. Board of Education*, their children went to separate and unequal schools. African-American children went to under-funded public schools with extremely low graduation rates. Whites went to private schools known as "academies."

It was rare for blacks and whites to drink and socialize together, although it was common to see warm, friendly conversations taking place between the races in the post office or other neutral settings. Legal segregation was long gone, but a strong tradition prevailed in both communities that it was best to live separately, and both black and white seemed to prefer it that way. You saw the races eating together at McDonald's and a few other places, but even there, they self-segregated to opposite sides of the restaurant.

In Leland, "Birthplace of Kermit the Frog"—Jim Henson had played here as a boy—we joined the all-white crowd for lunch at the Fratesi Brothers Grocery. The walls were hung with hunting photographs and taxidermied deer heads, and the food was excellent, reflecting the Italian heritage of its owners and the culinary updrafts from southern Louisiana. I had a New Orleans–style muffaletta sandwich (salami, prosciutto, mortadella, provolone, olive salad, onions, lettuce, tomato, mustard, mayo), and Martha had the fried oyster po'boy sandwich. The man next to us was working his way through a formidable creation called a Slap Yo Mama Po'Boy, with fried chicken tenders, ham, salami, jalapeno cheese, wine and cheese sauce.

Framed in plastic on the Formica table was a photograph of a locally famous elephant named Suzie. She had come through the Delta in the 1970s with a traveling circus, and a Chevrolet dealer called Trader John Weathersby had taken a shine to her. He persuaded the circus people to let him look after the elephant during the winter off-season. Unbeknownst to them, he started taking her on hunting safaris through Delta National Forest, riding on her back and shooting squirrels out of the trees.

We saved the Jim Henson Museum for another time and drove up through Heads and Helm to the small, broken-looking town of Shaw, where Martha became sad and upset. A wonderful Chinese couple had run a grocery store here for many years, but they had been murdered during a cash register robbery, and now Shaw had

joined the long list of Delta towns that had no grocery store and nowhere to buy fresh produce. One of the main reasons for the endemic
health problems in the region was that people had nowhere to buy
food except at convenience stores, gas stations, and maybe a McDonald's if they were lucky.

We stood in the wind on the corner of Chiz Street and Main.
There was a sign that read, "Let Shaw Be Seen as Neat and Clean." Behind it was an empty lot full of trash and rubble. Young men loitered
on the opposite corner. There was a barbershop that was also a bar
and snack counter, and stray dogs trotting through the ruins.

"The kids who live here have never seen one thing built," said
Martha. "They can't imagine building something themselves, or
someone else building it for them. When you grow up in the Delta,
everything around you is falling in, and emptying out, and it really
affects you. America isn't supposed to be this way."

We cruised on through an emptier flatscape, more cleared of
woods and swamps. Laser-leveled cotton and soybean fields ran out
to the horizon. People called the Delta the "Silicon Valley of agriculture," because farming here was so high-tech and state-of-the-art.
It no longer needed towns, or communities, or human beings, just
vast acreages and lines of credit and transportation links to global
markets. But human communities stubbornly persisted and stored a
deep rich culture.

Mound Bayou is the oldest all-black town in America, founded
by former slaves in 1897. For many decades it was a shining example
to oppressed, impoverished blacks all over Mississippi, with its own
black-owned credit unions, insurance companies, newspapers, hospital, school, zoo, and local elections. Theodore Roosevelt described
it as "the Jewel of the Delta." Now it was struggling with high un-
employment and poverty, drugs, gangs, a shrinking population and
tax base, sky-high rates of heart disease and diabetes. Yet, passing

through, people seemed friendly, not desperate or angry, and they were doubtless sustained by the deep religiosity of the black Delta. A population of 1,500, down from 4,000 in its heyday, supported fourteen churches.

Clarksdale, Mississippi, pop. 17,000, had all the same problems on a larger scale, with the highest per-capita murder rate in the Delta. But it also had a wealthy white elite, and a burgeoning new tourism industry based on the blues. At the Delta Blues Museum on Blues Alley you could see the shack that Muddy Waters had lived in during his sharecropping days, and other artifacts relating to the Delta's greatest and most influential art form.

At the crossroads of Highway 61 and Highway 49, a guitar-shaped sign commemorated Robert Johnson's deal with the devil. According to legend, the bluesman went out to a crossroads one night and sold his soul to Satan in return for mastery of the guitar. Blues tourists lapped up the story and could often be observed photographing each other underneath the sign. Tourism money had helped revitalize the old downtown, but many of the buildings had been left partially derelict for a hard-bitten bluesy look.

The actor Morgan Freeman, who spent most of his childhood in Mississippi, and came back in 2001, had opened a deliberately distressed blues club called Ground Zero, in partnership with a white lawyer, businessman, and political figure named Bill Luckett. Tourists could see live blues there every night, and also at Red's Lounge, one of the last surviving juke joints in Mississippi. Red's required no help from architects or designers to look broken-down, shabby, and authentic, and you could still see real-deal octogenarian bluesmen like T-Model Ford, Robert Belfour, and Leo "Bud" Welch playing there. But it no longer had the energy and atmosphere of a juke joint. Instead of dancing partying locals, the clientele was now dominated by reverential white tourists with cameras.

Without the tourists, the blues would have probably died out completely in Mississippi, as an art form connected to rural black life, and all these great musicians would be out of work. Younger blacks, by and large, had little interest in the blues or the bad old days that produced it, preferring hip-hop, pop, gospel, and the Southern retro R&B style known as soul blues.

We checked into the Shack Up Inn, a collection of old sharecropper cabins fixed up with plumbing, heating, and cooling and turned into a motel. It was founded on a bet by Guy Malvezzi and Martha's friend Bill Talbot, who we found drinking a beer behind the bar. A garrulous Delta storyteller with big sideburns, thick glasses, and an unruly shock of hair, Bill still couldn't believe how successful his scheme had been. "We're getting twenty thousand people a year through here now, and most of them are from Europe," he said. "The Europeans, and the Brits in particular, have done a lot to desegregate the music scene around here. They're always wanting to see the Delta black man in his natural habitat, so they started going to the juke joints, and the black folks got used to seeing white folks in there, and then the local white folks figured it probably wasn't that scary after all."

That night, after some bourbon drinking, I tried to get Martha and Bill to make sense of the weirdness in the Delta, the eccentric characters, the bizarre crimes in the local newspapers. Where did it come from? What did it mean?

"Isolation, humidity, toxic chemicals," Martha said. "With your eccentric white folks, a lot of it is idleness being the devil's workshop. And trying to sustain the genteel sophisticated thing in a depopulating, ghettoizing, slow-motion disaster zone."

"Hell, we pride ourselves on our eccentricity, and now more than ever," said Bill. "All the normal, sensible people have left the Delta and moved to places that are less screwed up. You've got to be at least half-weird to live here, otherwise you won't make it."

"Sometimes, I swear to God, living in the Delta is like being in love with a crazy person," said Martha. Then she lifted her glass up to the frog-croaking, mosquito-bitten, rotten-velvet Delta night, and called out, "I love you, bitch!"

THE NEXT MORNING, Martha wore her Key Underwood Coon Dog Memorial Graveyard T-shirt, and we went to breakfast at Chamoun's Rest Haven, "A Lebanese Tradition Since 1947." Fox News was playing on the television. The Ole Miss college football schedule was displayed next to a plastic camel and a Lebanese flag. Kibbe was on the menu, but we went for grits, eggs, and toast. The owner was a stout, swarthy man with a big head and no neck, smoking one cigarette after another at the cash register. "His daddy looked even more like a bear," Martha observed, lighting up one of her own.

Our next stop was Jonestown, pop. 1,200 and shrinking. We visited an old dusty ramshackle store, restaurant, and voter registration site called Uptown Brown's. On the wall above the door was a mural of a hot dog running down the road with its eyeballs bulging out, and the slogan "Home of the Original Jewtown Polish." On the side of the building, it used to say, "Home of the Polish Jew Dog," but the paint had now flaked and faded too much for that slogan to be legible.

Inside, there was a motley assortment of objects for sale: an old typewriter, a butterscotch suit with leopard-print lapels, Barack Obama's fake signature on a cotton sack with the slogan "No Mo Yasih Boss." I was hungry again, and went up to the cash register. An aged black man pointed at an aged menu encased in aged plastic. I surveyed my options, and said, "I'll have the Polish Jew Dog."

"Onions?"

"Yessir."

Two bites were enough. I stuffed the rest of it in a trash can outside, where loitering men murmured, "How you doing" without eye contact or a question mark. There was a barbershop where you could pay your gas bill, a pool hall, a defunct cotton gin, the usual boarded-up businesses and rotting buildings. We met a sweet woman named Levonn who ran a tiny store with one gas pump that dated back to the 1970s. When gas climbed over three dollars a gallon, she had to stop selling it, because the gauge on her old pump wouldn't go above $3.00—an unimaginable price in 1975. Now it was back down to $2.56 and she was in business again. "It's so impressive that she can get that gas out here and keep going," said Martha.

Inside the store, there was a forest of plants, and a mossy old tank full of minnows for sale. Her grandbaby was on the counter in a crib, next to the cash register. Martha asked about the nuns who had come down here from the Pacific Northwest to help out the community. Levonn said, "The sisters are so wonderful, and everybody loves them, but I don't know if they'll stay. One of our young men broke into the nun house to rob it, and he stabbed poor Sister Teresa. I felt so bad, but I've been praying, and I believe the Lord wants the sisters here. I believe He wants Jonestown to come back up, because this is really the greatest town in the world. We've been seeing some good progress lately. We had some dilapidated buildings. Now they're gone, praise Jesus. The county came and tore them down."

When we said our good-byes, she asked us to come back anytime. On the way to the car, Martha said, "You see, that's progress around here: tearing down a building. Not putting one up."

From Jonestown, we zigzagged around the Delta, following our whims. At Rosedale, by the great levee that holds back the mighty Mississippi River, I attempted to eat a Koolickle. This Delta delicacy is a dill pickle soaked in cherry Kool-Aid, and it tastes just like you might expect. Then we bought hot tamales from a roadside stand. A blend of ground-up meat, corn, and spices, wrapped up and cooked in a corn husk, Delta hot tamales are descended from milder Mexican tamales, and arrived here with Mexican and Mexican-American farmworkers from Texas. I preferred the spicier, juicier Delta version, but the Mexicans at the Pluto catfish farm thought they were a barbarism and a disgrace.

Because we liked the name, we visited the town of Grace, which was near Dahomy, Grapeland, Priscilla, and Meltonia. In Benoit, we puzzled over a sign at the Last Chance Bar: "We Sell Snacks To Kids Too [*sic*] Eat. Must Be 21 to enter." The multipurpose businesses kept coming throughout the day: "Meat and Furniture," "Fireworks and Deep-Fried Turkeys," "Fragrant Oil and Bait," "Limousine Services, Education and DJ."

The Delta has lost 50 percent of its population since 1940, which probably accounts for the doubling and tripling-up of local businesses, and nowhere has experienced more population loss than Issaquena County. "Let's go there and look at nothing," said Martha. "They got buckets of nothing in Issaquena County." In 1860 the county had 587 whites and 7,224 slaves. Now it had just 1,386 people in total, and 40 percent of them were living below the poverty line.

We came down through Onward, where a black man named Holt Collier had taken Teddy Roosevelt on a famous bear hunt. It was here that Roosevelt's refusal to kill a bear cub led to the invention of a soft toy called the teddy bear. Then we turned east through the tall trees and dark swamps of Delta National Forest, where Trader John the Chevrolet dealer had taken Suzie the circus elephant on squirrel safaris.

Martha was driving, smoking, drinking sweet tea, and telling stories about people called Rae Rae, and Mike Mike, and Stoner Huff, one of Tweetie Huff's daughters, and Crickett Sweeney, and a short-sighted lawyer named Whit Monger who always wore a seersucker suit in the summertime, and nurses who had worked with her father called Peaches Pepper and Cassandra Stiff. Midway through another story, she called up her mother Cindy in Greenwood, and said, "Momma, what's Dilapidated Housing Betty's last name?"

When Chesley Pearman called, Martha put him on speakerphone so I could hear one of his tirades. "There's only one way we're going to fix the poverty in the Delta, and everybody knows what it is," he said. "We've got to legalize that shit and grow the hell out of it. We'll be happy as clowns and rich as kings, but first we've got to get rid of these goddamn Baptists, Martha. They won't let us do nothing. I want to see bumper stickers saying, 'When We Outlaw Baptists, Baptists Will Be Outlaws.' We need to lynch 'em like horse thieves. They're a thorn in the Christ-side of Mississippi and I'm sick of them. Maybe I can rally my Episcopalians. They're a small but feisty group."

After he hung up, Martha said, "That's Chesley. He's small but feisty as they come."

WE SPENT THE night on Pluto, where Mariah had been staying in Louie and Cathy Thompson's house, and concluded our tour the next day in Greenwood. Martha showed me a sign hanging off a downtown building that said "DENTIST. Drink Coca-Cola," and pointed out that it was still a working dentist's office. We went to Kornfeld's clothing store to meet Maury "Bubba" Kornfeld, one of very few Jews still attending the Greenwood synagogue. He was an animated jovial character who delivered Yiddish-style comedy shtick in a Mississippi accent, rode a motorcycle, loved to hunt, and wore a Glock 9mm pistol on his hip. The store had been there since the 1940s, and it was stocked with work clothing, hunting gear, medical scrubs, Christian and secular biker gear, salves, ointments, shoelaces. Bubba Kornfeld specialized in big and tall clothing, which he kept in a separate wing of the store, and some of it was spectacularly huge.

"If you're easy to find, and hard to fit, we've got you covered," he said, snapping open a pair of jeans with an 86-inch waist. Then he reached for an unbelievable bra. "It looks like two elasticized bird baths," he quipped. Then came the pièce de résistance, a pair of Y-fronts with a 109-inch waistband. He held them up like a flag, stuck his head past them, and grinned. "I guarantee nobody's too big for our britches!" he said.

In the evening Mariah joined us for dinner at a strange and wonderful restaurant called Lusco's, dating back to Prohibition. It's on the south side of the railroad tracks, amid dilapidation and high crime rates. You park in a lot across the street, and a monosyllabic black man appears and escorts you over to the front entrance. If you've neglected to bring your own alcohol, he'll buy you a bottle at the Likker Legger down the block. The front door opens into a room full of moth-eaten taxidermy and faded memorabilia, then you go back into a warren of private cubicles, with curtains that pull across the entrances and buzzers to summon the waitresses.

Feeling conspiratorial, because no one could see what we were doing, and looking jaundiced from the peeling green paint on the walls, we feasted on onion rings, "wet Delta salad" (lettuce swimming in olive oil and vinegar), pompano fish, broiled shrimp, and the crunchiest, most succulent fried chicken I had tasted so far. "They used to have illiterate black waiters who could recite the whole menu in rhyme and memorize all the orders for a table of fifteen," said Martha. "Now all the waiters are white. People used to flick pats of butter up on the ceiling, and they would fall down later into somebody's plate with a piece of lead paint attached. People got really mad when they put a stop to that. Everything has gone on in these booths: sex, drugs, drunken-ass high jinks."

There was a rickety piano, where patrons sometimes played and sang, and a midden mound of oyster shells behind the mosquito-infested men's room. People felt secret and private inside their walled cubicles, and they tended to forget that the walls were made of plywood and didn't reach the ceiling, and that anyone walking past or standing outside could hear their conversations. It seemed like the perfect place to begin a disastrous affair, or hatch a doomed embezzlement scheme, or plan the kind of murder-for-hire that results in a live victim and a dead assassin, not that there's any evidence that Dr. Smith met with any of his conspirators at Lusco's.

Chapter 7

Elephant in the Room

THE BLACK DELTA was still a closed book to us. What little we knew of it was gleaned from fragments, clues, extrapolations. We were living in the blackest county in the blackest state in America—Holmes County was 82 percent African-American—and we still hadn't made any black friends. James Jefferson stopped by regularly to visit, but he still wouldn't come up on the porch, let alone into the house. Mariah seemed to make him especially uncomfortable, so she would stay inside, shaking her head over Mississippi's backwardness, while James and I talked by his parked truck.

Sometimes we'd talk for an hour or two, with James doing 95 percent of the talking. He would tell me about his hopes for his young son, what he remembered as the good old days on the plantation, and how much he loved it out here in the country where it was peaceful and beautiful and folks weren't robbing and shooting each other like they were in Tchula and Jackson. I was always happy to see him, and I took from the frequency of his visits that he enjoyed my company too, but we were not becoming friends in the normal way. The legacy of racial segregation and the Delta's feudal class system stood between us like a wall.

I kept inviting Monk and Lucy over for dinner, and several times we made enthusiastic plans, and then a message would go unreturned, or Monk's phone wouldn't be working, or something else would get in the way. I had some friendly phone conversations with gravel-voiced Lucy, who was hungry for any sort of news or gossip from Pluto, and disappointed to hear that none of the three Thompson sisters had their husbands lined up yet. "They better start getting it together and making me some grandbabies," she said.

"That's how you'll think of their children?" I said.

"Mmmm-hmmm. You tell those gals Lucy be ready."

Her friend Helen Malone started cleaning our house. She was a tall, strong, good-looking black woman of sixty, and she had grown up in a kind of mirror image of how white plantation children grew up in the Delta. At the age of two, she was adopted by Mrs. Fleming, a white woman whose husband owned the plantation where Helen's parents lived and worked in the fields. This was highly unusual. Helen didn't know of any other black children who were taken in by white mothers.

"I had a white mama, and a black mama, and I lived in the big house with my white sister, and Miss Fleming treated us both just the same," she explained, using "Miss" as an honorific in the Southern way. "My real mama lived right there in the quarters with my daddy, so I saw her every day. Mama would always say that Miss Fleming had taken me from her. Miss Fleming would always say that Mama had eleven kids and could spare one. Miss Fleming had two kids of her own, but one had died, so I filled that need for her. I liked it. I felt special having two mamas, and Miss Fleming was a wonderful lady. She loved me for real, and I loved her too."

When she was nine or ten, Helen remembers going to a segregated restaurant in Tchula with Miss Fleming. They walked in the front door marked "whites only" and were turned away because Helen was black. Then they went around back to the "colored" entrance and were turned away again because Miss Fleming was white.

"She didn't like any part of that and found us another place to eat," said Helen. "Miss Fleming didn't have no prejudice. Mr. Fleming didn't either, and that was real unusual back then. Other white folks would give him a hard time. They would say, 'Why you pay them so much? Why you treat them so good?' He would say, 'I get more work out of them,' but that wasn't it really. He was just a good man."

One day I was making myself a sandwich, and I asked Helen if she wanted one too. She said, "Yassuh Mr. Richard, I believe I will." I put the sandwiches on plates, and without thinking about it, I set the two plates down on opposite sides of the kitchen table. I sat down to eat and Helen picked up her plate, walked outside to the back porch, and ate there by herself, saying afterward that she had felt like some fresh air.

The next time I made her lunch, I sat down with my plate and put hers on the counter. It was raining outside. She took the plate and sat down diagonally across the table from me. Miss Fleming had been kind and loving, but evidently, Helen had been raised to know her place.

"Prejudice was real bad in them days," Helen said. "Black folks couldn't vote. On Election Day, the plantation owner would go down to the polling place and vote for all the black folks living on his plantation. Oh, it was bad. It's a whole lot better now. A *whole* lot better. But sometimes even now I go to a store and they tell me, 'Put your money down on the counter.' Isn't that terrible? If my money ain't good enough for you to touch my skin when you take it from me,

I'ma take it somewhere else. It's just skin. When you cut it, we all bleed the same."

A few weeks later, I put down her plate opposite mine, and again she moved it to the diagonal, and positioned the fruit bowl as a barrier between us. She would talk quite openly about race and racism. She put up a photograph of her granddaughter Tinkerbell, and would talk intimately about her family. But she wasn't going to eat directly across the table from "the boss man," as she sometimes referred to me. At least not yet.

MARIAH STARTED WORKING part-time at Turnrow Book Company in Greenwood, a first-rate independent bookstore in an old two-storey department store, set up and run by our friends Jamie and Kelly Kornegay. In Oxford's Square Books and Jackson's Lemuria, Mississippi already had two of the best bookstores in the country. In Turnrow, it had a third.

It was almost an hour's drive to get there in the morning, but Mariah looked forward to it because she liked her coworkers so much, it was a break from the isolation of the house, and as you might expect from a budding librarian, she loved being around books and book chat. The downside of working there, the thing that caused her real anguish, was the occasional racist customer, who couldn't even buy a book, or drink a cup of coffee, without making disparaging remarks about black people. Most of these customers belonged to the older generation who had grown up during the civil rights movement and its aftermath.

Greenwood had been a major battleground, and it was renowned among civil rights workers as the worst town in the Delta. When Bull Connor, the police chief of Birmingham, Alabama, used attack dogs and fire hoses to stop blacks from registering to vote, he was copying

Greenwood police, who had used the same tactics a few months earlier. Byron De La Beckwith, the white supremacist who shot civil rights leader Medgar Evers in the back, killing him in front of his family, was a Greenwood man, and after a white jury found him not guilty, he would walk around town openly bragging about what he had done. Four years after the murder, he ran for lieutenant governor on the slogan, "He's a Straight Shooter."

The White Citizens' Council, an organization formed to fight desegregation with intimidation tactics, had its national headquarters in Greenwood. Sidney Poitier and Harry Belafonte came here for civil rights rallies. Stokely Carmichael first called for Black Power in Greenwood. Martin Luther King was here shortly before he was assassinated. Bob Dylan and Pete Seeger performed here in support of local civil rights workers, who were getting beaten, abused, fired from their jobs, and insulted. A group of local whites brought a live chimpanzee to the courthouse and hung a sign around its neck that read, "I want to vote too."

The federal government prevailed against the segregationists, as it had prevailed against the secessionists a century earlier. Once blacks were able to vote in the Delta, they started to win public office, because they outnumbered whites three-to-one, and these days most teachers, principals, school administrators, judges, police officers, mayors, and city and county employees in the Delta were African-American. It was an unusual situation: whites still had the wealth, but blacks held the political power.

Many of the older whites in Greenwood pointed to the town's decay, its high crime rate, and its corrupt, nepotistic, failing public school system as evidence of what happens when blacks are in charge and proof that things worked better under Jim Crow. Furthermore, they often claimed to be the victims of racism now—since they were in the minority, and blacks were always demonizing them.

"So many white people seem to think nothing was wrong with the way things were back then," said Mariah one evening, after a bad encounter at work. "And they have no sympathy for African Americans, no understanding of what generations of racism and oppression does to people. It's just, 'Why can't they get their act together? Why do they keep saying it's my fault?'"

Mariah had been working there for a month when news came through that James Meredith would speak at the bookstore. In 1962, he made history as the first black student admitted to the University of Mississippi in Oxford ("Ole Miss"), over the livid objections of most white Mississippians and the segregationist governor Ross Barnett. The Kennedy administration sent thousands of US Marshals and troops to protect James Meredith, and when he arrived on campus to enroll, white students and segregationists staged a full-scale riot that ended with two dead and hundreds wounded.

In 1966, having earned his degree, Meredith went on a solo "March Against Fear" from Memphis to Jackson, to encourage blacks to stand up to white authority and register to vote. He set off from the lobby of the Peabody Hotel, wearing a yellow pith helmet and carrying an African walking cane. On the second day of the march, just south of Hernando, Mississippi, a white man from Memphis popped up out of the bushes with a shotgun, called out his name, smiled, and fired three times, hitting him in the back and the legs. While he was in hospital recovering from his wounds, Martin Luther King, Stokely Carmichael, and other civil rights leaders continued the march in his honor.

Meredith had always been a contrarian and something of an eccentric. He had never fit in with other civil rights activists, because politically he was a right-wing conservative. In 1967, he had actually campaigned for Ross Barnett, the racist governor who had tried to keep him out of Ole Miss, and he later worked for the arch-segregationist Senator Jesse Helms. Meredith didn't like the term "civil rights," because he thought it implied that black people needed special rights, and he had established a foundation to fight the use of Ebonics or black slang.

Now he had written a book called *A Mission from God*, and Mariah was excited that he was coming to Turnrow to promote it. The day before his arrival, one of the old white men drinking coffee said to Mariah, "Have you heard? JCPenney's running a special on white bedsheets."

Her blood ran cold. She felt frozen on the spot. Joking about a Klan lynching was something she couldn't compartmentalize, and didn't want to. Jamie Kornegay, the owner of Turnrow, said that the man wasn't actually as racist as he sounded; he liked to ham it up to shock outsiders. Mariah was not comforted.

James Meredith, wearing a blue pinstriped suit and a full white beard, stood up in front of about eighty people the following day, with whites slightly outnumbering blacks, and everyone welcoming and enthusiastic. It was a pleasant surprise to see he had so many white supporters in Greenwood these days.

After some introductory remarks, he launched into his speech. "Mississippi is the center of the universe," he said. "The two biggest issues in western Christian civilization are the white-black race issue and the rich-and-poor issue. Mississippi is at the apex of both. And if anybody in the world can solve the problem, it's Mississippi."

The core of the speech, and the subject of Meredith's new book, was the vital importance of the public schools to the black community. The reason for the continuing black poverty in the Delta was clear enough, he said. Whites had trained blacks to pick cotton; now the failing schools were not training blacks to do anything. The fact that he had integrated Ole Miss in 1962 was almost meaningless, because 98 percent of black high school students in Mississippi scored too low on standardized tests to get into any form of higher education. He said there was no point expecting politicians or whites to fix this problem. Nor was it their responsibility. It was up to the black community to put its own house in order. "We are the only ones holding ourselves back," he said, and repeated it several times.

He called on black church leaders to get more involved in raising children and influencing the schools. A year spent studying the Book of Deuteronomy had persuaded him there was no other way. "God told Moses to choose the right kind of leaders, and they must be from their own kind. You cannot have anybody else. I don't care how much they know."

It was a long and sometimes rambling speech that went on for nearly two hours and delved deeply into the Bible. His central point, that the black Delta was doomed unless the public schools could be improved, seemed unassailable. But was more church involvement the answer? Many in the crowd thought it was, and at the end of the talk, there were emotional calls to love the children like Jesus and begin a spiritual renewal in the schools and the community.

From what I could see, lack of religious faith was not the problem in the schools. In both Greenwood and Yazoo City, the public schools had received an F grade from the state education department, and in both places school administrators and community leaders had come up with the same solution: a big prayer rally, and no other changes in policy or personnel. Praying was also a way of doing nothing.

MARIAH AND I had never thought so much about race and racism in our lives. It was the great underlying obsession of the Mississippi Delta, the elephant in every room. Almost every charming, gracious, hospitable, generous white landowner we met came from a family that had profited from an American version of apartheid, or more accurately, a blueprint for the South African version. A delegation of Boers had visited Mississippi in the 1940s to see how white supremacy was implemented. Present-day Mississippi, especially in the crucible of the Delta, was in a kind of postapartheid situation, with wounds slowly closing and healing, but both races still highly suspicious of each other and haunted by the past.

Even a simple trip to the grocery store was fraught with racial undertones. If, as a non-Southern white person, you forgot to say "Sir," or, "Ma'am," to an older white person working a cash register, it was a slight rudeness, the sort of thing you could expect from Yankees and foreigners. If you neglected to use the same honorifics with a black person in the same circumstance, it would probably be taken as a sign of racism and disrespect. In the Jim Crow days, whites never used honorifics for blacks, and many whites in the Delta still reserved "Sir" and "Ma'am" for their own kind.

Eye games were commonplace. Sometimes black people looked you right in the eyes, to see if you would look back at them or avert your glance. This could be done as a simple test or an attempted intimidation. Sometimes a black person refused to look a white person in the eyes. This could be out of scorn and hatred, or because they were acting deferential. Fifty years ago, it was "uppity" to look a white person directly in the eyes, and men had been lynched for looking at a white woman in the wrong way.

Mariah realized that she'd never really thought about race until she came to Mississippi. It had been so straightforward in the laid-back university neighborhoods of Tucson, Arizona, where she grew up. Racists were bad, good people didn't associate with them, and that's about all there was to know. She had black, Asian, and Hispanic friends there, and it was no big deal. Here, race was so difficult and complicated. It was a kaleidoscope you could keep on turning.

One of our biggest surprises was meeting African Americans who

were against the civil rights movement and who blamed desegregation for the social and economic woes in the black community. It was
a minority viewpoint, but a significant minority that included some
prominent church, community, and political leaders. The argument
went like this: black-owned businesses were thriving under segregation, a black middle class had been rising under its own steam, the
community had been more tightly knit and mutually supportive than
it was now, and some good black schools had been forced to close
down when education was integrated.

"But, but, but," said Mariah, as we talked about it at the dinner
table. "They had to be totally subservient to white people, didn't they?
They couldn't vote. They had no access to political power or good
jobs. I don't get it."

When you heard older African Americans talking about the
good old days of racial segregation in Mississippi, you could put it
down to nostalgia for their youth. But there were young civil rights
denouncers too. Jelani Barr, the amateur theatricalist who was on Dr.
Smith's defense team, was one of them. He had just announced his
candidacy for mayor of Greenwood.

I met him for lunch at the Crystal Grill. This was a Greenwood
institution dating back to the 1940s, and during the civil rights era.
it had been a "whites only" private club. Now it was more comfortably integrated than most restaurants in the Delta. Jelani Barr came
through the door in Ralph Lauren sportswear, carrying an iPad, with
a cool, noncommittal expression in his eyes, and long curling eyelashes. He seemed to know all the staff and about half the diners, and
he greeted them with nods, handshakes, shoulder bumps, and chin
lifts.

He sat down and ordered a Coke, and I asked him how he knew
Dr. Smith. "Through my mother, Easter Barr," he said. "Dr. Smith
had treated her, and he became a friend of the family. When he got

arrested, his people asked me to look into some things, and I was happy to do it."

"What type of things?"

"Lee Abraham, Jim Hood, the Greenwood police department. How come Lee Abraham's buildings keep burning down, and he never gets investigated for arson. How come the crime scene at the law office is all cleaned up forty-eight hours after Byrd is murdered there."

"So what do you think happened that night?"

"Byrd went there wanting his money. Lee Abraham hired Byrd to murder Dr. Smith, and he would have finished the job if a car hadn't have came by on River Road that night."

"So why arrive at the law office wearing a ski mask and carrying a MAC-11, if he's just there to collect his money?"

He gave a derisive little laugh and stared at me like I was the biggest fool in the world. "Look," he said. "There's some shit you need to know. Lee Abraham is like Don Corleone around here, and Jim Hood is his bitch. He run Jim Hood. You think they don't know how to put a ski mask on a dead man, stick a gun in his hand, take a photograph whatever? Greenwood po-lice destroyed that crime scene, so who knows what-all they did."

After lunch, he took me on a tour of black Greenwood, and that's when he started laying into Martin Luther King and the civil rights movement. "MLK was good at integrating lunchrooms and bathrooms, but not social classes. Civil rights taught us that we deserved what the white folks have, and we don't have to build it for ourselves. It's a sense of entitlement: you did my grandmother wrong, so you owe me. That man sitting on the corner right there is a product of the civil rights movement."

The man in question was about forty years old, sitting on a street corner in the Baptist Town ghetto, staring off into space with all the time in the world. Paint was peeling off the shotgun shacks behind him, and chunks of the sidewalk were missing. We drove past shabby little liquor stores, Chinese-owned grocery stores, condemned buildings, empty lots full of trash. The young men standing on the street corners shouted out when they saw Jelani Barr rolling past with some white man in the car.

"They think you're with some ghetto improvement project," he said. "All kind of white folks have come down here with money to spend, and projects to build, and it just perpetuates the problem. Our people are so busy trying to get some of that money into their pockets, and get their nephews and cousins hired on, they can't see no further. It's just like James Meredith says. We're trapped in a four-hundred-year dependency problem. The only thing holding us back is us."

We passed the house of Senator David Jordan, a former civil rights leader who could always be relied upon to play the race card in local politics. The house was fairly modest, with a Cadillac parked outside it, and it set Jelani Barr off on a tirade. "The problem with him, and all those civil rights leaders, is they're so focused on sticking it to the white man, they forget about economics. They forget about job creation. They forget about the children. They want black supremacy—all black teachers and school boards, all black cops, all black city council, all black all the time. But our people can't read. We've run the schools into the ground, and parents are using them like day care. I love my people, man, don't get me wrong, but we can't keep yelling at the white man and acting like that's going to solve our problems."

As Jelani Barr went on, I couldn't help remembering a similar tirade delivered a few weeks previously by a professional exterminator who had come out to our house to tackle the rodent problem. He too said, "they use the schools like day care." He was a tall, lanky white man wearing a camouflage cap, and it didn't take him long to start throwing the n-word around. He was the first unabashed white racist I had encountered in Mississippi, and yet he and Jelani Barr were saying many of the same things. The difference was in tone. The exterminator was bitter, sneering, hateful. Barr was sad and regretful. "Too many of our people, all they want to do is drink and get high, fuck and fight, and wait for the next welfare check," he said. "We got the highest teen pregnancy rate in the nation, right here in the Delta, and three out of four kids got a single mom. And all our leaders do is to say, white man this, white man that, and keep collecting their paychecks."

Listening to Jelani Barr, my first thought was that he had a case of internalized racism, a self-loathing planted there by white racism, and then deflected outward against his own people. Then I felt horribly patronizing, as an ignorant white foreigner, for presuming to know what was in his heart.

Maybe he was right in a blunt overgeneralized way. He certainly knew a lot more about the problems of the black Delta than I did. But if he was right, that meant the racist exterminator was also right, and that was extremely shaky and uncomfortable ground to set foot on. It was much easier to label Jelani Barr as naïve, especially in light of his other views. Surely it was absurd to say that the civil rights movement had done more damage than Jim Crow. He was defending a madman in Dr. Smith, and his mayoral campaign was haphazard to say the least. It consisted mainly of lengthy soliloquies posted on YouTube and a proposal to turn downtown Greenwood into an entertainment district with bars and nightclubs.

In some ways, he seemed eccentric, but as we were shaking hands good-bye, he said something that seemed to cut right to the heart of things, "The whole problem in this Delta is that nobody can see past black and white. Very, very few. So all our energy goes into stopping the other ones, blaming the other ones, trying to get what they have. It's so obvious that we need to work together, but we can't get out from under that other shit."

"You mean the history of this place?" I said.

"I mean racism," he said. "On both sides. You think white folks got a monopoly on that shit?"

Chapter 8

Deer Season

AT THE HOUSE, we were starting to feel slightly more at home, less embattled, less ignorant of our surroundings. We knew what poison ivy looked like now and no longer blundered into it by accident. We had learned to smear a paste of baking soda on fire ant stings as soon as possible. Mariah had been bitten so many times by mosquitoes that she was no longer having an allergic reaction, just the usual itching with unusual burning, and she kept a tube of hydrocortisone cream in her purse to deal with that.

Mariah had relented slightly in her organic purism. She was now spraying a Roundup product on the poison ivy, and allowing me to dust the fire ant mounds with poison, since the boiling water treatment just seemed to move the ants to a new location. Having endured the painful sting of red wasps, yellow jackets, and hornets, she had given me permission to zap their papery nests in the porch eaves with an aerosol bug-killer.

I had now shot more than thirty armadillos around the house and learned to dump the corpses in a watery channel we called "the ditch of death." If I threw them in the bushes, or in the woods, Savanna would invariably find them and roll joyfully in the rotting stinking remains. One armadillo must have crawled into the shed to die, because Mariah was startled to find a vulture in there one day. The bird tried to hide from her, and seemed uncertain how to escape. "You know you're living out in the country when there's a vulture stuck in your shed," she said, and I had to agree.

When a family of raccoons started eating our figs, I should have shot them, but sometimes I got tired of all the killing I had to do. I'd decapitated several cottonmouths with the garden hoe, shot a harmless water snake by mistake, hacked up an equally harmless rat snake in a panic because it fell off the shelf in my writing studio and was nearly six feet long. I'd emptied dozens of mousetraps, stomped, slapped, and swatted an uncountable number of spiders, cockroaches, and winged biting insects.

We'd already gorged ourselves on the delicious figs, and Mariah had made ten jars of fig jam with balsamic vinegar—excellent with cheese and crackers or stuffed inside a pork tenderloin. So we let the raccoons have their turn, and they stripped the huge tree bare. They must have eaten two hundred figs in two days, and we couldn't help wondering if they got catastrophic diarrhea.

A tractor driver named Charlie, working in the fields around the house, was incredulous that we'd (a) allowed the raccoons to eat our figs, and (b) missed a golden opportunity to feast on all that good raccoon meat.

"Y'all never ate no coon?" he said. "He eat better than a squirl."

"I've never eaten squirrel," I said.

"How bout possum? He good."

"Nope."

"Well goddamn, that ain't right! Here what I'ma do. I'ma kill a coon and a squirl and a possum, and cook em up for y'all. We drink some beers and have a good time."

That was a feast that we kept finding reasons to postpone. Mariah didn't want to eat the raccoons, because they were cute and furry with human-looking hands, and she didn't want to eat opossums because they were creepy and weird, with their snaggleteeth, rodent eyes, patchy fur, and leathery tails, and their tactic of playing dead when they felt in danger. The prospect of eating squirrel was a little more appetizing, but what she was really starting to crave was Asian food, Mexican food, tapas, the soba noodles at that place down on Delancey Street.

"And just once, I'd like to go to work without seeing a dozen dead animals on the road," she said one evening. "Although you can't beat the variety. This morning it was two dead otters, a cat, two dogs, a raccoon, a couple of turtles, a skunk, and a big old wild hog."

If the old house had been less charming and handsome, if the setting had been less spectacular and the neighbors less like family, we might have tried to sell it, because it wanted all our time and money. One of the two central air-conditioning units we had inherited was now leaking beyond repair. The torrential Delta thunderstorms were still finding a small leak in the roof, and two different roofers had failed to locate it. The boards were rotting in the walls of my writing studio, eighteen windows needed reglazing and repainting, I still hadn't gotten under the house to tear out the collapsing insulation. The corner boards were rotting, the bare walls were crying out for art, the living room needed a couch and rugs and more chairs, and we needed another vehicle. The good news was that the racist exterminator had poisoned out the mice and rats, although the downside to that was the stench of rotting rodents inside the walls. Such were the Delta's powers of decomposition that the smell didn't last more than a few days.

Fall came like a blessing in October. The heat and humidity dissipated, the light became crisper and less gauzy. We started wearing jeans again. The war against vegetation reached its annual ceasefire. Then the insects laid down their arms, the snakes went into hibernation, the leaves started turning red and gold, and it became unusual to see any human male, black or white, who wasn't wearing camouflage clothing. The great annual rite of deer season had begun.

It was also commonplace to see girls and women coming out of the woods in camo outfits, carrying rifles and compound bows, sometimes with a deer strapped on a four-wheeler. In the gun shops and hunting stores, we saw women wearing camo with immaculately styled hair and full Southern makeup. The *Yazoo Herald* ran a photograph of a female bowhunter named Tracy Paul smiling proudly over a fourteen-point buck she had killed. "I was really excited about starting to bow hunt," she told the *Herald*, "but I think I got more excited when my husband made me some arrows with pink zebra fletching."

On the opposite page, managing editor Jamie Patterson wrote a column about squirrel hunting with her new pink Ruger .22 rifle, "a pretty pink in honor of breast cancer awareness." Leave it to Southern women to feminize hunting, we thought. Then the newspapers, and the social media networks, started to fill up with photographs of camo-clad children, some as young as four and five, holding up the ears or the antlers of the deer they had just shot and killed.

We couldn't afford to buy a deer rifle, so Martha's husband Donald lent me a bolt-action 30.06 he wasn't using, and Cadi Thompson lent Mariah her .243. We took the rifles down into the pasture by the river and kept practicing until we could hit a small target from a hundred yards away. Both of us had a horror of wounding a deer and then having to follow a blood trail to end its agony, and this was a real incentive to improve accuracy. But even if the death was quick and clean, we still didn't know how we'd feel about it.

"If a deer comes into my gun sights, and in that moment I'd rather see it live than kill it, I'm going to let it walk, and that'll be the end of it," I said to Mariah. It was the first cold night, and we were sitting by a fire in the rug- and furniture-starved living room.

"Same here," she said. "If I don't want to do it, I'm not doing it. But if it's a clean kill, and done with reverence, and it gets us enough meat to last through the winter, I think I'd feel proud of myself."

I WAS THE first to get up an hour before dawn, put on several layers of warm clothes, drink strong black coffee, gather up the gun, the bullets, the binoculars, a knife for skinning and gutting, and an orange nylon vest to wear over my jacket so no other hunters would mistake me for a deer. This was the absurd thing about the camo craze. Deer hunters were required by law to wear solid orange over it, so it didn't actually provide any camouflage at all. It was a fashion and lifestyle statement, a way of showing solidarity to the hunting tribe.

It was still dark when Mike Foose arrived to pick me up. "Are you ready?" he said.

"I think so," I said. "We'll have to find out."

He drove down the levee to Joseph Brake, and we parked and loaded our guns. Mike said, "You know where that tree stand is in front of the ditch at the north end? Why don't you go there, and I'll be at the other end of the brake. Now remember, you want to aim right at the center of the shoulder, so the bullet will break down that shoulder and go through the heart and lung area. That's going to be the quickest, most merciful death, and if you do it right, that deer won't be able to run more than a few yards, if at all."

Trying not to make too much noise in the dry leaves and twigs, I made my way through the woods, using a small flashlight as little as possible. I felt nervous and clumsy. I found the stand and climbed the ladder to a small platform with a bench to sit on and a rail around it to prevent falls. Deer don't look up for danger, so a tree stand offers concealment, assuming that you don't make any noise and the wind doesn't blow your scent toward the deer.

The woods were cold and still and silent. In the first gray opaque light, the silhouettes of trees took shape. Thick vines hung off them in loops and coils. Then the full range of colors appeared, and small birds started singing and hopping about in the brown and gold leaf litter. My ears strained into the silence, listening for the rustle of hooves in the dry leaves. My eyes scoured the woods through my binoculars, which I'd bought six years ago for watching birds and wildlife, never imagining that I would one day use them for hunting. The thought of shooting an animal for meat, or any other reason, had been unthinkable then.

There was a small clearing about sixty yards away, and I imagined a deer walking into it. I raised the telescopic sight to my right eye, braced the butt of the rifle against my shoulder, and rehearsed what Mike had taught me: aim at the center of the front shoulder, inhale, exhale slowly, gently squeeze the trigger.

I sat there motionless for two hours, studying the woods more intently than I'd ever studied my surroundings before, imagining deer, hallucinating deer, trying to conjure up deer, but catching not a single glimpse of a living deer. Mike Foose didn't see one either, but when he described the experience as "a wonderful morning's hunting," he wasn't being sarcastic. The light had been gorgeous filtering down through the autumn foliage, and he had seen two pileated woodpeckers—huge, magnificent birds—a number of interesting waterfowl, and a four-foot alligator that he had never seen in the brake before. I had seen a rabbit, an armadillo, many different birds, many shifting arrangements of light and leaves, and with my senses focused so acutely on my surroundings, I had altered my normal consciousness. I had done the thing that modern life conspires against. I had fully inhabited the present without distraction.

THAT AFTERNOON, MARIAH went off to a deer stand with Cadi Thompson, thereby signaling a dramatic breakaway from her past. Mariah used to be a vegetarian, although she was eating red meat with enthusiasm by the time we met. If I'd told her then that she'd be living in Mississippi and hunting deer with a young Republican that she adored like a sister, she'd have told me to shut up.

Cadi had been going into deer stands since she was six years old. Louie would bring a sleeping bag for her and wake her up when a deer appeared. Sometimes he lined it up in the scope and let her pull the trigger. Cadi's older sisters, Carmen and Julia, also had plenty of childhood exposure to deer hunting, but they hadn't taken to it like Cadi. Nor did they catch alligators like Cadi, or go out into the swamps at night to grab bullfrogs with their bare hands like Cadi. She was the fearless tomboy sister, the closest thing Louie had to a son.

Cadi, now twenty-two, had several female friends and relatives who liked to hunt as much as she did; one of them had deer tracks tattooed around her torso. When girls went hunting together, especially when they were teenagers, the temptation to chat was strong, but it was necessary to be quiet in a deer stand. So what some girls did was sit quietly and text back and forth until a deer appeared, whereupon they'd put down their phones and pick up their guns.

That wasn't how it went with Cadi and Mariah. They gave in to the urge to chat, along with the urge to eat all the chocolate that Cadi had brought along. They saw some deer, but they were too young to kill, and Mariah got a little bored watching them graze for three quarters of an hour. She thought Cadi was too flippant and irreverent about the act of hunting. Cadi thought Mariah was a bad influence, because normally she didn't talk so much, or eat so much chocolate in a deer stand. This didn't stop them going hunting again.

AN HOUR BEFORE dusk, Mike and I crawled along a low ridge, careful not to skylight ourselves. We lay down on the cold muddy ground behind some bushes and looked out over a long field bordered by woods. "There's a weed called henbit growing in that field, and the deer love to eat it," Mike whispered. "You watch this side and that far corner. I'll be over there." He crawled about twenty yards away and took cover behind a different bush. A soft intermittent breeze was blowing into our faces, right where we wanted it.

Half an hour went by. I watched honking flocks of snow geese trail across the sky in wavering V-formations, and the setting sun paint the autumn trees. Then four deer emerged from the woods at the far end of the field. One was a spike buck, and the others were yearlings—all too young to kill. A few minutes later, a doe sprang out of the woods about eighty yards away. She snorted loudly and leapt into the air, kicking up her hind legs like a bucking bronco. I watched mesmerized through my binoculars, aware that I should be looking through the scope of the gun.

She leapt again, and a third time, and then settled down to feed. My heart was hammering away in my ribcage. I picked up the gun and looked at her through the scope. Was she big enough to kill? I thought so, but I wasn't sure. I crawled over toward Mike, and said in a loud whisper, "Should I shoot her?"

The doe saw the movement, or heard the whisper, and bolted off into the woods.

"Next time just use your judgment and don't bother asking me," Mike said. "She was plenty big enough. You had a nice shot at her. Why didn't you shoot?"

"I've never seen a deer leap and buck like that," I said. "I wanted to see what she'd do next."

Two days later, I came back to the same place by myself. I waited for an hour and the same doe came out of the woods at the far end of the field, maybe a hundred and eighty yards away. Lying on my belly, with my elbows propped on the ground, I got her lined up in the crosshairs, although she was too far away to see the exact center of her shoulder. Adrenaline was coursing through me. Slowly I squeezed the trigger and BOOM! She leapt and turned and ran off into the woods.

I charged down through the briars and across a ditch into the field. I found the deep tracks in the mud where she had landed and spun, and I followed those tracks into the woods, looking for blood spots. I couldn't find any. I hadn't wounded her. I had missed her completely.

MIKE FOOSE, THE purist, thought that modern deer hunting involved entirely too much shopping, dressing up, playing with gadgets, stacking the odds, and not enough patience and woodcraft. The modern hunter could shave, shower, and shampoo with a wide range of scent-masking bathroom products. Then he, or she, could put on several hundred dollars' worth of insulating, wicking, scent-reducing, high-performance camouflage clothing. Most hunters didn't like walking, so they drove a four-wheeler to their deer stand, which was quite possibly heated with a comfortable chair and a portable toilet. Handheld devices indicate which way the wind is blowing and how far away the hunter's scent cone is detectable to a deer.

What they called hunting was more like farming. People planted clover or other food plots for the deer, at a nice comfortable shooting distance from their deer stands. Others used an automatic feeder with a digital timer to throw out feed corn at certain times of day. Salt and mineral licks were used to attract deer, and so were all kinds of products made from doe urine and estrus to attract bucks. Motion-activated tracking cameras recorded the movements and numbers of deer, and interfaced with computers and smartphones. All over the Delta and beyond, men were whipping out their phones and showing each other night-vision images of the big buck they intended to kill that weekend.

I had no interest in killing a big trophy buck and hanging its head on my wall. I preferred them to keep breeding, and passing on their fine genetics, but this was very much a minority viewpoint. In the hunting magazines, websites, TV shows, and in the cluster of men at the local hardware store, the talk was all about trophy bucks, not just how to kill them, but how to grow them. People were putting down supplemental feeds, vitamins, and minerals to make the horns grow bigger. They were culling out males with small or misshapen horns, so they didn't spread their bad-horn genes through the herd. There was an elaborate scoring system for the horns, with all the tines mea-sured and counted according to a special formula, and this was how trophy hunters competed against each other.

Mike Foose used to be a trophy hunter, and he had brought back some impressive horns from Africa. If a big trophy buck showed up within range, he was definitely going to shoot it, but he was perfectly happy to shoot does for meat, especially since there were so many does around. And I was actively after a doe, because people said they tasted better.

With so much hunting going on, you might think deer would be getting scarce, but that wasn't the case at all. There were more whitetail deer than people in Mississippi. The numbers were so high that the state allowed each licensed hunter to kill three bucks and five does a year. And nationwide, the whitetail deer population was exploding. In 1900, it was 500,000. Now it was up to forty million, and the herds were destroying crops, degrading forests, and acting as a kind of mass transit system for the ticks that cause Lyme disease in humans. In the Northeast and Midwestern suburbs, which were literally teeming with deer, professional hunters were being paid with tax dollars to cull their numbers.

Mariah and I went together to the ridge where I missed the doe. She took cover behind a bush, and I inched my way as quietly and smoothly as I could down the slope of the ridge, to get myself thirty yards closer to the far end of the field. Just before dusk, three young deer came out of the woods at the far end of the field. Then the doe. She was a hundred and fifty yards away. I took aim at her front shoulder, exhaled slowly, and with a pounding heart and blood ringing in my ears, I squeezed the trigger.

BOOM! She dropped and lay there without moving. I expected to feel some sadness and regret at erasing her life, but instead I felt elated and hugely relieved that I had killed her so cleanly. When we got to the body, we saw that the bullet had hit her slightly higher than I had intended and shattered her spine behind the neck. Death must have been instantaneous. Seeing her up close, so beautiful and so dead, the eyes already clouded over, Mariah and I felt gratitude, and rested our hands on her still-warm flank. I called Louie Thompson, who came with a four-wheeler to get her out of the field.

"It's the ultimate sacrifice," he said, taking a look at her. "She's a mature female, probably raised a couple of sets of fawns. She's had a good life. Look at all the fat on her rump."

We took her to the Pluto farm shop and hung her upside down with metal spikes through her legs. Louie led me patiently through the skinning and gutting. I expected to feel queasy, but that didn't happen. Instead I felt a responsibility to do the job right and not spoil any of the meat by nicking the bladder or the guts. Louie had been carving up deer for forty-five years and he'd never seen one with so much fat. Great white slabs of it lay under the hide and all around her heart.

We cut out the beautiful lean dark meat of the tenderloin and the backstraps. I sawed off the shanks for venison osso bucco and sliced away the scrappy flank meat, which we would stew slowly with Mexican spices and make *barbacoa*. We threw out the guts and organs for the local wildlife to eat. The next day I took the shoulders and hindquarters to a husband-and-wife deer processing team, who turned them into delicious sausages (adding pork fat and spices), smoked sliced sandwich meat, and tenderized steaks. It cost $103 for sixty pounds of this processed meat. Teresa Milner, who swiped my card on her phone, said that patience was essential in her job, because every single hunter wanted to tell her the story of how they got their deer. She thought she'd heard them all until a man told her one about using his leg to try and wrestle a deer to the ground, and then riding it like a horse through the woods until he cut its throat.

"I'm not saying I believe it, but I do admire it as a story," she said.

"It's human nature, I suppose, for hunters to tell stories about their kills," I said.

"No, honey, it's the South," she said. An alarm went off from one of the ovens, and she started pulling out freshly cooked venison summer sausages. I commented on how good they smelled, and she said, "I can't sell them, I'm afraid. But here, have a taste." She carved me off a slice. It was studded with flecks of cheese and jalapeno, and tasted so good that I let out an involuntary moan. "You can have the rest of it," she said, putting the foot-long sausage in my bag.

FOLLOWING A RECIPE by the Texas chef Jesse Griffiths, who specializes in wild game, I marinated the tenderloin for a couple of hours with olive oil, salt, pepper, fresh thyme, sage, rosemary, and oregano. I built a fire from a fallen oak tree that I'd cut up and split, and Mariah pulled a lettuce out of the garden. When the fire had burned down to hot ashy coals, I put a grill over it, and laid down the tenderloin, turning it every few minutes until the meat was slightly charred on the outside and still rare on the inside. While the meat was resting, Mariah dressed the lettuce with salt, olive oil, and lemon juice, and made a sauce of sour cream, horseradish, lemon zest, and parsley. I sliced the tenderloin into round discs and poured us both a glass of good red wine, and we gave thanks to the deer.

The meat wasn't gamy at all. It was rich and delicate and exquisitely delicious. The doe had fed to her heart's content on clover, henbit, acorns, wild plums, corn, soybeans, and grasses. She had led an incomparably better life than any factory-farmed animal, and now she had become meat. The wolves and panthers were gone now, and the humans hunted with high-powered rifles instead of handmade bows and arrows, but the deer's position on the food chain had not changed over the millennia. If she had reached old age, her teeth would have worn away, and she would have starved to death. Coyotes and vultures would have eaten her. Instead she died instantly, provided us with meat for the next nine months, and one meal that we'd never forget.

Chapter 9

92 in the Shade

SINCE I ARRIVED in the Delta, I'd been trying to visit the blues singer T-Model Ford. We had a history together, and something like a friendship. But it wasn't easy catching up with him. His phone had changed. He'd moved house. Messages went astray. Then he was in the hospital, having suffered a stroke. Finally, I got hold of Stella, his long-time girlfriend and newly married sixth wife, and she gave me their new address in Greenville, which had once been the grandest town in the Delta and was now one of the most dilapidated and crime-ridden.

"T want to see you," she said. "And if you can help any with these hospital bills, we sure would appreciate it." In her accent, it sounded like *whore-spital beals*, and it took me a moment to understand what she'd said. Then I told her I'd do what I could, and I was afraid it wouldn't be much.

"That's fine," she said. "You just come on and visit, and don't bring no whiskey. He ain't allowed it no more."

Ten years ago, after the breakup of my marriage, I needed a place to hole up and lick my wounds for a few months. My friend Bruce Watson from Fat Possum Records offered me his trailer in Water Valley, Mississippi. He was recording the last of the raw, unvarnished, real-deal Mississippi bluesmen in a studio next to the trailer, and he warned me to expect rowdy company from time to time.

James "T-Model" Ford, who was in his early eighties then, and his mentally impaired drummer Spam, were the most frequent guests in the trailer that summer. They would pull up outside in T-Model's powder blue 1979 Lincoln Continental. I would help Spam, a tall, gap-toothed figure in his fifties, carry in guitar equipment, boxes of fried chicken, and the inevitable bottle of Jack Daniel's, while T-Model got himself out of the driver's seat and standing upright with his walking cane. Then he would flash his pearly-dentured smile, with a gold star inlaid in one of the front teeth, and deliver a kind of declamation:

"Ooo-wee! Look out now, cause here come ol' T-Model again. I'm the Taildragger from Greenville, Muzz-sippi, and I make the pretty womens jump and shout! Yeah! They took my gun, but I got my knife, and I'll cut a motherfucker too, and that's the goddamn truth. Can't read, can't write, I don't argue with folks about the Bible, but I love the womens! I love em cause of that little split they got. I got three womens right now and they won't let ol' T-Model *alone*. I'm a bad man! I can't get around like I used to, but if I can reach a motherfucker, look out! I knocked out Winehead Jones with this."

He would raise up his clenched right fist, which looked as though it belonged to a strong man in his fifties, and invite me to punch it as hard as I could. It was like hitting a brick. T-Model had worked most of his life in logging and sawmill operations around the Mississippi and Arkansas Delta, and dug ditches on the chain gang while men around him died of heatstroke and snakebite. He was discovered by Bruce's partner Matthew Johnson, the founder of Fat Possum

Records, who found him playing his rough exuberant blues in a shabby little club on Nelson Street in Greenville, aged seventy-three. Fat Possum recorded him for the first time and turned him into an internationally renowned blues artist, who had toured Japan and Australia and all over Europe.

When T-Model referred to Winehead Jones, he was talking about his fellow Fat Possum bluesman Paul "Wine" Jones. T-Model had indeed punched him out during an argument about women after a show, not that Jones seemed like a hard man to knock into unconsciousness. By the time I met him, Jones was a sick, dying man who couldn't hold his wine anymore. When he came to stay in the trailer, T-Model would crow over him unmercifully and invite him to look time and again at the mighty fist that had knocked his lights out.

I was a sorry heartbroken wreck that summer, and the bluesmen would pour me whiskey and give me their best advice. Paul "Wine" Jones said I should go to a whorehouse in Memphis where the women could do tricks with ping-pong balls and shoot them through miniature basketball hoops. "If you got money, that place will fix any man's blues," he said.

Spam, who was setting out on a tour of Europe with nothing but a change of underwear and a can of Vienna sausages (pronounced *Vy-eena* to rhyme with "hyena"), said I should be careful of sporting women. He held up his hand, and I saw the fingertips were missing. His crack whore girlfriend Francine had sliced them off with a box cutter.

"And you still ain't broke up with her!" yelled T-Model.

"Yeah I did," said Spam.

T-Model turned to me, livid with rage, and pointed a long quivering finger at Spam. "There he go, telling lies again!" he growled. "If there's one thing I hate worse than a fool it's a goddamn liar. Spam, I seen you and Francine on Nelson Street just the other day! You stupid, lying, fool-ass motherfucker, you make me mad as *hell*."

Spam looked glum. I said, "T-Model, quit giving Spam such a hard time. You know he can't help it."

"Goddamn rooster got more sense than that big ugly motherfucker," he said. "I should kick the shit out of his dumb ass. He knows I can too."

T-Model was bothered by my condition. He hated to see a man with his spirits down because of a woman. The remedy, he said, was to be like a tree. "When my sister died, I prayed to God to let me be like a tree," he said. "A tree don't let nothing get him down. A tree just keep growing and growing. He don't give a shit about them other trees around him. But when he die, he gone fall and knock those motherfuckers *down*!"

Matthew Johnson liked to describe T-Model Ford as "the happiest friendliest psychopath you'll ever meet." He was certainly a strange old man, with a streak of mean, belligerent anger that he directed mainly at poor, undeserving Spam, and sometimes at Stella, who would give it right back to him. But when you knew about all the horrors and hardships that T-Model had lived through, it was his happy, outgoing, joyful side that was the most striking and remarkable. He had a real love of life, and it shone right out of him when he smiled.

His sharecropper father had beaten him viciously all through his childhood and choked his brother to death. When T-Model was eleven, his father beat him between the legs with a piece of wood, injuring him so badly that he lost a testicle. Afterward, as he stood there with blood running down his legs, his father ordered him to put some pants on, get out in the field, and start hoeing. He went out there and sat down naked in the cool earth to get some relief from the burning pain. His father later stole T-Model's first wife away from him, and what hurt most was how willingly she went.

He found work in a Tennessee logging camp, and that's where he got his nickname. His last name was Ford, and he was hardworking, consistent and reliable, like a Model T car. One night in a juke joint near the sawmill, he got into a fight over a woman, and a jealous man stabbed him in the back. T-Model opened his pocketknife with his teeth—an operation he could still perform at lightning speed—and stabbed the man to death.

That got him ten years on the chain gang, of which he served two. You could still feel the indentation in his shinbone from the ball and chain. A fellow prisoner named Elephant, for his size, taught him how to fight, and how to take a beating without getting your spirit broken. To punish the prisoners, the guards would tie them over a wooden barrel and whip them like slaves. Elephant made T-Model a ring from a fork that he still wore sixty years later.

There was a scar on T-Model's neck where one of his wives had attempted to slash his throat. He watched another wife drop dead on the kitchen floor after she drank poison to induce a miscarriage. He had been shot, stabbed, pinned under a fallen tree, crushed under a car he was working on when the jack slipped. He had twenty-six children that he knew about, but he doubted that was all of them.

One of his sons had broken a chair over his head, and he was hard of hearing in one ear as a result. Another son had stolen his pistol, used it to kill someone in order to steal his sneakers, and then been sentenced to life in the notorious Mississippi state penitentiary at Parchman. I asked T-Model how that made him feel. He said, "I miss that pistol. It was a long-barreled .38. Hard-shooting mother-fucker."

His motto, often repeated, was, "I don't let *nothin* get me down." Most people can't do this—stay happy, no matter what—but T-Model Ford, by his superhuman strength of will, and extraordinary powers of denial, was able to pull it off. Sometimes it was disturbing to see how easily he shrugged off tragedy and horror. An elderly white woman in Greenville had taken it upon herself to teach him how to read and write. T-Model had really appreciated it, and he enjoyed the woman's company. But before he learned to make his letters, thugs broke into her house, raped her, and killed her.

I saw him two weeks later. He said, "I felt bad when I heard about it. She was a good ole white lady. But I ain't gone let it get me down. I don't let *nothin* get me down. I play the blues, but I don't ever get the blues. I won't allow it."

There was no sadness in his music. It was rough, raunchy, juke joint blues, played on an electric guitar that he called Black Nanny, and backed up by Spam pounding out caveman rhythms on the drums. Sometimes it was angry, sometimes it was mad, sometimes it was so raw that it sounded like punk rock, but it always sounded bold, proud, triumphant.

His fifth wife gave him his first guitar when he was fifty-eight, shortly before she left him. He didn't know how to tune it, so he came up with his own tuning system. "I play in the key of T," he liked to say, or, "I play in the key of my woman left." He found a way to copy his favorite Howlin' Wolf and Muddy Waters riffs, and then he started improvising licks of his own, and making up his own lyrics. He loved playing guitar. In the trailer, he would play for two or three hours straight, smiling and grinning, pausing to swig from his bottle of Jack Daniel's, occasionally singing a few lines, "Rock me baby, till I drop dead in your arms . . ."

NOW HE WAS eighty-nine years old, or ninety-one, or possibly ninety-two, living in a scruffy little rented house in a bad part of Greenville. When I arrived, Stella came out of the front door and told me not to leave anything valuable in my truck. She was bigger than

I remembered her, with dyed orange bangs, green fingernails, and a leopard-print top, and she also looked calmer, happier, more confident of herself, more worldly. I asked her how long she and T-Model had been together now. She said, "Twenty-five years, and married since May. A white lady told me to get married to him, or I wouldn't get nothing when he died."

"How's he doing?"

"He cain't hardly get out of bed, or do for his self. I been bringing a preacher around."

It was early afternoon on a Tuesday, and the living room was full of grown men and women watching TV. They were Stella's children and grandchildren and cousins. They murmured monosyllabic greetings when I said hello, and didn't take their eyes off the afternoon soap. The house smelled of old fried fish and stale beer. Stella opened the door to a small bedroom.

T-Model was sitting on the bed with his legs hanging down, wearing a red hooded sweatshirt and pajamas, looking like a shrunken, ancient version of his old self. There was still some wattage in his smile, and strength in his handshake, but he looked uncertain and afraid, and this was shocking, because he'd always been so confident. Well-wishers had sent cards and letters from all around the world, and although he couldn't read, he enjoyed showing them to me. I read out some of the messages, "We love you T-Model Ford! Get well soon! Love, Annika. Berlin."

"Hey T-Model! Wishing you well from Melbourne. Come and visit us again down under."

"Dear T-Model, we are sorry to hear about your illness. We are praying for you . . ."

He smiled and nodded. "Plenty those people sent money too," he said.

I talked about the old days in the trailer, and how we used to ride around Water Valley in his Lincoln Continental, and visit his friend whose wooden leg kept falling off. "He dead now," said T-Model. "Spam dead. Winehead Jones dead."

He gripped my hand. Tears formed in his eyes. "I been crying all the time," he said. "Cry and cry and cry. It just got next to me."

"What did?"

"I'm scared. I don't want to go down there. I'm in the hands of the Lord now, and I believe he'll take me home. But it gets next to me."

Black Nanny, his guitar, was at the foot of his bed. I asked him if he was still playing. "I won't play no blues," he said. "The preacher been coming around. He says it's devil music. I don't drink no more. I don't smoke. I don't cuss, try not to. No more chasin womens. I'm with the Lord now, and believe He'll take me home."

He smiled bravely, then his smile seemed to crumble apart, and he started crying. "I'm scared," he said, and it was clear that he was scared of going to hell. I wanted to tell him that hell didn't exist, but that called heaven into question too. I said, "Don't worry T-Model, you're a good man, look at all these cards, people love you, you don't have anything to worry about."

He said, "All I play is church songs now. I got a new CD. I recorded it with Bruce and them. Sound pretty good. It's in there. Just hit play."

He pointed to the boom box on the table. The CD was paused on track 2. I pushed the button and heard drums and blues-gospel electric guitar. T-Model grinned and nodded along to the music. "Yeah!" he said. "When I hit the guitar, it sound good!" Then the vocals came in, and his voice sounded amazingly strong.

Stella came into the room to check on him. T-Model was grinning and moving his head and shoulders to the music. "I sound pretty good," he said.

Stella said, "That ain't you, baby." She picked up the CD case and showed it to us. It was *You Can't Hurry God* by the Reverend John Wilkins. A confused smile came over T-Model's face. Then there was a knock on the bedroom door. His physical therapist had arrived. She was a good-looking white woman, and T-Model, who used to flirt compulsively with any woman of any race, size, or appearance between the ages of sixteen and seventy-five, did not even attempt to catch her eye.

As I was leaving, I gave Stella sixty dollars to help with the bills. She thanked me and said, "You be careful in this neighborhood. Don't stop for nobody. They rob you quick around here."

THE FOLLOWING DAY I paid a visit to Sam Olden, the ninety-three-year-old intellectual terror last seen at Butch Gary's dinner party. He greeted me on the front porch of the house in Yazoo City that his grandfather had built in 1894; in 1994, he had thrown a hundredth birthday party for the house with a hundred guests. Sam clasped me firmly by the shoulders and told me I was looking even more handsome than he had remembered. He said he'd been suffering from a mild but persistent dizziness, but it hadn't stopped him from driving to Jackson and back the day before, a round trip of a hundred miles. Nor had it prevented him from reading the entire *New York Times* that morning, followed by half of *The Economist*.

We sat in the living room, with the curtains half drawn against the bright sunlight, and a clock ticking quietly. History books and magazines and a fat leather-bound Bible were on the floor next to his reclining armchair. Sam launched into a lengthy critique of the conventional wisdom regarding the future of the former Soviet territories, studded with facts and quotations retained from his morning's reading, underpinned with historical details regarding place names, treaties, ex–prime ministers. At ninety-three, there was no question that his brain was sharper and more lively than mine. He asked what I'd been up to, and I told him about my visit with T-Model Ford.

"I despise the blues," he announced. "I know that some people claim to find some musicality in it, but all I can hear is sadness and a very primitive technique. Of course, classical music is what I love. Opera. I suppose you'd say my tastes are too refined to appreciate the blues, but there's more to it than that."

Sam's loathing of the blues began when he was a child. In the 1920s and early 1930s, while T-Model Ford, or "Son" Ford as he was known then, was getting beaten by his father and working in the fields, Sam Olden was growing up in the bosom of white privilege and gentility. His grandfather was the biggest cotton planter in that half of Yazoo County, and he had bequeathed a plantation to each of his nine children. Sam was born on Coon Camp, a plantation that derived its name from an abundance of raccoons, rather than negroes.

When he was a young boy, his parents moved to Yazoo City, where he and the other white children in the neighborhood were looked after by black maids/nannies that they called nurses. The children adored them and thought of them as family members. These women would leave their houses early in the morning, walk north across the railroad tracks, light fires in their employers' houses, and start cooking breakfast and cleaning. During the day, they would sometimes need to go back to their own houses, to pick up things, or check on people, and the question arose: what to do with the white children they were looking after?

"They couldn't leave us with our mothers, because our mothers weren't there," Sam recalled. "Coca-Cola had just been invented, and our mothers were all off drinking it at the soda fountain. So the nurses would get together and round up all the white children, and we'd all go together. You'd have three or four black women, and five or six white children, and we'd walk in a little tribe across the railroad tracks to the colored part of town.

"I remember it clearest in winter. That's when it was at its most grim. The streets were mud, people were living in these ramshackle houses with newspapers on the wall for wallpaper, and an outdoor privy. Every one had a pig in the backyard, and cabbages rotting on the stalks, and the smell was awful. I absolutely hated going over there, and every time I did, there would be an old Victrola somewhere playing blues. It was the tune of squalor for me. To this day, I cannot hear the blues without smelling pig slop and rotten cabbages."

Margie was the name of the black woman who looked after Sam and his sister Sis. Sam's mother hired her when she was eighteen years old, and she stayed with the family for the rest of her life. "Me and Sis never thought of Margie as being black," said Sam. "She was just like another mother to us, as important to our lives as any member of our family. But it was unthinkable to seat her at the dinner table when there was company over. That simply wasn't done."

In the summers, they would pack up and go to his grandmother's plantation Linden, where Sam's two best friends were black boys his own age. As soon as they heard the car coming, they would leave the tenant houses and run up to the big house to play with him. "Despite the rigid segregation of that era, it was perfectly normal for white children to have black playmates," he said. "They were our buddies, just as if they were white. We felt bad about how poor they were, and one year I remember me and Sis filled shoeboxes full of Christmas presents for Sonny Man, which was one of the boys—I always loved that name—and his two brothers."

I had just been reading William Faulkner's essay "Mississippi," in which he describes his quasi-fraternal friendship with a black boy who was born in the same week as him. They were "suckled together at the same black breast," he writes. Whites wouldn't drink from the same water fountain as colored, but they were happy for their babies to have a black wet nurse. It was a mark of social status.

Young Faulkner and his friend slept and ate and played together every day. As they got older, they reenacted Civil War battles with sticks and chips as soldiers. Faulkner claimed the right to be a Confederate general because he was white, but his black friend refused to play unless he was allowed to be general in one game out of three.

"I hadn't heard that story, but it sounds exactly right for that era," said Sam.

"Whatever happened to those black playmates of yours?" I asked.

"I lost touch with them, simply because we stopped going out to Linden."

"When did you become aware of racism?" I asked.

"Oh, fairly young," he said. "It was so ingrained in the older whites, and it was inherited from their forbears who had lived in slavery times. It was ingrown and innate in even the finest white minds, like Washington and Jefferson, who judged a black man to be a quarter of a person. It was a sense of arrogant superiority, a total lack of respect, and I felt it strongly from my adored grandmothers. They didn't hate blacks, or even dislike them, but thought they were absolutely inferior to whites, and here to serve us. My father and mother inherited it too, but they were kind people and never showed any disrespect."

"And what about you and Sis?"

"When we started to understand it, we were horrified, mainly because we loved Margie so much. We thought it was so terribly wrong, and we tried to make up for it by doting even more on Margie, and being as nice as we possibly could to all the black people we came into contact with. Segregation was enforced so rigidly here. It pained me particularly that blacks weren't allowed in the library. It was horrible really, the strength and depth of that feeling, and all I can tell you is that it was inherited."

"So you and your sister were unusual?"

"I suppose we were, although we never talked about it with our friends. When any of us talked about blacks, it was usually because we found them somewhat amusing. Awful really, but there were a lot of jokes and stories, and we participated in them."

When the civil rights movement came to Yazoo City, and was met with staunch, angry, and sometimes violent white resistance, Sam was living in Peru and Spain. "I am eternally grateful that I missed the entire thing," he said. "My sister was here and she had a hard time of it. She was horrified that our close, close friends were joining the Citizens' Council and things like that. Mercifully, it was all over by the time I came home."

Like his dear departed writer friend Willie Morris, Sam had high hopes for black Mississippians after the victories of the civil rights movement. "I really thought that once the schools were desegregated, and they had the vote, black people would thrive here. It saddens me tremendously that more blacks didn't take advantage of the new opportunities. The schools have let them down. Drugs have exerted such a malign influence. We're still seeing this terrible violence with stabbings and shootings. I really thought that would become a thing of the past."

The telephone rang. Sam said, "Excuse me, would you mind passing me the phone?" He answered it and delivered a burst of Italian. Then he said, "Francesco, it's wonderful to hear your voice, but I'm afraid my Italian is rusty, so I'm going to have to trouble you to talk in English . . . Yes indeed . . . Why, of course, I'd love to take your scuba-diving classes, but I won't make it there this summer."

After hanging up, Sam said, "Francesco is from Livorno. I met him in an underground winery in Moldova. I haven't seen him in years, but he calls me faithfully."

I brought the conversation back to Margie. Nowhere else in

America had been as rigorously segregated as Mississippi. Nowhere else had fought the idea of racial equality so viciously. And nowhere else had I heard so many stories about loving, quasi-familial bonds between whites and their black servants and employees. "Margie was with my mother until she died, and when Margie died, right over here at the King's Daughters Hospital, I was at her bedside," he said. "Me and Sis were listed on the program at her funeral as 'adopted children,' and that's exactly what we were."

The telephone rang again. "Ah, Velma, how wonderful to hear from you," he said. A brief conversation ensued. Sam told Velma about his doctor's appointments, and inquired after people called Junior, Robert Earl, and Little Wilson. Then he said, "I do have some company here at the moment, so I'm going to say good-bye now, and we'll talk again soon."

Velma was Margie's niece in Detroit. Margie had never had children of her own, but in addition to Sam and Sis, she also thought of Velma as her child. When Sis outgrew her clothes, they went straight to Velma, which meant that she was one of the best-dressed girls on her side of the tracks. Sam, Sis, and Velma all felt a close kinship that came from having Margie as a mother figure.

"We're still close to this day," said Sam. "Velma calls me every week or two, and she comes down to visit me and Sis periodically. I have no doubt that she'll be at my funeral, and I trust that won't be any time soon. I would like to make a hundred, and I have to say, apart from this dizziness, I feel pretty good."

He was sleeping extremely well, and waking up feeling refreshed, energized, and full of enthusiasm. He had some skin problems on his legs that required driving to a doctor in Jackson once or twice a week. "The only other thing I've noticed is a tendency to wander off the point when I'm talking," he said.

Wander was not the right word for it. When he was talking, Sam strode off on vigorous detours. I mentioned that I'd been enjoying the meat from the deer I killed, and that reminded him of the time he had eaten elk meat at the palatial country home of Om Vera Sager on her 3,000-hectare estate of pure virgin forest near the small town of Mullsjö in central Sweden. Om, of course, is Swedish for Madame, and quite a lady she was, being the daughter of a Russian czarist diplomat who was serving in Stockholm in 1917 when the revolution broke out and made it impossible for him to return home. She had been extremely good to one of Sam's dearest friends, the Rumanian Prince Alexandre Ghika, the last reigning prince of Wallachia, whom he met in Paris in 1954, where he was employed on the Quai d'Orsay and dealing principally with Balkan refugee affairs.

So began a story that lasted the better part of an hour, delving into the history of the Swedish crown, the influence of Russian and French culture in Swedish affairs, the shifting diplomatic alliances in central Europe during the Second World War, the diplomatic career of Prince Alexandre Ghika, the Russian invasion of Rumania, the life and times of Om Vera Sager. The most remarkable thing about the story was not the command of historical knowledge that it demonstrated, but the way that it never lost sight of where it was going, which was the dinner table at Margretenholm, that glorious forested country estate in central Sweden. An ample glass of vodka was already in place by each plate as a prelude to the elk meat, and Om Vera, who knocked hers back in one gulp, insisted that everyone speak French to keep any secrets from the servants.

A FEW WEEKS later, Stella invited me to a fund-raising party at the house in Greenville. T-Model was going down, she said, and the medical bills were stacking up. It was a two-hour drive across the flatscape, and I listened to prewar Delta blues all the way: the raw growl of

Charley Patton, the slashing guitar and anguished wail of Son House, the spooky moans of Rube Lacy. And I thought of Sam Olden as a boy walking across the tracks and smelling that pig slop and rotting cabbage.

The sky was gray and stormy, and a cold wind whipped across the bare, muddy fields. Charley Patton's woman had a heart made of railroad steel. Son House got a letter and how do you reckon it read? It said hurry, hurry, the gal you love is dead. So he grabbed up his suitcase and took off down the road. When he got there, she was laying on a cooling board. Well, the minutes seemed like hours, and the hours seemed like days. His good gal was dead and she'd stopped her low-down ways.

I thought of T-Model Ford, renouncing the blues as the devil's music and making a last-ditch attempt to get to heaven after all that drinking and fornicating and killing a man—two men if you count the one he ran over in his Pontiac. Johnny Farmer, another Fat Possum discovery, quit making blues records after he shot and killed his wife by accident, mistaking her for a deer. He blamed the entire incident on the fact that he'd been playing the devil's music.

R. L. Burnside, Fat Possum's best-selling artist, shot a man who died from the bullet wounds, but denied that he had intended to kill him. I remember asking him about this, and he said with a smile, "I just meant to shoot the motherfucker in the head and two times in the chest. Him dying was between him and the Lord."

R. L. was dead now. So was Junior Kimbrough, my favorite of all the Fat Possum bluesmen. He played a hypnotic driving trance blues from the north Mississippi hills and left behind thirty-six children. T-Model Ford and the Fat Possum bluesmen were the last gasp of a musical tradition that had clearly traceable roots to West Africa, but it was really a twentieth-century phenomenon, born in the Delta and not in the way that most people assume.

In most of the Deep South, the ordeal of slavery had run straight into the misery of sharecropping, but that wasn't how it happened in the Delta. After the Civil War, hundreds of freed slaves voluntarily migrated to this swampy new frontier, because it was the only place in the South where they could rent land, clear it, sell the crops they could raise on it, and work toward owning their own land. By 1900, two-thirds of the Delta's farm owners were black.

That all changed during the next twenty years. White planters and corporations exerted their power and, crucially, their access to credit, to dispossess black farmers of their land and establish large-scale plantations. Many disenfranchised black farmers now found themselves sharecropping on the new plantations, in a new era of stricter white supremacy, and often moving from one plantation to another, searching for better treatment and a fairer deal. This was the era that gave birth to the blues. It was not an ancient ancestral moan but the cry of alienated, uprooted modern man, craving independence and strongly individualistic in a way that African music had never been.

Playing the blues was also a way to make money, attract women, have fun, and escape hard work in the cotton fields. Those early musicians thought of themselves as entertainers, and when they were playing a house party, or a juke joint, or a street corner, they played pop and folk standards, as well as the blues. The mournful anguished ballads that we think of as the essential Delta blues were sung in more private settings and heavily recorded because labels were always looking for original material.

THIRTY PEOPLE, BLACK and white, were gathered in T-Model Ford's front yard. Smoke was rising from a big barbecue rig, coolers were stocked with ice and beer, and a bottle of moonshine whiskey was making the rounds. Stella, in an orange flowered muumuu, was greeting the guests and accepting their cash donations. T-Model was asleep in a wheelchair on the front porch, with blankets piled up on his lap, oblivious to the shouting children running in and out of the front door next to him. Stella soon wheeled him back inside.

There was some awkwardness between the black and white partygoers, expressed as formality and politeness, a slight tension in the body language, a reluctance to make eye contact. It went beyond the fact that we were also strangers. Lightnin Malcolm, a big-jawed, redheaded white bluesman from Missouri, who had toured extensively with T-Model Ford, plugged in his guitar on the front porch. T-Model's adopted grandson Stud got behind his drum kit. Lightnin Malcolm stood at the microphone, and said, "This here's my thing, y'all. I love to play a yard party, and don't be in no hurry to leave. I might just play all night long."

He started playing the Junior Kimbrough song "All Night Long" in the hypnotic hill country style, with drone notes on the bass string, repeating lead patterns, and a stomping driving rhythm. Essentially, he was playing bass, rhythm, and lead guitar, all at the same time, and fitting them into Stud's syncopated drumming. The first person to dance was a black man in a fedora hat, far gone on moonshine. Then the women started dancing. A couple of black women playfully showed some moves to a couple of white women, and the white women playfully tried them out. Then more men started dancing, and it became clear black men could dance with white women without anyone frowning or getting offended. Helped along by beer and liquor, the awkwardness was dissolving, and fun was emerging.

Some teenage boys from the neighborhood gangster-limped into the front yard, wearing baggy hip-hop clothing, gold jewelry, and box-fresh baseball caps. Stud started beating out hip-hop rhythms, Lightnin Malcolm played choppy funk licks, and called them up to the microphone. They took turns rapping and cracking each other up. They threw out hand signs, shouted out to the neighborhood, and made their exit laughing and grinning. The music reverted back to hill country blues. The dancers kept on dancing.

I was standing by the barbecue smoker with a big, effusive man named Bill. He was turning out succulent slabs of ribs, smoked chicken, homemade sausages, and he'd made a big vat of barbecue beans with molasses and chunks of charred rib meat. "It's a great day to be in Mississippi," he said. "Our food, our music, our people, black and white, having a *good* time. Mississippi got its problems, but fuck all that shit, cause we know how to live, man. We have good times like a muh-fucker. I wouldn't want to be nowhere else."

"Me neither," I said, and I clanked my beer can against his. It felt like it mattered more in Mississippi, that black and white could have such a good time together. Everywhere you looked, people were smiling, laughing, drinking, dancing. It felt like old taboos were falling and progress was being made, and it was also an occasion of great sadness.

From time to time, Stella would wheel out T-Model Ford into the middle of all that music and revelry. Knowing how much he would have loved it, it was heartbreaking to see how unresponsive he was. When he did manage to get his eyes open, he would blink a couple of times, look around with a puzzled expression, and then slump back into unconsciousness.

Chapter 10

Po Monkey's

WE WERE EXPECTING winter to be mild and short-lived at this semitropical latitude in the Deep South. There were palmetto palms in the woods, a teeming abundance of reptile life. New Orleans was only four hours down the road. The first frosty morning came in late November, and the day before it, a swarm of several hundred ladybugs arrived at the house. They crawled inside through cracks in the window frames, and gaps under the doors, and took up residence in the high corners of the warmest rooms. "They're lucky they have those cute little polka dots," said Mariah. "If they were gray, or dark brown, I'd be up there with the vacuum cleaner."

The first hard freeze came in early December. We covered our winter vegetables with bedsheets, and on Louie's advice, ran all the taps in the house to keep the pipes from freezing. Then came an ice storm that knocked out the electricity for twenty-four hours, followed by long weeks when the temperatures fell into the teens and twenties, and a vicious wind came raking across the Delta from some frozen quarter of hell.

Winter was desolate and monochromatic: lifeless brown fields, skeleton trees, pewter gray skies. The only green in the landscape was the occasional field of winter wheat, and the only visual drama was provided by enormous flocks of snow and specklebelly geese. Thousands of them occupied the muddy field in front of the house, and Savanna learned the giddy joy of charging toward them and making them all scatter into squawking flight. Some of the lettuce and kale in the garden grew slowly and valiantly, and we ate it with gratitude. The rest of the vegetables were stunted little sprigs, not quite freezing to death, but unable to grow. We should have put them out of their misery, but we kept thinking the weather would warm up.

The house had a propane-fueled central heating system, and Mike Foose had warned us that it was expensive to use in such a big, old, drafty, high-ceilinged house. For the first month of winter, we set the thermostat at 57 degrees and were never warm in the house. Then we received a propane bill of $804. So we stopped using the central heat altogether, lived in long johns and multiple layers of fleece and wool, bought electric heaters for the bathroom and bedroom, and huddled around the living room fireplace.

Winter was a test of our relationship. Mariah grew up in the desert heat and joke winters of Tucson, Arizona. She got cold easily, and she hated being cold. Winter in New York had been okay, because all the buildings were so warm. It was one thing to bundle up to go outside, and another to wear four or five layers of clothing inside the house. Since it was me who had gotten her into this situation, without fair or adequate warning about the cold, it was at least partially my fault.

I certainly felt responsible for her discomfort, and somewhat ashamed. A man who couldn't keep his woman warm in winter wasn't much of a man at all. Sometimes, as people will, I rearranged these feelings, and decided that the real problem here was her attitude. I started to say things like, "Well, I'm fine, but I've got on more layers than you," and, "If you're cold, you're obviously not wearing enough clothes."

During one particularly cold snap, when the temperature got down to nine degrees outside, and thirty-four degrees inside the house, I tried to turn it into an adventure. "Just pretend we're camping," I said cheerily, as I carried another load of firewood through the house into the living room, tramping in dirt and spilling little pieces of debris everywhere. I was wearing a heavy fleece-lined Carhartt jacket, a wool cap, two pairs of socks, long underwear, a wool shirt, three sweaters, and a scarf. She was bundled up in sweaters and flannel-lined trousers, with a heavy Pendleton blanket pulled around her.

"I don't want to be camping *inside* my house," she said. "That's the worst thing you could have said. I want to be warm and comfortable inside the house. I want it to feel like a home. I know we can't afford the propane. I know it doesn't make the house warm anyway. I understand the situation, but please don't remind me that we're basically camping here."

The electric heaters were a big disappointment. The rooms were too big, the ceilings too high. Cold air whistled in through gaps in the window frames. We had a plan to abandon three-quarters of the house and move into the kitchen and the master bedroom, both of which had wood-burning stoves. The problem was that the stove-pipes were rusted out and needed replacing. Two handymen had already tried and failed, because they couldn't find the right parts. Wood-burning stoves were on the way out, they told us. They advised us to replace the sagging underfloor insulation ($8,000), add more insulation in the attic ($6,000), and buy much bigger electric heaters ($1,500 + much bigger electric bills).

I drove to hardware stores all over the Delta, and down in Jackson, looking for the right diameter stovepipe, the right elbows, and two new insulated thimbles to join the interior pipe with the exterior pipe. I managed to pick up the elbows and some lengths of pipe. Then I went online, wrestled with confusing specifications and measurements, and ordered some more parts that weren't quite right. Our friend Doug Roberts found the rest of what we needed in Grenada, Mississippi, and he came down for a frustrating weekend of trying to fit them together. The male and female pipe ends didn't match up, but finally he managed to crimp, bend, force, tape, and whack the goddamn things together with torrents of foul language.

With fire extinguishers at the ready, we lit the first fires. Smoke leaked out in a few places, and we sealed them up with aluminum tape. Then a nasty brown liquid started dripping on the floor from the kitchen stovepipe. The firewood wasn't properly cured, I guessed, and moisture was condensing and puddling in a horizontal section of pipe. No amount of tape could stop that leak, so we put a big cooking pot underneath it and learned to live with the sooty smell. The bedroom stove, however, was a champion. The day after Doug left, I built a big fire in there, adjusted the dampers, and got the temperature up to eighty degrees. For the first time in many weeks, I saw my girlfriend naked.

My life became dominated by splitting wood, snapping fallen branches into kindling, carrying and stacking wood, kneeling in front of stoves and blowing, stoking, damping, raking, and carrying out ashes. I resented the time it took away from reading, writing, and research, but I didn't mind the work itself. It was satisfying to swing a big axe on a frosty morning, and get warmed twice by the wood: once by the effort of splitting it, and once again when I blew it into flames.

Mariah really appreciated it too. She would come home from work, park behind the house, catch a brief blast of icy wind on her way across the back deck, and then enter a warm kitchen, with deer sausage frying in the skillet, sweet potatoes in the oven, perhaps some cabbage from the garden shredded up and cooking in chicken stock and thyme. To be able to change her clothes in a warm bedroom now felt like an unexpected pleasure, rather than a basic human right. She became adept at lighting fires too, and found some pride and satisfaction in this new skill. But it was still a smoky, smelly, troublesome way to get warm, and it seemed like winter would never end.

MARIAH STILL DIDN'T like being alone in the house when I was gone. Although I had promised to quit traveling, our bleeding finances required me to go out into the world and commit acts of journalism. Louie and Cathy's house was as warm and welcoming for Mariah as it could possibly be. They kept the thermostat in the seventies, and Louie built a big fire in the living room fireplace every night. Cathy hugged Mariah like a fourth daughter when she arrived, and Savanna got on well with the Thompson dogs.

There was good Southern food for dinner every night, cable television, soft, comfortable furnishings, and the warm feeling of coming into a happy, relaxed family household. Occasionally politics would come up, but not in a confrontational way. The Thompsons made a polite, sincere effort to understand why Mariah thought the way she did about certain issues, and she did the same. They were conservative Bible Belt Republicans, and she was an urban liberal Democrat, except it wasn't like that at all, because no one was defining or judging each other by their politics.

Perhaps no woman on earth loves babies more fiercely than Cathy Thompson, who spends her days bringing them into the world as a labor and delivery nurse in Jackson. She was putting the pressure on her daughters to get married and start giving her some grandbabies. As an adopted daughter, Mariah was catching some of this pressure too.

"We need a baby on Pluto," Cathy told her. When Mariah said she wasn't sure about having kids, Cathy reminded her that she was thirty-four years old, her reproductive system was getting old, and if she wasn't going to have a baby right this instant, it was definitely time to freeze her eggs.

Mariah and I swung back and forth on the subject of having children. Our teetering finances were one big obstacle. Cathy joked that Mariah could be a welfare queen like all those black women having babies in Tchula and Thornton, and it was a sign of how close the two of them had become that Mariah didn't get offended.

When I returned from my trip, she looked so warm and content and comfortably nestled into the Thompson household, and I felt bad about taking her back to the cold, drafty, half-furnished house down the road, with its premodern heating system. With an hour until bedtime, and no split firewood or kindling in the stack, there was no point even trying to warm up a room. It was time to get back into our long johns, sweaters, scarves, and hoodies, and then dive under the comforters, quilts, and blankets.

MARTHA STAYED UP in Greenwood for most of the winter and seldom left the house. One day I went over there, and she was watching a Sundance-award-winning documentary called *Zoo*, about a man who died after having sexual relations with a horse. She was scandalized, and the man's choice of cocktail only made it worse. "You do not drink a daiquiri before being penetrated by a trained horse," she said. "Parasol drinks and bestiality do not go together, and they never will. If you're going to have sex with a horse, drink a beer, or a whiskey drink. I mean, come on."

She was between book projects, waiting for a royalty check, and trying to write an essay that she called "Loaves and Fishes." Her husband Donald was no longer baking his excellent bread. The Viking Range Corporation, one of Greenwood's largest employers, had been sold off to a corporation from Chicago. The new bosses had laid off 20 percent of the workers and closed down the bakery where Donald was working.

"The thing that gets me is that none of it was Donald's fault," she said. "All he was doing was baking really great bread, and selling all of it every day to people who loved it. Now everyone in Greenwood has to eat crappy bread, because that's what the bottom line has dictated, and we're supposed to think this is some kind of progress."

Louie Thompson, having kept it secret from Cathy and everyone else, had just revealed that his catfish hatchery was losing money, and he would have to find a job. Martha said, "Louie has worked in that hatchery all his life. He belongs on Pluto, wearing an old pair of shorts and a fishing shirt. It breaks my heart to think of Louie putting on a pair of khakis, and lacing up a pair of sensible shoes in the morning. And just like Donald, it wasn't his fault. Delta farm-raised catfish is a great product. Louie is one of the best there is at producing it. And the market says he can't produce it anymore. It's the winter of Loaves and Fishes."

Donald got a nice severance from Viking and was happy to take it easy for a while and not hear the alarm go off at 3:00 a.m. Louie was going to try raising bass in his ponds, to stock ponds and waterways for fishermen, and look around the Delta catfish industry for a salaried job. As a former president of Catfish Farmers of Mississippi, and a universally liked and well-respected man, his chances seemed fairly good.

We had our own worries. Mariah wasn't earning much part-time at the bookstore, and with the Viking layoffs, the future of the

bookstore was uncertain. We were spending far more than we expected to spend, and the old house always seemed to have its hand in
my pocket. Gasoline was a big expenditure. We had bought an ugly
used hatchback so I could get around while she was at work, and
between the two vehicles, we were spending nearly as much on gas
as she was earning.

She was driving ninety miles to get to work and back. I was doing
the same to buy groceries at the Walmart on Highway 82, which was
the nearest place to buy organic produce, imported cheeses, and
prosciutto. It was also the only place I knew that reflected the true
demographics of the Delta—majority black, minority white, with a
smattering of Mexicans, Chinese, Lebanese. No one was immune to
its lure, and it was a great place to eavesdrop and people watch. You
could see the whiskey-sodden cotton gentry buying ammunition
at the gun counter, as camo-clad lesbians shopped for arrows and
teenage mothers wheeled past with their shopping carts. You could
see lawyers and politicians, preachers and construction workers, the
morbidly obese chuffing past in motorized shopping carts, a black
man in a yellow suit buying a green lawnmower and a jug of doe
estrus.

When Walmart first arrived in the Delta, in the 1980s, there was
a great wailing and gnashing of teeth among writers, photographers,
and aficionados of the old, crumbling, picturesque Delta, where there
were no corporate businesses, and it was all Mom-and-Pop old-
school Americana. Walmart was destroying the regional uniqueness
of the Delta, they said, and making it more like everywhere else in
America.

Martha didn't see it that way. "Walmart came in here, and we
turned them," she said. "There's nothing more Delta than a Delta
Walmart." It wasn't just the accents and mannerisms of the customers, but a quality of lax and haphazard disorganization. Products

were often stacked in the wrong places and mislabeled. The store would run out of things. The checkers were nearly all black women, and sometimes they questioned my food choices.

"You sure got a lot of vegetables," said one. She was in her mid-twenties with a hairstyle that would take many sentences to adequately describe and long fingernails painted purple and gold. "You really gone eat all that?"

"Sure," I said. "What's wrong with vegetables?"

"Uh uh, I don't eat none of that rabbit food," she said. "I eat like folks."

She picked up a bundle of asparagus. "Now what this is?" I told her, and she called across to the neighboring cashier, "Code on this? Sparrow-guts or something."

Another time, a cashier held up an avocado, and said, "What this is? Look like it fell out of a elephant."

I was buying groceries there one afternoon when I heard a woman wailing and screaming in the clothing section. Disgracefully, I did not rush toward the sounds of a woman in distress, but carried on shopping and tried to pretend it wasn't happening. The wailing continued. A few minutes later an ambulance crew came rushing through the front doors with a stretcher, and I watched them wheel out a young teenage girl who'd gone into labor. She was a black girl no more than fifteen years old, and she looked so frightened with her huge pregnant belly sticking up from the stretcher.

Later, after I'd told the story a few times, I started leaving out how frightened the girl had looked, and how upset I had felt. I turned it into a tragi-comic welcome-to-the-Delta anecdote; we had the highest teen birth rate in the nation, after all. I realized that I'd taken on Martha's philosophy, which was laughter to keep from crying. People needed tools to cope with all the poverty, tragedy, and dysfunction in the Delta, and the most popular ones were denial, religion, gallows humor, drugs, and alcohol. All these tools have warping effects on the clear rational mind, and they seemed to feed the weirdness.

I had met plenty of Deltans who drank modestly or not at all, but I'd still characterize it as a hard-drinking place, and it certainly thought of itself that way. Nowhere else in the world had I seen such gigantic measures of liquor poured, such widespread enthusiasm for Bloodies and Mimosas on weekend mornings, or such firm insistence on giving sixteen-ounce Styrofoam cups loaded with iced liquor to guests leaving a party, so they might have a "traveler" for the drive home.

At a bar in Yazoo City, the bartender asked me if I wanted to "go tall" with my bourbon on the rocks. I didn't know what he meant, but it sounded encouraging. "Sure," I said, "Let's go tall." He filled up a pint glass with ice. Then he filled it to the brim with bourbon. When I got up to leave with about half the drink gone, he poured the rest of it into a Styrofoam cup, assuming I would want a traveler.

No, this was not legal. Drunken driving is against the law and heavily penalized in the Mississippi Delta like everywhere else. But people here were more willing to take their chances, or less willing to let the law cramp their style, and some of them could barely conceive of going down the road without a beer or a traveler. As one man explained to me, "You never know what's going to happen, especially at night. You might end up in a ditch, and damn sure need a drink of whiskey."

The same man told me a story about a police officer who was notoriously hard on drunk drivers. He had arrested his own brother for DUI, scandalizing the community, and made himself even more unpopular by lying in wait outside the local bar with the lights off in his cruiser. One night, a man came staggering and stumbling out of the bar. He fumbled with his keys trying to get the door of his truck open. Finally he got in the driver's seat, drove away from the bar, and then remembered to turn on his headlights. The cop pounced.

"Have you been drinking?"

"No sir, I haven't."

"I saw you staggering out of the bar. Step outside the car."

The cop got out his Breathalyzer machine. The man blew a 0.00. The cop assumed there was a malfunction and fetched a new machine. Again, the man blew 0.00.

"What's going on here?" said the cop.

"I'm the DD," said the man.

"The designated driver?" said the cop.

"The designated decoy," said the man.

His drunk friends in the bar had waited for the cop to pull him over, before getting in their trucks and driving home. This was a typical Delta story, although I can't guarantee its full veracity. It contained mischief, alcohol, clever whimsical use of language, and the humiliation of a tight-assed authority figure. As such, it was also typical of a story you might hear in Ireland.

MARIAH WOULDN'T DRIVE after a single drink, so if we went for an evening out, I was usually the designated driver, although not always entirely sober. Driving fifty miles home on a long, straight, empty road with the moonlit fields streaming past, hoping not to run into a stray dog, or a deer, or a DUI checkpoint, became a familiar experience, as it was for many people here. It's always a long way in the Delta, they said, but never too far to get there.

In the nineteenth century, Delta planters and their families were famous for making forty- and fifty-mile horseback journeys in order to attend parties and balls. They were gregarious people who lived in a place where human settlements were spread out and isolated. Once the Delta was cleared and tamed, its geography was determined by the requirements of large-scale plantation agriculture, rather than human sociability and convenience. Today, with disappearing towns, shrinking populations, and mechanized agriculture, that was even more true.

It was forty miles one way to Club Ebony in Indianola, a famous African-American nightclub founded in 1948, and well worth the journey if Super Chikan was playing. He was a virtuoso electric bluesman who built his own guitars out of cigar boxes, auto mufflers, rifle butts, and other found objects. It was forty-five miles to have cocktails at the Alluvian Hotel bar in Greenwood, followed by sensational fried chicken in a booth at Lusco's, or James Beard Award–winning contemporary Southern fare at the Delta Bistro.

It was a 160-mile round trip to Po Monkey's on a Thursday night. You drove north to the small town of Merigold on Highway 61, then turned on to a gravel road that ran parallel to a bayou in pitch blackness unless the moon was out. You kept going, wondering if it was the right gravel road, until you saw a small dim light in the darkness up ahead, and then a long row of old rectangular American cars and pickup trucks, and a few newer ones, parked on the edge of a field.

Then you walked up to an ancient-looking sharecropper's shack, built from unpainted cypress boards, patched up with pieces of plywood and corrugated tin, and covered in hand-painted signs and drawings. One depicted a man in a backward baseball cap, with the words "not like this" written next to it. Another drawing showed a pair of male buttocks with the pants sagging below them, with the words, "and not like that." That was the dress code and above the rickety-looking front door, another sign read, "NO beer brought inside. Please NO drugs or Lounld [sic] Music."

There used to be juke joints like this all over rural Mississippi, but Po Monkey's was almost the last one left. It was popular with blues tourists, and it had been officially designated as a cultural landmark in the National Register of Historic Places. It was in the process of being commodified and preserved as a museum version of itself, but it wasn't there yet. Most of the clientele was black and local, and they were here to drink and dance.

Monday night was "grown folks night," which meant strippers. Thursday night was "family night," which meant no strippers. It was five dollars at the door, and then a moment of adjustment as you tried to process the sensory bombardment. The floor wasn't level; it had a definite tilt sloping down from the pool table to the kitchen. Dozens of toy monkeys hung from the ceiling, and some of them were augmented with phallic plastic bananas and sex shop dildos. Also hanging from the ceiling were strings of colored lights, pieces of tinsel, naked plastic baby dolls, a revolving disco ball, and a perennial sign scissored out of paper that read SEASONS GREETINGS.

There was floral wallpaper and reflective foil on the walls, people dancing to loud funky music, a few white tourists sitting at tables and standing against the walls. Some of the dancers were fantastically overweight; the Delta's obesity problem was shaking it and grooving.

Nothing was more eye-catching than the proprietor Willie Seaberry, Mr. Po Monkey himself. A big, tall, sixty-seven-year-old tractor driver, he worked in the surrounding fields for a corporate farm, slept in a tiny room behind the dance floor, and owned more than a hundred zoot suits. The first night we went there, he was wearing a bright red suit, a crazy wig, and a peculiar little apron, behind which swung an enormous rubber penis. Po Monkey found the most innocent-looking white girl in the room, a young Italian woman, who was sitting down watching her boyfriend shoot pool. Po Monkey stood in front of her, and then snatched the apron aside, and grinned with delight as her hand flew to her mouth.

On the walls there were photographs of high school graduations, hunters with trophy bucks, glossy promos signed by professional strippers. A small hatch in the wall went back to the kitchen and the beer cooler. Beer was the only drink for sale, but you could bring your own bottle of liquor and buy a "set up": glasses, ice, mixers. The DJ was playing a mixture of old-school soul and the newer, funky soul blues coming out of Memphis, and it all sounded great on the big bumping sound system, except to those few tourists who were expecting to hear Delta blues.

Some of the white people, ourselves included, felt slightly inhibited and out of place. The locals weren't unfriendly by any means, but we lacked their ease and comfort and flamboyance. Our clothes looked drab by comparison. Our body language was a little stiff and awkward. Then the door swung open and in came a group of white Delta frat boys—pastel-colored fishing shirts, bowl haircuts with the bangs flipped to the side, pudgy cheeks. They were immediately at home, dancing and high-fiving, cracking jokes with the men, flirting with the women in a way that didn't upset anyone. And they had real moves on the dance floor.

I needed plenty of alcohol before I felt loose enough to dance, and that was problematic. Po Monkey's was best if you got at least half-drunk and did some dancing, but then you were looking at an illegal eighty-mile drive home, white knuckles on the steering wheel when you saw a police cruiser, and the extremely sobering possibility of a night in a Delta jail. Still, it was worth the risk occasionally, because after a big blowout night out at Po Monkey's, you left convinced that it was the greatest nightclub on earth.

I ALWAYS BOUGHT the local Delta newspapers when I saw them, and I started following five or six of them online. They were run on very limited budgets, and usually included Bible homilies, a hunting columnist, and a political commentator who bellowed like a wounded buffalo. Weirdness was almost guaranteed in the news section. Greenwood had started promoting itself with the slogan, "That's So Delta!" and that became a category for some of the news stories I was collecting in my files.

The police announced that motorists should not stop for police. Armed bandits were posing as police officers, and until they were apprehended, motorists should ignore any police officers who tried to stop them on the highways. Several months after this announcement, a man in a police uniform, standing in the road by a parked white hatchback, aggressively flagged me down, and I swerved around him.

In Itta Bena, the ex-judge was refusing to leave office, even though he was no longer getting paid. The new judge was drawing a salary, but she was unable to hold court, because the ex-judge was still in there hearing cases and refusing to budge. Then the chancery clerk, Larry Buffington, discovered that neither of them was authorized to be a judge, because it was an elective position, and both of them had been appointed. So years and years of legal decisions in Itta Bena were now vulnerable to appeal.

In Drew, the new mayor gave a speech in which he described whites as "the opposite race" and stressed that there was no need to "exterminate" them. In the same speech, he pleaded with the citizens of Drew to stop robbing the Dollar General, because it was the only store left in town, and they were robbing it blind. If they kept it up, he said, the store would surely close.

A pack of feral dogs near Vicksburg was increasing in size and boldness; the city had been trying to catch them, without success, for more than two years. Here in Holmes County, former supervisor Norman Cobbins was sentenced to prison for swindling county money. Our congressional representative, a white man named Jason White, ran as a Democrat, presumably to get black votes. Once elected, he declared that he was a conservative man of God, and that his code of morality required him to switch sides and join the Republican party.

Up in Southaven, Republican mayor Greg Davis, who was elected on a "family values" platform, was indicted for misusing $170,000 of taxpayer money. Among his illegal expenditures was $67 spent at Priape, a business that described itself as "Canada's premiere gay lifestyle store and sex shop." Davis claimed he was being "persecuted" for his fiscal conservatism.

The medical profession was beset with scandals. One doctor was convicted of watering down chemotherapy drugs. Another was caught bribing a county supervisor in an elaborate fraud scheme. In Clarksdale, a heart doctor called Roger Weiner was running for mayor, despite the fact the FBI had accused him of offering money for sex to women on a website called sugardaddyforme.com.

Over in Tupelo, outside the Delta but firmly in Mississippi, a Wayne Newton impersonator and martial arts expert had mailed packages of ricin, a deadly poison, to President Obama and other politicians. Inside the packages there were written notes intended to frame his archrival, an Elvis impersonator obsessed with the alleged black market in human body parts in north Mississippi. Also mixed up in their feud was a gloriously profane mortician who served as Tupelo's congressman.

A *Rolling Stone* journalist covering the story wondered "if the air down here perhaps contains an element that causes dreams to ignite and burn hotter and stranger than anywhere else in the world." Mariah and I had speculated along the same lines. Or maybe it was the farm chemicals raining down from the sky into the ground water. Mississippians could be the nicest, kindest people in the world, but when they felt grievously wronged, their thirst for vengeance could drive them into insane feuds. When the ricin story broke, we thought immediately of Dr. Smith and Lee Abraham—another half-baked attempt to destroy an archrival that backfired disastrously.

Chapter 11

Death Row Valentine

MARIAH DOESN'T DO Valentine's Day. She doesn't believe in it, or care about it, and she was genuinely unconcerned when I told her that I had inadvertently lined up a Valentine's Day outing for Martha and me. I had requested us a tour of the Mississippi state penitentiary and penal farm at Parchman, and the approved date came back as February 14th.

Parchman Farm first sent a chill through me when I was a young record collector in London. The bluesman Bukka White had a grim dirge that began, "Judge gave me life this morning, down on Parchman Farm." The white jazz singer Mose Allison, who grew up in the Delta near Parchman, also sang about it, "Well I'm putting that cotton in an eleven-foot sack / With a twelve-gauge shotgun at my back . . ."

Most haunting of all were the Alan Lomax recordings of the prisoners singing as they toiled in Parchman's cotton fields. They were call-and-response work songs, like the slaves used to sing; one visitor to Parchman said the swelling power of the chorus almost knocked you off your feet. The convicts called the sun "Ole Hannah," and in the long, hot days of summer, they begged her to move faster, "Been a great long time since Hannah went down. Oh, Hannah, go down." There were songs about everyday life at Parchman, about women, mules, bad luck, crime and punishment, and they often contained a dose of sarcastic humor, "Oh wasn't I lucky when I got my time / Babe I didn't git a hundred, got a ninety-nine."

Alan Lomax was there in the 1940s, when Parchman was the closest thing to slavery left in the South, with notoriously harsh and brutal conditions. Discipline was enforced with a fearsome leather strap known as Black Annie, and the prisoners would chant a cadence along with the whippings, "One . . . he's a gitten' de leather. Two . . . he don't know no better. Three . . . cry niggah, stick yo' finger in yo' eye . . . "

The white superintendent lived in a three-storey antebellum-style mansion with spindles and gables and a wraparound porch, and his job was to produce as much cotton as possible with his unpaid labor, which was overwhelmingly African-American. Unlike most prisons, which drain the public coffers, Parchman was highly profitable. It was making a million dollars a year through the 1940s, and the money went straight into the Mississippi state treasury.

Not much changed in the 1950s and 1960s. It wasn't until 1971 that the US Justice Department ended the worst abuses, and there have since been further reforms and modernizations. Since the 1980s, most of its vast acreage had been leased out to private farmers, but many convicts still work in the fields, and it's still reputed to be a very tough prison indeed. When Mississippians say "Parchman," the word is laden with dread.

•   •   •

MARTHA HAD GONE there once before on a school trip, designed to scare teenagers into obeying the law and staying out of prison. One of her classmates asked a prisoner what was the worst thing about being there. "The first time they fuck you in the ass," he replied, and this was the first time that she and her classmates learned about that kind of rape.

She wanted to go again for two reasons. Like most Deltans, she had a morbid fascination with the place. And as a writer, she was interested in the fact that the prison produced so much of its own food. Parchman was one of the largest farm-to-table operations in the country. "You know how to show a girl a good time on Valentine's Day," Martha said when I picked her up at her house in Greenwood on a cold bright morning. She was wearing a black leather jacket with a Los Angeles Museum of Art Security Officer patch on the shoulder, and for some reason she couldn't stop sneezing. "Ooh, excuse me," she said. "I must be allergic to the cell phone in my rectum."

We'd both been following the newspaper stories about the brisk trade in cell phones inside Parchman, and the creative ways of smuggling them in. The entire Mississippi prison system was run by gangs, and riddled with corruption, with the guards bringing in most of the drugs, weapons, and cell phones. Another persistent problem was female guards having sex with male prisoners, and getting pregnant as a result.

We drove through the bleak winter fields, passing the small town of Schlater, which was pronounced "Slaughter." Martha said, "I've only got one question about Parchman: is it true that they bury their dead prisoners standing up in the peach orchard? That's what I've always heard, and I always wonder about it when I bite into a peach."

It was an unusual prison in so many ways, and one of them, we discovered, was the absence of a perimeter fence. By the time we saw the gatehouse and a long horizontal sign saying MISSISSIPPI STATE

PENITENTIARY, we were already on the prison grounds, but we'd seen no demarcation lines or fences. Parchman was so big, isolated, and remote—18,000 flat and virtually treeless acres in the middle of Delta nowhere—that it had never needed fences. Where could a prisoner run to? Where could he hide where the bloodhounds wouldn't find him? He was imprisoned by space, emptiness, and distance.

A smiling, friendly black female guard gave the car a cursory search without looking under the seats. She told us to report to the main building, and said, "Y'all have a nice visit now." The superintendent was waiting for us. He was a thin, dapper black man from Clarksdale named Earnest Lee. He wore a light gray suit with a tangerine shirt, a gold tie, and brown shoes with long, extended, squared-off toes. A bulge in the small of his back suggested a pistol. "What exactly is your interest here?" he asked. I told him I was writing a book about the Delta, and Parchman was obviously a big presence in its history and consciousness. Martha said she was interested in the food they were growing and serving to prisoners.

"Well," he said. "We farm 5,569 acres. We produced over four million pounds of vegetables last year, valued at $1.3 million. We raise chickens for the eggs. We used to raise hogs, but too many were going out the back door, instead of coming through the front door. We don't even raise cotton no more. We got out of that business."

He took us through to a conference room and gave us a presentation that displayed his excellent head for figures. "We have a 4,648 capacity, with 3,382 offenders today," he said. "We have 868 staff, with 661 on security. Our inmates are sixty-seven percent black and thirty percent white."

He summarized the history of Parchman with a slide show. We looked at a photograph of a black man in a striped prison uniform, pointing a shotgun at black prisoners. This was a "trusty-shooter," a Parchman innovation. Rather than pay guards to watch the prisoners and make them work, the white sergeants would get prisoners they trusted to do the job. The sight of black convicts armed with shotguns never failed to astound visitors, but the system worked well, because the trusty-shooters were given an automatic pardon if they managed to kill or wound an escaping prisoner. They seldom tried to escape themselves, preferring to rely on their marksmanship to get out of Parchman free and clear. Ordinary convicts were known as "gunmen," because they worked in the fields under the gun of a trusty-shooter.

Parchman was also unusual in allowing conjugal visits for its prisoners. "It started in 1918, only for black inmates, and for better productivity," said Superintendent Lee. "In the 1930s, all inmates were allowed conjugal visits. Today, it's only for minimum-custody or medium-custody inmates who are legally married. They can get it four times, or two times a month, and we have conjugal visit apartments for them."*

A photograph flashed up of the Freedom Riders, who were arrested in 1961 for promoting civil rights, and locked up at Parchman, where the guards stripped them, mocked them, and blasted them with fire hoses. Then came a photograph of black prisoners in striped uniforms chopping cotton in a line, being eyed by a fat white man in a short tie and a boater hat. I kept expecting Superintendent Lee to express some sign of disapproval of the old days at Parchman, when black men were treated like slaves, but he did not.

When the presentation ended, I said, "What's the biggest problem Parchman faces today?"

"Staff," he said. "So many of our staff get caught up in illegal activity."

"Why is that?"

---

*Conjugal visits have since been banned by the state legislature.

"To work here, you need a high school GED and no felony conviction. We give you a four-week training course, and the pay is twenty-two thousand dollars a year and benefits. In the Delta, that means you get predominantly black females with previous work experience at McDonald's, Burger King, and Walmart. Too many of them don't have what it takes. Dealing with criminals, trying to outsmart a convict, it's too much for them. You've got to have character and integrity. We had that in the old days here."

"Why is it predominantly females?" I asked. "Men don't want to work for those wages?"

"Too many of our young men drop out of high school, or get a felony," he said. "Too many come in here as offenders."

Incarceration was now the second biggest industry in the Delta, after agriculture. Twelve new prisons had been built in twenty years. If you grew up poor with limited employment opportunities, as most people did in the Delta, prison was always on the horizon. If you graduated from high school, and stayed out of trouble, you could get a job in prison that paid more than Walmart and had benefits. If not, there was a good chance you'd end up there anyway, on the other side of the bars.

WE GOT IN Superintendent Lee's car and embarked on a six-hour tour. Parchman was a huge operation. The farm grew all the vegetables for the entire state prison system, and had the capacity to grow a lot more. The only problem, said the manager at the packing plant, was that most prisoners these days refused to eat vegetables. "Fast food is all they know," he said. He encouraged us to look around and told us not to worry about the dozens of inmates working there, because they were all minimum custody. Nonetheless, we were unnerved to see a line of unguarded butcher knives hanging up in a side area. It was the same in the prison kitchens: knives and scissors lying around.

At the mechanic's shop, inmates were servicing and repairing various vehicles, four-wheelers and boats belonging to prison officials. "We still have a few horses around here too, but most of our staff are black now, and they don't want to ride," said Superintendant Lee. We went to machine shops, adult education classrooms, flower gardens, dog training facilities for the famous Parchman tracking hounds, peach and pecan orchards, where he assured us that no dead prisoners were buried standing up.

"This is where we used to do all our executions at," he said, showing us the old gas chamber. "We have used hanging, the electric chair, gas chamber, and now we have the lethal injection table. So far we have executed seventeen inmates by lethal injection, all for murder."

"Do you honor their last meal requests?" said Martha.

"Within reason," he said. "Me, I wouldn't even want to eat."

"It'd be a tough call for me," she said. "Maybe pancakes and bacon."

As we approached the maximum-security unit that contained death row, he said, "Now we fittin to go to the real penitentiary, yes sir!" He opened the first door, and a female guard gave him a two-second pat-down. "I got pat down better than that on my vacation to Thailand," he said. The guard didn't pat down me and Martha at all. We hadn't been searched since we'd arrived.

We went through the heavy gate leading into the death row unit. It opened automatically and closed manually. But it wouldn't close because it was broken. Superintendent Lee wrestled with it for a while and then put through a tight-lipped call to maintenance. With the door lolling open, we went into a waiting area, where two young female guards were sitting down by a small table. One had orange braids swept up like a pineapple. She was eating fried chicken. The other guard was eating from a bag of Valentine candy.

The superintendent said under his breath, "Every time I come here, somebody eating." He addressed the guard with the candy. "You eating again, Jellybean Fingers?"

She gave him a sulky pout. He said, "I can tell you didn't get nothing for Valentine's Day."

She sassed him back, saying suggestively, "And I can tell you did."

Both of them tried to stifle their laughter at that one, and the guard eating fried chicken let out a snort.

"Sergeant, it's that time," he said to her, holding his arms slightly away from his body.

He wanted her to follow protocol and pat *everyone* down for weapons and contraband before allowing them to enter death row. She looked at him blankly.

"Well, Sergeant?" he said. "Are you going to put your chicken grease all up on my clothes?"

"Nawsuh, I wouldn't do that," she said, licking the grease off her fingers. "You always dress like a G."

He said, "What about you, Jellybean?" She started licking her fingers too.

"Never mind," he said. "We're going in."

Inside the door was a stack of plastic riot shields, and a young male guard with an innocent boyish face. He tried to find a riot shield that wasn't broken, but there wasn't one. So he picked up the best of the bunch, put his arm through one strap, and held the dangling broken strap with his other hand. There were two tiers of cells, containing forty-seven murderers. Most of them gave us one look and turned away. Some glowered. None threw feces. The superintendent pointed to a Chinese murderer on the upper tier. "Him up there got the same name as me, but he's Chinese. Yes sir! His name's Lee."

•   •   •

THAT WAS AS close as we got to the real penitentiary. We weren't allowed to interview any prisoners about the conditions, the gangs, the extraordinarily high rate of violence, or anything else. Aside from that brief, weird glimpse of death row, we weren't allowed inside any cell blocks. But it wasn't a slick public-relations exercise. Superintendent Lee didn't try to cover up the corruption among his staff.

"Cell phones, we can't control it," he said. "They're worth fifteen hundred dollars each in here, and the staff brings them in. Since we went tobacco-free, tobacco is worth more than marijuana, and a potato chip bag full of marijuana goes for a thousand dollars. The staff brings it in."

He seemed resigned to the shortcomings of the institution that he ran, most of which were outside his control, and nostalgic for the old days at Parchman. "These young thugs we get now, they don't want to work," he said. "They just want to eat, raise sand, and watch TV all day and all night. It ought to be, if you don't work, you don't eat. We can't force them to work, or threaten them with real punishment, because the ACLU put all these stipulations on us. We don't have the power anymore to run this place right. We used to, but not no more."

"But wasn't it terribly racist and brutal back then?" I said. "People said it was worse than slavery."

"Some of it went too far, but you had more structure then," he said. "Staff was more committed to doing what's right, and the prisoners knew how to work. Black Annie made them work, but we can't use Black Annie no more."

We thanked him for spending so much time with us, and made a dazed exit through the gift shop. "Oh my stars, what a weird day," said Martha, holding up a prisoner-made kitchen apron.

"Didn't you feel like something could go badly wrong at any time?" I said.

"What, you mean a big old line of butcher knives just hanging there? The busted door to death row? Sergeant Chicken Grease and Jellybean Fingers? That baby-faced kid with the janky-ass riot shield? We didn't get searched once all day! It was just so . . ."

"So Delta?"

"Yup."

ON THE WAY back to Greenwood, Martha started telling me what she knew about "Henry," a convicted murderer who was sentenced to life at Parchman, and somehow spent forty-seven years working for her great-aunt Kerry, and living in her back garden. "Have you seen *Driving Miss Daisy*?" she said. "That was Henry and Aunt Kerry, inseparable, devoted to each other, up to a point." Then Martha decided that she didn't know enough to do the story justice and said I should talk to her mother, Cindy Foose, who had known Henry well.

A small, energetic woman with glasses and curly hair, Cindy is a needlework guru who flies around the country teaching classes and seminars on rarified sewing techniques. Like Martha, she's a wit and a storyteller. A few days after the Parchman visit, she sat me down in her front room in Greenwood with a glass of iced tea and apologized for the mess, which I hadn't noticed and still couldn't detect—was it the fabric and sewing supplies stacked neatly on the table? She told me she'd be delighted to tell me about Henry, because he was one of the most wonderful men she had ever met, and his story was so unusual,

"His name was Elijah McGee, and the first time she met him, Aunt Kerry said, 'I can't ever remember that, I'm going to call you Henry.' He couldn't read or write, but he was smart as a whip. Today he'd be diagnosed as ADD, because he couldn't sit still. He was always on the go. He was missing part of his thumb and finger, and he never told us how it happened.

"He was from Hazlehurst, south of Jackson, and when he was sixteen, his mama had a boyfriend who beat her, and 'attacked' his sister. That was the way he put it. The only way to stop him was to murder him, and he knew that led straight to the penitentiary. So he murdered him, and went straight to the sheriff's office, and told the sheriff that the man had needed killing, so he'd gone ahead and done it to protect his mama and his sister. Sure enough, they sent him straight to Parchman.

"When he got there, the superintendent pulled him out to be his wife's yard man, I think because he was so young, and the superintendent could see that he didn't belong there. He grew roses, and chopped cotton, and after a few years of that, he stepped off the end of a cotton field and walked all the way to Memphis. He trapped a bird, ate some acorns, stole some clothes from somebody's wash-line, and hopped a freight train all the way to Wyoming. I asked him once why he went all the way to Wyoming, and he said he wanted to see how far that train would go. You know, they never really searched for him around Parchman, and I think it's because the superintendent and his wife liked him. Anyone could see that he was a good man. It just shone right out of him."

Elijah McGee spent five years in Wyoming, growing cabbages for a rancher. Then the Social Security Act was passed, requiring everyone in America to be registered and numbered. He knew the authorities would track him down, so he told the rancher that he was an escaped prisoner. The rancher turned him in, after the cabbage crop was harvested, and Parchman sent a sergeant who brought him back to Mississippi on a passenger train. The same superintendent was still there, and his wife was thrilled by the return of Elijah McGee. She immediately commandeered him to work in her flower garden, which he did until 1946.

At that time, there was a serious labor shortage in Mississippi because the Great Migration was in full swing. Thousands of blacks were fleeing poverty and racism in the rural Deep South for factory jobs in Chicago and other northern cities. To address the labor shortage, the state of Mississippi came up with something called the Wage Hand Program. If you were a landowner, you could go to Parchman and pick out a prisoner to work for you. These prisoners were called "wage hands," but you didn't have to pay them. You just had to feed them and clothe them and give them a place to live. They were, in fact, slaves, and many were horribly abused.

"So Uncle Junior, who was kin to William Faulkner and had a small farm at Vaughan, Mississippi, went up to Parchman to get a yard man for Aunt Kerry, who was crazy about her roses and irises and daylilies. Uncle Junior walked up to the superintendent's house, the big old mansion that was there, and he saw Henry working in the flower beds. Henry looked at him and said, 'Boss, are you looking for a hand? If you take me, you won't ever be sorry.' Uncle Junior said, 'Are you good with flowers?' Henry said yes, and showed him all the flowers he'd been growing. So Uncle Junior went to the superintendent, and the superintendent said, 'My wife is going to kill me, but that man has no business being here. Take him.'"

And so it was that "Henry" moved into a little backyard shack at the Heard family farm in Vaughan, where he lived for the next forty-seven years as Aunt Kerry's yard man and inseparable companion. "She was never out of his sight," said Cindy. "They went everywhere together, with Aunt Kerry driving, and Henry riding in the backseat. He took to carrying a pistol, even though he was a convicted felon, and he kept it on the floorboards of the car. She bought him that pistol. She bought him a shotgun, clothes, and a TV, which he loved, but as far as I know, she never paid him a dime."

"Wait a minute," I said. "So this is a faithful slave story?"

"Well, I suppose he was, in a sense, but he was also a convicted murderer who was much happier being with Aunt Kerry than at Parchman. Later, we got him pardoned, and then he was able to draw Social Security. He and Aunt Kerry had a joint bank account, so he could spend money, but she never paid him. I'm sure of that."

"So how would you characterize their relationship?"

"They were crazy about each other, but there was a line drawn between them that was never crossed. Henry had his own chair, plates, cups, and saucers, and he would sit at his table in the pantry. She'd be eating at the kitchen table, and they'd have these long conversations, but they wouldn't ever look at each other."

"They wouldn't look at each other?"

"Absolutely not. That would mean they were eating together, which was a big taboo in those days. They had a great mutual admiration, but they could never acknowledge it. When *Driving Miss Daisy* came out, I took Henry to see it. He was very nervous about being there with me, and I couldn't get him to sit next to me. He sat behind me. But he loved the movie. Afterwards he told me, 'You know, Lil Miss, the only difference between that man and me is that I ride in the backseat, and Miss Kerry drives.'"

During the civil rights era, Cindy asked Henry if he wanted to register to vote, and offered to take him, but he had no interest in that. She tried many times to get him to ride in the passenger seat of her car, but he would always say, "No ma'am," and get in the backseat. Once she piled up the backseat with boxes and clothes, forcing him to ride in the front. Of course, he saw straight through that ruse and called her out on it.

Being an intelligent man who couldn't read or write, television was a lifeline. He watched as many news and current affairs programs as he could, and he would give Aunt Kerry a synopsis of world events every morning. She never got the hang of television, and preferred to hear the news from Henry. He was a fantastic gardener who grew tomato plants so tall he needed a ladder to reach the top of them. He won flower contests for Aunt Kerry and coaxed record harvests out of the peach and pear trees.

"He was beloved by everybody," said Cindy, and I couldn't help thinking about all the discredited white Southern mythology around the figure of the faithful slave, and then wondering if I was belittling his individuality and dignity by thinking in those terms.

"What did they love about him?" I asked.

"You couldn't be in a room with him for ten minutes and not feel good. He had that exuberance. He was the most steadfast, giving person. He was an expert hunter and fisherman, always had a bird dog, and he taught all the white kids for miles around how to hunt and fish."

When Uncle Junior died of lung cancer, Henry told Cindy, "You'll never have to worry about Big Miss. I'll never leave her side." In her latter years, Aunt Kerry's eyesight deteriorated badly, and when she was driving, Henry would call out directions from the backseat and tell her to steer more to the left or the right. She had his shack moved closer to the house, and a buzzer installed. She could push the button above her bed, and it would buzz at Henry's house. But she insisted on a fence between their two houses, and she would never cross it.

As Henry aged, he got cancer of the bladder, and she put him in hospital. The staff were puzzled by the constant stream of white visitors at his bedside—all the young men that he'd taught to hunt and fish, all of Aunt Kerry's friends and the ladies from her Methodist church, and a nun from St. Dominic's who came to pray over him every day. Henry had never seen a nun before, and he told Cindy, "I wish her church would take up a collection and get her some clothes. She wears the same ones every day."

When she finally had to accept that Henry was dying, Aunt Kerry bought him a new suit to be buried in and went to the best black funeral home in town. She asked the funeral director, Mr. Peeples, to spare no expense, and she wrote him a big check.

"When they called to say he was ready, I went down there," said Cindy. "Mr. Peeples met me at the door and said, 'We've got him all fixed up.' I went back there, and I almost had a heart attack, because they had him winched up and sitting bolt upright in the coffin. I just about died. He looked like he was fixing to say something! I said to Mr. Peeples, 'This can't be. You're going to have white ladies fainting and having heart attacks left and right. You've got to lay that man down.'

"He said, 'But that's how we always do it.'

"I said, 'You have got to lay him down flat, and close that casket up.'"

The funeral was the following day. The magnificent casket was closed and decorated with a glorious display of Henry's favorite flowers. The pallbearers were the young white men he'd taught how to hunt and fish. "These were good ole boys from out in the country," said Cindy. "Big strapping corn-fed guys, and they were nervous about being at a black funeral home in this scary neighborhood. Mr. Peeples started giving them these short white gloves. He said, 'We don't handle caskets with our bare hands.' Oh Richard, it was such a scene! Aunt Kerry was like the widow, talking out loud and carrying on, and these big ole pallbearers with their little white gloves. There must have been a hundred people at that funeral, and the only black person there was the corpse."

After they'd buried him in the Yazoo City cemetery, Aunt Kerry had his shack torn down, saying she couldn't stand to look out the window anymore. Henry had been gravely concerned about how she would react to his death, and his worries were justified. Aunt Kerry was never the same again.

Cindy was going through Henry's things when she found a book of Polaroid photographs. She started turning the pages, and found photographs of his flowers, his bird dogs, various white children, and many photographs of the same black woman taken over many years.

"None of us knew a thing about her," said Cindy. "He had never mentioned her. We tried to find her, but we didn't know her name. We just had to hope that they'd found happiness together."

When "Henry" died, he left all his possessions to Cindy, except his shotgun, which he gave to her then-husband Mike Foose, and his bed, which he left to Martha.

Martha put the bed in her son Joe's room. Named after Joseph Newton, the revered black man who also gave his name to Joseph Brake, Joe slept in the bed of a black murderer, yard man, and shadow family member who was equally revered.

Chapter 12

Separate and Unequal

JOE WAS TEN years old with a shaggy mop of thick dark hair, bright blue eyes, and big feet that turned outward. He had a vivid imagination and was developing a talent for smart-mouthed sarcasm that came straight down the mainline from his mother. Although he was not above shooting raccoons in the butt with his BB gun for fun, his ambition was to be a zookeeper, and he had a tame squirrel named Rocky that would perch on his shoulder.

Sometimes Joe grumbled about being "the only human kid on Pluto," but he had a thriving social life in Greenwood. There was often a pack of cousins and other kids milling around in Martha and Donald's backyard, and his best friend, Edison, was a frequent visitor. It was hard to visit Edison because Edison didn't have a house. He lived with his father and grandmother in a small grocery store in the Baptist Town ghetto, and he slept in a small side room behind the meat counter. They were Chinese Americans, recent arrivals in the Delta. They hadn't picked up the drawl yet, although you could hear it beginning. Like Mariah and I, they were starting to use "y'all," without even thinking about it.

Joe met Edison at Pillow Academy, a private school just outside the Greenwood city limits. It was founded in 1966 as a way for white families to escape the coming horror of racially integrated public schools; one of Pillow's founders was also a founder of the White Citizens' Council. These "segregation academies," as they became known, popped up all over the Delta, and more sparsely in other parts of the Deep South. Until very recently, the student body at Pillow was 100 percent white. Now it was admitting a few black and Asian students, although still 96 percent white.

Martha and Donald grudgingly sent Joe to Pillow. It cost nearly $6,000 a year, the academic standards were not that high, and they disapproved of segregated education. They wanted to send Joe to the high-performing, racially integrated public elementary school six blocks from their house, but Joe wasn't allowed to go there because of the way the school district lines were drawn. His assigned elementary school was on the other side of downtown. It was 82 percent black, which they didn't mind, and showing poor test results, which was the deal-breaker.

Edison's father preferred to raise him in a grocery store rather than send him to that elementary school. Doing without a house was how he managed to pay the fees for Pillow. When I asked him about it, he put his hand on Edison's shoulder and drew him closer. "Without a good education," he said, "how can he succeed in life?"

That, in a nutshell, was the tragedy of so many children growing up in the Delta. The Greenwood public school district was rated F by the Mississippi Department of Education. The surrounding school district of Leflore County was also rated F. Holmes County managed a D. So did Clarksdale. Yazoo City rated F. The Delta counties of Humphreys, Coahoma, and Bolivar were all rated F.

The wretched state of the public schools was a constant topic of conversation, argument, blame throwing, and handwringing. It was the main reason why young families, black and white, were leaving the Delta, and it was a massive impediment to any hopes for the future. The Delta's leaders were trying hard to persuade manufacturing companies and other businesses to move to the region, but it was a very tough sell once the executives saw those awful school grades and learned that the academies cost six grand or more. They'd rather locate their businesses in Oxford, or Tupelo, or the better neighborhoods of Jackson, where their children could attend good free public schools.

I opened my *Yazoo Herald* one morning to find a special graduation edition, with color headshots of all the graduating students in the area. At Yazoo City High School, all 119 faces were black, and many had the creative names that were getting so popular: Cubdeerix, Darshavious, Divirious, Dequintance, Dantonieon, Dietrecanna, Stevondria, Teairra, Xzeavius.

At Manchester Academy and Benton Academy, all the students' faces were white, except for one Hispanic girl and one Asian boy. There were boys named Thad, Will, Hunter, Gage, Blanton, Parker, and girls with pearl necklaces named Cole, Crosby Ellen, Annandale, and Nora Grace.

Yazoo County High School was more mixed. Alongside Demonparis Williams, Katavious Williams, and a friendly-faced girl called Shitorial Demus, were Billy Jenkins, Tyler Lynch, Leigh Cupples, Heather King, and other white students whose parents probably didn't have the money to send them to one of the academies. But still, sixty years after the US Supreme Court ordered the South to integrate its schools, education in the Mississippi Delta was almost entirely segregated by race.

FROM 1954 TO the mid-1960s, the Delta counties, along with the rest of the Deep South, dawdled and delayed with increasingly far-fetched legal gambits. In the late 1960s and early 1970s, when a series of legal decisions finally forced the white Delta high schools to start admitting black students, most people expected a massive white flight into the newly built segregation academies. But that's not how it happened. Some white parents did send their children to the academies, but most did not. Slowly and gradually, with only a few black students at first, and a few more the next year, the Delta's public schools began to integrate. There were some ugly incidents, but it went far better than most people had been expecting.

There was a sweet spot in the 1970s, when most Delta public schools managed to deliver a good education to black and white students, but that all changed in the 1980s. The balance of black and white reached a kind of tipping point. White parents and grandparents could tolerate a certain number of black students in the classrooms, and the bathrooms, but once black students were in the majority, and black administrators started hiring black teachers, it was too much for them, and that's when whites fled en masse to the academies.

If whites had stuck with the public school system, things would be very different now in the Delta. When they removed their children, they also removed their money, influence, experience, and personal investment in the public school system. In rushed the influence of poverty. The Delta public schools started to experience similar problems as schools on Indian reservations, in crime-ridden inner cities, and the poorest, most isolated counties in Appalachia. All of the

worst schools in America, without exception, are located in the highest areas of poverty, just as all the highest-performing schools are in
the wealthiest zip codes. Statistically speaking, poverty produces bad
parents and bad students, and the good ones are exceptions.

One famous study on the subject found that poor children on
average hear thirty million fewer words than rich children in the first
four years of their life. Closing that gap is extremely difficult, especially when you factor in all the social ills associated with poverty in
America. The poorest Americans have the highest rates of alcohol
and drug abuse, violence against children, sexual abuse of children,
neglect of children, illiteracy, mental illness, teenage pregnancy, de-
linquency, incarceration.

Approximately three-quarters of the Delta's public school students today have unmarried mothers. More than 80 percent qualify
for the federal free lunch program, meaning that they live below the
poverty line. Some children are arriving at kindergarten not knowing
how to hold a pencil, not knowing their colors or their numbers, and
in a few cases, not knowing their names. Poverty, and the culture that
poverty builds around itself, is the biggest challenge faced by Delta
educators, but persistent funding shortfalls by the state are certainly
not helping. Neither are the chronic problems with mismanagement,
nepotism, and corruption in the Delta school districts.

In F-rated Leflore County, things got so bad that the state board
of education had to take over the school district and fire the superintendent and all five school board members. "I've never in my life
seen anything like this," said Robert Strebeck, the veteran conserva-
tor sent in to straighten out the mess. The school district had almost
twice as many employees as it was supposed to have. The district had
been without a business manager for seven months, and its finances
were in complete shambles. "They just continued to spend, spend,
spend without any knowledge of what they had," said Strebeck. While

fighting a legal battle against the takeover, the school board hired yet more people and awarded a round of pay increases. One thing they did not spend money on was maintenance of the school buildings, many of which were in terrible condition. In a long speech to the county school board and its employees, Strebeck had to stress several times that the purpose of schools was to educate children, not provide jobs to adults.

The Yazoo City school district also appeared to be bloated. It was spending $8,841 per student, well above the state average, and almost double what the private academy spent per student, yet only 43 percent of its employees were teachers. Meanwhile, the ex-superintendent of the Greenville school district, Harvey Andre Franklin Sr., was going to prison for embezzlement. He agreed to pay his friend and former colleague Edna Goble $1.4 million of the district's budget to get her Teach Them to Read program into the Greenville schools. In return for this huge overpayment, she agreed to pay off $36,000 on his truck loan, $9,400 on his home improvements, and $1,900 on his American Express bill.

So it went on. In Clarksdale, where the school board president had got caught shoplifting from Fred's Super Dollar, there was a big cheating scandal, with teachers feeding answers to students, and then a clumsy attempt at a cover-up. It was so easy to believe that the situation was hopeless, that the children were doomed to a bad education, that the Delta's public schools were trapped in a perfect quagmire of underfunding, poverty, mismanagement, corruption, and social dysfunction. And all too often, the only solution offered by local leaders was to keep on praying, more fervently than before.

THE SCHOOL THAT gave me hope was up in Quitman County, one of the poorest, most depopulated counties in the Delta. Only eight thousand people were left in the county, with a median household income of $20,000 a year. The county seat was the small, scruffy town of Marks, which was visually dominated by a grand old courthouse that stood like a monument to the past. Lettered into its stone was a dubious claim from Jim Crow days: OBEDIENCE TO THE LAW IS LIBERTY.

A few miles south of Marks, on a highway dotted with abandoned buildings and front-yard junk shops, was Quitman County Elementary School, "Home of the Wildcats." It was a low-slung red brick building put up in the 1950s, and in bad need of structural maintenance, or tearing down and replacing. Rainwater seeped into the classrooms, and the interior walls didn't reach the ceiling properly. One hundred percent of the students were poor enough to qualify for a free federal lunch, and 97 percent were African-American.

Three years ago, the school was a borderline F, and the state was ready to take it over. Test scores were abysmal. A fifth of the students had been retained in their grades. The school had gone through four principals in five years, and the staff was thoroughly demoralized. Teacher absenteeism was a big problem. Much as the students disliked going to the leaky, old, failing school, they had a better record of attendance than some of their teachers.

Into the breach stepped an Oxford-based organization called the Barksdale Reading Institute (BRI). Founded in 2000 by Jim Barksdale, the billionaire CEO of Netscape, its mission was to raise educational standards in his home state of Mississippi, with a particular emphasis on reading. Barksdale himself had difficulty learning to read as a child, until an inspirational teacher came along and turned him into a lifelong book lover.

In return for autonomy in running the school, BRI offered to pay the salaries of a new principal and vice principal, and bring in other staff and supplies. This was a new approach for the Barksdale do-gooders, born of disappointment. They had tried putting reading coaches in schools, and setting up model classrooms, in the hope they would inspire and replicate. The limited impact of these programs persuaded them that you couldn't change a school without a change of leadership.

"One night I woke up and said, 'Let's do this,'" said Claiborne Barksdale, Jim's brother and CEO. "Let's go hire some really good principals. Let's grab these schools by the throat and see if we can do it."

For the beleaguered, perennially broke Quitman County school district, the Barksdale offer represented a huge budget windfall and a way to avoid state takeover. The new principal, chosen by Barksdale, was Michael Cormack, an African-American educator from Oregon, highly trained, motivated, and energetic. His vice principal was Cytha Stottlemyer, a white woman from Pennsylvania with similar qualities. In less than two years, they turned the school around.

When they arrived, 38 percent of the students were at the national average for reading. Eighteen months later, that number had jumped to 59 percent. The improvement in math was even more dramatic, rising from 30 percent to 83 percent. The overall index of academic achievement at the school rose from 104 to 151. The state raised the school's grade from borderline F to C, and standards continued to improve.

HOW DID THEY do it? Could the same methods be replicated in other schools? If you could improve a school that quickly and dramatically in the Mississippi Delta, it seemed to me, you could do it anywhere. I walked up to Quitman County Elementary School's front door, where BOIL WATER ALERT signs were taped on to the glass. Basic infrastructure was disintegrating all over the Delta, and these signs were commonplace, indicating that the water supply was contaminated. Inside the lobby was another sign: "If you live in any of the following situations: in a shelter, car, park, abandoned building, you may qualify for certain rights or protection."

By the front reception desk, a big colorful Mood Meter chart invited children to identify their happiness and energy levels every morning. It was part of the Barksdale push for "emotional literacy" among the students. They're taught how to recognize their emotions, understand where they come from, and regulate their moods as a way to break the cycle of acting out and getting punished. Teachers also encourage them to show compassion, at school and at home, and reward them for acts of kindness and understanding of others.

As I chatted to the friendly secretaries and waited to meet Cytha Stottlemyer, a first-grade class exited a classroom and came down the hallway. They were strikingly well behaved, walking in single file at a medium pace, with their hands in their pockets (reducing the temptation to poke, grab, etc.), and bubbles of air in their mouths (to keep from talking, shouting, etc). Pawprints painted on the floor indicated the correct path of travel, on the right-hand side of the hallway.

The school was orderly without being strict. The overall atmosphere was happy, fun, welcoming, full of pride and enthusiasm. Looking into classrooms, I saw rapt young faces, hands shooting up to answer questions. Despite the shortcomings of the building, great care had been taken to decorate it. There were photographs on the walls of high-achieving students, and frequent reminders of the school slogan, "We are Readers, Writers and Problem Solvers."

The children had made posters illustrating and describing the books they had read, and these were all over the school. *The Very Hungry Caterpillar*, for example, had carefully handwritten entries under headings of plot, characters, setting, publication date, purpose, tone, conflict, and resolution. When the new regime took charge, very few children enjoyed reading. Now the whole school is excited about books. The revamped library is one of the most popular places to hang out during recess, and the children covet the special red T-shirts they get for reaching their reading goals. When the new Book of the Month is announced, the whole school and many parents and grandparents assemble for a rally. Children perform a play based on the book, and there are dance performances, competitive cheering contests, prizes awarded to the best readers.

Ms. Stottlemyer sat me down in her small windowless office behind the secretaries and poured some coffee. She was in her early thirties, I guessed, with an air of calm assertive confidence, and absolute dedication. "What, out of everything you've done, has made the most difference?" I asked.

"We have very high expectations for all our students, and a real sense of urgency to get them there," she said. "They understand that we really care about them. All that makes a big difference, but there's no magic bullet. It comes down to the effort we've put in. People have worked tirelessly in the face of very real challenges, and we've done it as a team, which wasn't always the case here."

The first step was to motivate the teachers. Rather than fire most of them, based on their poor performance, Michael Cormack took them away on a team-building retreat and got to know them. He discovered that most of them were perfectly competent, a few were outstanding, and all of them felt underappreciated. The administrators, they said, were in the habit of mocking and belittling them. Bitterness was the prevailing mood at the school, trailed by hopelessness. The state and federal government were imposing more and more tests, as if more testing was the way to improve test scores, and the school had lost sight of any larger purpose.

Cormack brought new energy and vision. He was able to inspire the teachers with a sense of mission, and he was nice to them. He remembered their birthdays, and kept track of their health concerns and family members. He invited them to break bread together at staff dinners and weekend barbecues, and rewarded their achievements with small prizes and acknowledgments.

He also required them to work harder, with more discipline and urgency. Two veteran teachers, stalwarts in the local community, refused to work harder, and he had to fire them, which cost him a lot of political support. A few more teachers didn't renew their contracts, and he hired some replacements from outside the school district, losing a little more support.

When Cormack announced that children would no longer be beaten at the school, the community was aghast; perhaps no cultural group in America is more strongly in favor of corporal punishment than African Americans in the South. "I had a real problem with it," said Ricardo Sacks, a math teacher who spoke to me between classes. "They whupped my tail at school. Why shouldn't these kids get it too?"

Instead of beating badly behaved children with a paddle, the new administration took away their privileges and socially isolated them. They lost recess time. They were banned from talking to other students at lunchtime. Each student's behavior was tracked throughout the day on a multicolored board. At the top was black, indicating perfect behavior, and reinforcing the idea that black is beautiful. At the bottom was the red zone, where students lost all their privileges. "I was skeptical at first, but the kids have bought into the system, and there's no question that it works better than the paddle," said Sacks. "I would say discipline has improved dramatically."

All over the school, small, clever ideas have been put into action. Colds and other illnesses have been greatly reduced by installing hand sanitizers and giving frequent reminders to "wash your paws." When the bathrooms got dirty, the school held a contest between boys and girls to see who could keep their bathrooms cleaner. It worked like a charm, and the boys won, which shamed the girls into trying even harder. In addition to sending notes home if a child has done poorly or behaved badly, the school started sending positive notes home with children who'd had a particularly good day at school.

Meanwhile, the Barksdale institute was pumping in money for library books, computers, learning software, reading coaches, speech and behavior therapists. A prekindergarten program was introduced and expanded with federal funding, and this has made a big difference in kindergarten. Some children arrive knowing almost nothing. A nine-year-old showed up who didn't know his name properly, and he was a joy to the teachers, because no one else made so much progress or was so pleased about it. The transition from second to third grade is proving problematic, as books get longer and more difficult and social life gets more involved and distracting, so the school is now working on building up more "reading stamina" in second grade.

THE BIGGEST CHALLENGE has been political, and it has come from the school's own board. When Michael Cormack announced that he was leaving the school to become the new CEO of Barksdale, the school board was expected to approve Cytha Stottlemyer as the new principal, in order to continue the partnership with Barksdale and keep the progress going. But the board members voted against Stottlemyer by a majority of 3 to 2. They gave no reason for the decision, which took place in executive session, but it was an open secret what lay behind it.

The three board members, and a faction of the community, were resentful of the well-heeled outsiders who had come in and taken over their school. The autonomy required by Barksdale, especially in hiring and firing, was a direct challenge to the traditional power of the school board. For one member, this resentment was severely aggravated by the fact that Cormack and Stottlemyer hadn't picked her granddaughter as Homecoming Queen. Not only that, but they had reduced Homecoming from a week of celebrations, in which no learning took place, to less than a full day. Perhaps inevitably, Stottlemyer's race was also a major factor. During one of the meetings, someone came right out and said it, "We don't want white people telling our children what to do."

Most parents and teachers, however, supported Stottlemyer, and they raised such an outcry that the board was forced to hold an emergency hearing. More than a hundred people attended. The board refused to let any parents speak, but Cormack was able to show a video reel of testimonials about the progress the school had made. Again, the board voted no, even though it meant saying good-bye to approximately $400,000 a year from Barksdale at a time when the school district was deeply in debt.

Families camped out on the lawn of one of the school board members and refused to leave. Stottlemyer supporters wouldn't stop calling his phone. They wore him down, essentially, until he agreed to change his vote to yes. That gave Stottlemyer majority support on the board, and she was duly sworn in as the new principal. It was a hurtful experience for her, but she dusted herself off, and according to everyone I talked to at the school, she has done a fine job, and increased her support in the community.

"First, God made idiots," wrote Mark Twain. "This was for practice. Then He invented school boards." When I offered this quote to Stottlemyer, she smiled politely and changed the subject.

•   •   •

THE STORY PROVES that money and leadership can transform a Delta school, but Quitman County Elementary is a small island in a rough sea. These eager, well-behaved, book-enthused children will move on to middle and high schools that do not have the benefit of private money or principals trained at the nation's top academies. Expectations are lower, urgency is less, corporal punishment is the main disciplinary tool, and the trials of adolescence will be taking place at the same time. Stottlemyer, recently married and getting used to the last name Guynes, is trying to build bridges to those schools, and help them improve, a process that requires delicate political footwork. If the perception builds that she's a bossy white lady who thinks she knows better, she's not going to get anywhere.

Some of her students will hopefully make it through and go on to college, and then you have to wonder if they'll ever come back to Quitman County. At present, the biggest employers in the area are the state penitentiary at Parchman, the big private prison at Tutwiler, and the floating casinos at Tunica on the Mississippi River, all of which lie outside the county limits. Inside the county, the biggest employer is the school district.

As I drove home through torrential rains, I pondered the economic significance of the schools. In the Delta, where poverty is so extreme and job opportunities are so scarce, people look at schools as a source of employment, first and foremost. School board members and superintendents run for election, and once in power, they tend to distribute jobs as patronage within local kinship networks, shoring up their support for the next election. Educating children becomes a secondary concern.

Outsiders had come in and transformed a school, filled hundreds of children with new enthusiasm for learning. A majority of the school board saw this as a threat, and an echo of white supremacy. How dare they come in here, to our community, and tell us what to do? The most encouraging thing about the whole story was the persistence of the parents and teachers, who kept tugging and pulling at the school board until it came plopping out of the mud.

Chapter 13

Rites of Spring

THE YAZOO RIVER formed the boundary line of our property, and if you didn't mind the snakes and mosquitoes, or the briars and the mud, it was restful and therapeutic to spend time there on the riverbank, watching the occasional alligator holding itself motionless against the current. All that murky brown water, almost chocolate-colored in a certain light, flowed down to Vicksburg at the southern tip of the Delta, and then joined the Mississippi and flowed on to New Orleans. Many times I had stood there and fantasized about making that journey in a raft or a canoe. So imagine my surprise when I went down to the river one morning in spring and found the water flowing in the other direction.

Half the North American continent had poured its snowmelt and spring rains into the Mississippi, and by the time the big river reached Vicksburg, it was so huge and powerful, and the Delta so low-lying and flat, that its outswelling waters pushed back the Yazoo and caused it to flow backward for more than a hundred miles. If I launched a raft now, it would float upstream to Greenwood—a very strange thought indeed.

The backward-flowing river was also increasing in volume. It drowned its banks, and then the long riverside pasture where Mike and Beth had kept their horses. Big fish were swimming and jumping in the horse pasture now. Alligators were coming in to hunt them. Beavers were using the high water to reach trees that had been too far away and gnaw them to death.

One morning I watched a six-foot alligator sunning itself on a piece of dry ground about forty yards from the back door. Another was floating in the horse pasture. They weren't dangerous to humans, unless you stumbled on a female guarding her nest, but they were a real threat to a dog, especially a bold, reckless hooligan of a dog like Savanna.

She now had the full freedom of a country dog, and used it to chase deer for miles and miles through the swampy woods, limping home after dark with torn-up pads, a coat full of burrs, her face covered in cuts and scrapes. Once she came home with her face clawed open by a raccoon. Another time she returned with a sucking chest wound, having been gored by a wild hog.

She was killing the occasional rabbit, squirrel, and chipmunk, judging from the tails on the lawn, and I saw her grab an armadillo by the tail, drag it into a ditch, and half-drown it while chewing its belly open. She was a heavily-muscled seventy-five-pound German shepherd mix in her prime, and although she was afraid of thunderstorms, and brooms, and clicking thermostats, and pieces of paper that blew about unexpectedly, she would stand her ground and bark at coyotes, who didn't think she was worth it.

Savanna's worst habit was chasing vehicles. She would bark and snap at the front wheel, actually getting her fool head in front of it if the vehicle was going slowly enough. It looked like a vet bill or a heartbreak waiting to happen, and I was trying to train her out of it. One spring morning I was on the front porch with Savanna when a battered old burgundy truck came toward the house, towing a long, clattering metal trailer. I told her to sit. She sat. Her hackles were fully raised, and she was trembling with barely contained desire. In my most decisive voice, I said, "Stay." She was a coiled spring, and as the truck came past the house, she launched herself off the porch and charged after it. I saw the truck stop on the levee road behind the house. A man got out, Savanna started barking at him, I ran over there.

He was a scruffy black man in his late thirties or early forties, and he was doing exactly the right thing, standing calmly without moving, angled slightly sideways, as the dog barked and lunged around him. I got her under control and apologized profusely. He said, "It's alright. I know dogs. She big, but she ain't mean."

He had lively bright eyes, several missing teeth, and a wiry medium build. Something more than the missing teeth, and difficult to describe, suggested hard drugs in his past, but maybe not anymore. We introduced ourselves—I'll call him B—and he pulled off his glove to shake my hand. He was here with the farm's permission to haul the old scrap metal out of the woods and sell it in Greenwood. In the old days, he said, people would just dump their old cars, appliances, leaky metal roofs, and broken equipment in the woods, and there was good money to be made if you didn't mind going in there and dragging it out. "I can make hun-fitty [$150] a day, and that's good money for a black man in the Delta," he said. "Snakes is bad though. I be killing six, seven snakes a day."

He lived in the nearby hamlet of Thornton with his wife and three children. He told me where their trailer was, but all I knew of Thornton was a few brief glimpses from driving through. There was a neat little whitewashed church, a derelict cotton gin, scattered trailers and falling-down buildings, a permanent cluster of men under the crooked rusty awning of a bar with no sign. I stopped for ice and gas sometimes at a ramshackle little store across the highway from Thornton. It also sold beer, cigarettes, crickets, minnows, rolling papers, crack pipes, and a few essential food items like Vienna sausages and milk.

"Tell me about Thornton," I said. "How is it there?"

He said, "It's like this: we poor, but we raised to be poor. It's all we know. Lord knows we need money, but I wouldn't live anywhere else. I love the country, the peace and quiet, the hunting and fishing. I know airbody, and airbody know me. We all kin. We poor, but our spirit is strong. That's why we sing so good. And some of these country ladies out here look so good it make you bite your finger."

"Have you ever lived anywhere else?"

"Uh-uh. Look at me. If I move to the city, I ain't be staying in some nice residential neighborhood. I be up in the ghetto where all the robbing and shooting is at. If you rob me, I got to shoot you, and I don't want to do that. So I stay out here in the country, and I try to do right. Lot of people around here sling rocks [deal crack]. They do it cause they lazy. But I don't mind hard work, or honest work. I like it, and it keep me out of trouble."

He was in the woods for a few hours. When his trailer was full up with scrap metal, he drove back past the house and stopped to talk some more. He asked where I was from, and what I did, and how come I was living in Dr. Foose's house. He pronounced it, "Dot-to-Foo how," without the apostrophe. I thought back to when I first arrived and could barely understand the dialect at all. Now I could get nearly all of it. We talked for about half an hour, and then he said, "I can see you ain't from around here."

"How's that?" I said.

"You look me straight in the eye when we talking, like it ain't no thang. White folks around here, it ain't like that. Very few. You smoke weed?"

"Sometimes," I said. "You want some?"

"Well sure."

There was a lot of it about in the Delta, like everywhere else. The difference here was that people kept giving it to me. Leaving their houses or parties, they would slip a joint or a bud in my pocket, or bring a little gift when they came to visit. Since I was a very occasional smoker, and a complete lightweight who never took more than a hit or two, the stuff was starting to stockpile. I gave B a few buds to take home, and he said, "Now I know you my friend." He wrote down his phone number, and said to come over to Thornton and have a drink sometime.

"Ain't no need to worry," he added, observing a trace of anxiety in my face. "I'm always packing [armed]."

I paused for a moment and said, "That's good to know."

AFTER A LONG, cold, muddy beginning, the Delta spring came on with a rush, and soon there were ten, twelve, sixteen different shades of green in the landscape again. Wildflowers carpeted the roadsides. The light reacquired its honeyed quality, and for the first time we saw the spring flowers that Mike and Beth had planted and nurtured all around the house. After the early daffodils came the yellow irises, the purple bearded irises, a riot of blue spiderwort. Every few days, there was another gorgeous surprise. A smallish tree we had never really noticed suddenly burst out with purple flowers and revealed itself as a Japanese magnolia.

It was almost frightening to see how fast the bamboo was growing. We had inherited two large groves of bamboo about sixty feet

high. One was green, the other was a rare black bamboo. Every morning we would kick over twenty or thirty new shoots that were trying
to colonize the lawns and the levee banks. Left alone, they grew ten
inches a day.

From the mud at the bottom of the ponds, where they had survived the winter on the oxygen stored in their lungs, turtles swam
up to the surface and then hauled themselves up on to the banks
to soak up the warmth of the sun, as their ancestors had done 175
million years ago. On the front porch, lime-green lizards appeared.
The males had bright pink throats that expanded into a bubble. Then
green tree frogs came out of hibernation, followed by small black
lizards with midnight blue tails, and huge croaking bullfrogs. The
spring bird migration brought ruby-throated hummingbirds, blue-
birds, mockingbirds, orioles, spectacular warblers and buntings, and
many other species into the yard.

We decided to celebrate spring with a big house party. Invitations
went out and were accepted in London, New York, Philadelphia, Arizona, New Mexico, California, Singapore. Most of these people had
never been to Mississippi before, and all they knew of it was horror
stories and stereotypes. It didn't help when I advised them to steer
clear of politics and religion, and added that race relations were a
touchy subject, and yes, the Civil War was still a big deal down here,
and Northeasterners should expect to get called Yankees. In fact,
Mariah was often called a Yankee, even though her hometown of
Tucson was down near the Mexican border. If you were from a state
that didn't fight for the Confederacy, you were a Yankee.

Meanwhile, our neighbors were going into full Southern hospitality mode. Cathy Thompson ferried over extra beds, mattresses,
sheets, blankets, quilts. John Newcomb offered to put up more guests
in a charming two-bedroom cabin that he called The Shack. Louie
said he'd cook a big vat of New Orleans–style red beans and rice for

Friday night. Donald and Martha organized a traditional crawfish boil for Saturday. I went down to the Blue Front Café, a juke joint in Bentonia, and hired the proprietor, Jimmy "Duck" Holmes, to play a set of his ethereal blues.

We were all worried about the huge old dying pecan tree in front of the house. It was hollowing out, listing slightly to the side, and if it went down in a storm, or a spring tornado, it would batter its way right through the roof of the house and into the living room. Louie called Charles Henry Shelton, the president of the local power company, last seen at the Pluto dove hunt, and Charles Henry called me back. As always, he was long-winded and time-consuming, but there was an odd sort of music in Charles Henry's slow, precise, carefully enunciated drawl, and I could have listened to him all day.

"I have a guy," he said. "He's the best I've ever seen. He might be the best there is. I'd put him up against anyone, anywhere, at any time. I'm talking about he's good in a tree. Real good, and he specializes in big trees. Hairy trees. What diameter are we talking about?"

"It's about three and a half feet thick, and seventy or eighty feet high."

"That's a big tree. Sure is. That's a hairy tree. He'll probably have to rope it down in pieces. What we need to do is get *him* out there to give *you* an estimate. But I'll have to call him. You won't be able to understand him. It's hard enough face-to-face, and dang near impossible on the phone. But I can communicate with him. His name is Eddie Earl Douglas, and he's dumb like a fox. You know I'm talking about?"

"Dumb like a fox?"

"That's right. He might seem dumb. He might act dumb. But I promise you he ain't dumb. He's dumb like a fox, but I don't believe he'll fleece you. You might not understand him at all when he gets there. If that's the case, here's what you need to do. You need to call *me*, and put me on the phone with *him*. That way I can be the interpreter so that *y'all* can understand each other. I'm telling you, he's real difficult to understand. And he's real good in a tree."

So Eddie Earl came out to take a look at the tree. He was a small-ish, square-shouldered, strong-looking man in his fifties, wearing his power company uniform and cap. He was cheery and friendly, and at the same time, he was somewhere far away, off in his own world. I could just about understand his accent, and he could just about understand mine. He walked around the tree. He gazed up at it with his hands on his hips. "Big tree," he said. "I can take it down for you."

"How much would you want to do it?"

"How much you think it's worth?"

"I don't know."

"If it fall, it a cost you plenty."

"I know."

"I can do it Saturday."

"I've got a house full of people on Saturday. But what's a fair price to take it down?"

"Fo hunna."

"That seems like a lot."

"It ain't."

"Okay. Four hundred. Can you do it another day?"

"Not this month."

"Well, alright then. You might have a bunch of hungover people watching you work."

"Heh heh," he chuckled. He said, "I'm used to that with these yere tractor drivers around here."

In his accent, tractor drivers sounded liked *trat-drahs*.

•　　　•　　　•

ALMOST WITHOUT EXCEPTION, the newcomers were stunned by the beauty of the place, as we had been when we first saw it. "Magical," was the word they kept using, and ultimately it referred to the light, the way it fell through the cypress trees into the cathedral of Joseph Brake, the rolling mists that ghosted out of the sloughs into the apricot dawn, the shimmering cotton fields and painterly sunsets.

Our friend Paul, a British ornithologist who works at the American Museum of Natural History in New York, saw fifty-eight different species of birds. Our friend Micaela, a photographer from London, saw twelve alligators, a pair of bald eagles, dozens of snowy egrets, and an uncountable multitude of the giant invasive swamp rats called nutria.

Micaela came a week in advance of the party, and arrived as a jabbering, exhausted, stressed-out wreck. After a few days of sleeping, reading, going for walks, and sunbathing on the front porch, it all melted away, and she felt more like her own true self than she had done in years. "It's so peaceful and calming here," she said. "You could charge people for this." She was leaning back against one of the old wooden pillars on the porch, watching the basking turtles on the banks of the ponds. Savanna was stretched out asleep on the freshly mown lawn, about ten feet away, and the air was full of chirping birdsong.

Suddenly Micaela jumped up and levitated backward, and then I saw it too: a fat cottonmouth slithering out of the flower bed on to the lawn, where the dog still slept oblivious. I couldn't see the garden hoe so I rushed inside for the .22, clattered outside again through the banging screen door, and shot the snake three times. Still it writhed, and displayed its white mouth. I lowered the rifle to its head for the coup de grace and it struck at the end of the barrel. I found the garden hoe and chopped its head off. Still the body coiled and uncoiled, and the gaudy orange and black pattern of its scales reminded us of a Russian gangster in a bad shirt. Micaela kept saying, "Jesus!" and going into fits of panicky laughter.

Ten minutes later, as we drank cold beers to calm ourselves down, another cottonmouth exactly the same size came out of the same flower bed and poured itself up on to the porch. For a moment, I thought it was the first snake come back to life. I grabbed again for the garden hoe, and then used it to carry the two still-twitching corpses to the ditch of death.

By Friday afternoon, all the foreigners and out-of-staters had arrived, and been warned about snakes, fire ants, and poison ivy. Most of them had already been plied with Pluto hospitality, shown around on boats and tractors and four-wheelers, invited into various houses for drinks and snacks. They had noted the Confederate flag flying from Bobby T's carport, and visited his ninety-year-old mother next door. Louie and William Thompson were her other sons, and she had raised two daughters too.

She was known as Aunt Mary, or Nonnee. She was getting a little deaf and slightly vague now, but still able to carry on a lively conversation and charm the birds right out of the trees. She served the visitors white wine and spicy Mississippi cheese straws, asked about their lives with genuine interest, told some sweet funny stories, did her impersonation of a wide-mouthed frog, and when the visit was over, she scrunched up her face slightly into the cutest smile, and said, "Well, toodle-ooh! Y'all know where to find me."

Louie and Cathy brought over the red beans and rice at sunset. John Newcomb arrived with top-shelf bottles of rum and Scotch, and we had already laid in plenty of beer, wine, and bourbon. Donald and Martha arrived with a dozen people, and wheeled Bobby T up a ramp that Mike Foose had built at the back of the house. Bobby T had been the wildest of the three Thompson brothers until two highway accidents put him in his wheelchair. Now he spent most of his time carving wooden crosses in his workshop.

When we moved in, he carved us a beautiful wooden replica of Richard the Lionheart's coat-of-arms and lent me some books he thought might be useful. One was a fascinating scholarly analysis of the Delta after the Civil War. The other had a Confederate flag on the cover, and was titled *The South Under Siege, 1830–2000*. It was a defense of slavery, a denunciation of Lincoln's War, and a call for Southerners to defend themselves against the Northern liberal plot to impose totalitarian socialism on the old Confederacy. The flag on his carport had already given some of the Yankee visitors pause, and now he arrived at the party with a big pistol in the pouch of his wheelchair and an ancient sweat-stained original Confederate battle hat on his head.

Mariah and I got on just fine with Bobby T. We compartmentalized what we didn't agree with, and focused on the things we liked about him: a generosity of spirit, a ready sense of humor, a talent for coaxing beauty out of dead trees, and the way he always made us feel completely welcome at his house, and on his family's land. And because we were so close to the Thompson family now, we felt a loyalty toward him that ran deeper than the desire to be good neighbors.

News of his pistol traveled rapidly through the party, and I wondered how my friend Jordy would react. A lawyer who worked in New York and lived on Long Island, he was virulently anti-firearms, believing that no one should be allowed to own guns except law enforcement and the military. He looked over at Bobby T and said to me, "Hey man, I'm not going to come down here and tell anyone what they should do with their guns or anything else." When I asked him if he wanted to do some shooting tomorrow, he laughed, and said, "Come on, man. Of course I fucking do."

The series of school massacres that had hardened Jordy's gun control views had produced an ammunition shortage in Mississippi. People were afraid that the government was about to ban guns and ammunition, and they had gone into a panic-buying frenzy. At the gun shops and hardware stores in the Delta, and even at the Walmarts, it was hard to find bullets in any caliber, and they would only sell you .22 bullets one small box at a time. "All these Yankees down here, and we're out of ammunition," joked Louie. But he did have some ammunition put by, and he invited the Yankee visitors to come and shoot it with him the next day.

My friend Tim Hower was an Ohioan living in New York, a self-described Double Yankee. He had an Internet preacher's license and played music as the Reverend Timmy James. He came up to me during the party and said, "I've been getting some good advice on predicaments I never even imagined. I should watch out for Belzoni women, find a Cajun if I need a turtle butchered, and never underestimate the impact of a well-aimed piece of meat."

Michael Thompson, William's son who ran the day-to-day farming on Pluto, had been telling a story about a Delta card game about to boil over into violence,

"It was a bunch of big ole young guys around a card table, and they were drunk, and starting to square off, and you could see what was about to happen. So Will Jones, who was on the other side of the room, picked up the hindquarters of a deer, which happened to be there cause it was hunting season, and man, he launched that thang. You could see the fat glisten as it grazed past the light fixture, and BAM! Here it lands, right on the card table. It totally defused the situation. I mean it just changed the whole damn subject. Hindquarters landing on a card table will do that every time."

It was a night of flowing bourbon, and flowing stories, and my friend Tom Vaught, an actor-bartender from New York City, could more than hold his own in both these departments. He had a full graying beard, and was about to launch a product called T. Vaught's Beard Oil—For the Rugged Gentleman. The Mississippians weren't used to the idea of a hearty, bearded, bourbon-swilling raconteur who wasn't a Southerner, and they kept questioning Tom about his origins. "Are you sure you don't have any kin down here?" said Cindy Foose, a keen amateur genealogist. "Because I'm from Vaughan, Mississippi, and that's pretty close to Vaught. Maybe they used to be Vaughans, and then changed it to Vaughts. Now, wait a minute! Ole Miss plays football at the Vaught-Hemingway stadium! So there was definitely a Vaught down here."

Accompanied by the Reverend Timmy on his National guitar, Tom surprised them further by singing a repertoire of old Delta blues songs in a big, growling, booming voice, and then improvising new lyrics about the people he'd just met. The ornithologist pulled out a harmonica, a Mississippian started playing the spoons, and rest of us stomped our feet on the wooden planks of the back deck. Friday night was supposed to be the warm-up for the real party, but it generated so much energy that it rolled deep into the night.

WHEN EDDIE EARL DOUGLAS arrived with his teenage son the following morning, there were still comatose bodies strewn around the house, but most people were drinking coffee on the front porch. English children were practicing their Southern accents. A German was playing an acoustic guitar. A New Mexican hydrologist compared hangover notes with a New York lawyer. Others were emerging from bedrooms, and tents on the front lawn, and soon all faces were tilted upwards, watching Eddie Earl climb the tree.

There were no concessions to modern protocols of health and safety. He didn't wear a harness. At no point did he secure himself with rope. He sat up there in a fork of the tree, about thirty feet off the ground, and started yanking on the cord of his chainsaw, having trouble starting it. Once he got it going, he used it one-handed, hanging on with the other hand, and the lower limbs started to come crashing down on the lawn, to big cheers from the porch. He climbed higher, with the chainsaw whirring in one hand, and cut down some more limbs. If you've ever tried to wield a small chainsaw with one fully extended arm, you can appreciate the strength it took to do that with a big chainsaw, while perched on a tree limb forty feet off the ground.

One huge limb overhung the roof above the living room. When he got to it, everyone retreated to a safe distance on the lawn. He tied a rope around it, and then, using some kind of genius eyeball physics, he got his son to wind the rope a few times around the main trunk, at just the right height, so when he cut through the limb, it swung away from the house and landed with an immense thud exactly where he wanted it to, just missing a wooden fence on one end and a flower bed on the other. Roars and whoops from the lawn. Eddie Earl broke out into a grin.

Then Louie and Cathy Thompson arrived unexpectedly with big glass pitchers full of Bloody Marys and ten pounds of pulled pork barbecue. That brought another cheer. Then John Newcomb and Lisa Barker arrived with side dishes, freshly baked cakes and pies, and two more pitchers of Bloodies. "Alright, we got us a tree-felling party," said John. "After we get through with this, we'll go out on the lake in my boat. We've got her all gassed up, and full of cold beer."

Jordy said to Mariah, "My god, is it always like this here? People just show up and bring you food and cocktails?"

"Pretty much," she said. "A Southern woman's not going to show up empty-handed."

So we drank Bloodies, and ate pulled pork, and cheered Eddie Earl as he brought that big hairy tree down, limb by limb, and then one chunk of trunk at a time. It took him four hours, and afterward he looked exhausted. I asked him what he wanted to eat or drink, and he said, "Water. Cold water."

That reminded him of a joke he wanted to tell. "Get your woman," he told me. "It ain't no bad story. She'll like it." I fetched Mariah, and a few other people came over, and Eddie Earl told one about an old man who invited his daughter and grandchildren over for a special meal. He had made pulled pork and ice cream. He told his grand-daughter to get a plate from the draining board and fix herself some pork. She got the plate and told her mother it was dirty. The old man overheard her, and he said, "It's just as clean as cold water can get it. Now rinse it off, and fix yourself a plate." The same thing hap-pened with the ice cream course. The little girl said the bowl was dirty, and her grandfather said, "It's just as clean as cold water can get it." Then they went outside and a big black dog jumped up and licked the granddaughter all over her face. The grandfather said to the dog, "Cold Water, you get offa her."

Eddie Earl hooted with laughter, and then told two more jokes of a similar style, but harder to understand. One concerned a black boy who avoided certain death while flying an airplane because he knew how to ride a mule, and a white boy who crashed and died in the same situation. The other one I couldn't really understand at all. Then he got in his truck, with his shy silent son, told us all to have fun, and drove back to Yazoo City with four hundred bucks in his pocket. He was right. Considering the risks, the expertise involved, and how disastrous a mistake would be, four hundred was a fair price, and I hadn't bargained for the entertainment value.

BY SUNSET, THERE were ninety people at the house, and nearly all the new arrivals were Mississippians. A couple of them had set up a skeet-shooting range in the horse pasture, and the antigun liberals were over there blasting away with borrowed shotguns. We set out a long table on the front lawn, covered it with newspaper, and stationed trash cans and rolls of paper towels at each end. Then Martha and Donald arrived, and dumped out a hundred and fifty pounds of boiled crawfish on the table. Mississippians cook them in the same way as Louisianans, boiled up with hot peppery spices and chunks of sausage, potato, and sweet corn. Cadi Thompson showed us how to eat crawfish: pinch the tail, suck the meat through the head, take a swig of cold beer.

The bluesman Jimmy "Duck" Holmes arrived in a crisp white shirt and a very sharp tweed jacket, worn with a baseball cap and sunglasses perched on the brim. He was with a woman called Thelma, and I felt a little awkward that they were the only black people here. I had invited others, from T-Model's party, from Yazoo City, but none of them could make it. I had invited some of the local farm workers, but they said they couldn't party if the bossman was going to be there, and that made it difficult to invite Monk. We were becoming friends, but I didn't want him to be the lone black guest. So in the end, the only black people there were a hired musician and his girlfriend.

During the First World War, a black soldier from Bentonia, Mississippi, had gone to France and learned an open minor tuning for the guitar. He brought this tuning back to Bentonia, where the blues legend Skip James learned it and developed a new style with it, with droning bass notes and an ominous eerie feel. Two other Bentonians learned it from Skip James, and one of them passed it on to Jimmy "Duck" Holmes. He mastered it as a young man, but it wasn't until he was in his sixties that he made his first recording, or started playing live shows. I asked him why not. "I didn't figure anyone wanted to hear that old-time stuff," he said.

Now he was making records for a small label called Broke and

Hungry, and touring all over the world. He'd just canceled a date in Tel Aviv—"Too much commotion"—and was flying out next to Switzerland.

He set up his amp and microphone on the front porch, fiddled with its settings for a long time, and then began to play. His thumb played a monotonous droning bassline, and his fingers played a complementary rhythm, sliding up the fretboard, flicking across the strings, leaving long blue notes hanging in the air. Then he started to sing and his voice was a pure soulful ache. Shivers climbed my spine. It was hard to believe such a masterful musician was playing on my porch. Some of the Mississippians came closer, and one set up a video camera, but most of them drifted away. They'd been around the blues all their lives and it was no big deal. For the foreigners and out-of-staters, it was a rare treat, and afterward we bought up all his CDs, and people made plans to see his upcoming show in New York.

I was worried that too much party energy had been expended on Friday night, but the influx of new people, and the bonds forged the night before, and the magic that alcohol can work under the right circumstances, made for another flat-out king-hell raging all-night blowout. We lit bonfires and sent blazing lanterns sailing away across the Delta. Tim got out his flashing steel guitar, and Tom picked up a stick from the firewood pile and held it up like a microphone. "Well I got drunk this morning, and I got drunk this afternoon," he sang, improvising the words. "And all the women I meet tell me I come too soon. Now I'm out here on the sidewalk all alone. It's just me and this Mississippi Microphone . . ."

It was a cathartic night, with broken furniture and hurried sexual trysts, dancing, drinking, howling, so much laughter, so much hugging and goodwill among people who had arrived as strangers from different cultures.

When all the dust had settled, and the wreckage had been

repaired, the goodwill did not fade away, or get forgotten. For many of the Mississippians, the Yankees arrived as Yankees, and left as Tom, Tim, Jordy, and so on—guys you could have fun with, and who came down here and treated everyone with respect. The party also shattered Northern stereotypes about Mississippi, and the Deep South. The Brits, coming from an island where genuine hospitality is in short supply, assumed that much of what they experienced was a gesture or façade of friendliness. But when they got home and checked their devices, there were emails, and social media messages waiting for them, and these were not gestures either, but the beginnings of lively, lasting friendships.

Louie and Cathy decided to take a vacation in New York City, and the New Yorkers they had met, captained by Tom, were determined to show them that Northerners knew something about hospitality too. They went to a friend's bar and restaurant in Brooklyn, and for Louie and Cathy, it was drinks on the house, complimentary appetizers, a big feast, and then a walk back across the Brooklyn Bridge to see the glittering spectacle of Manhattan at night.

Tom took them around his favorite joints in the Lower East Side and Chinatown, introduced them to all the bartenders and maître d's, ordered them cocktails and ethnic foods to sample. Cathy came back to Mississippi telling all her friends and relatives how much she loved New York City, and how wonderful and welcoming the people were there. That was something about New York that many of them had never heard before.

I was left with that same feeling I'd had in T-Model Ford's front yard, that drunken revelry could make a difference, that it was good for different cultures to come together, and chip away at human prejudice one party at a time.

Chapter 14

Holmes County Miracle

AFTER A FEW more roadside conversations, I got to know B a little better and arranged to meet him at his trailer for a drink. His truck wasn't there when I arrived, and a pit bull was sitting on the doorstep, unconstrained by fence or chain. I could hear a TV going inside, and children squealing and yelling. I called his cell phone. It was out of service again. I honked the horn. The door remained closed. I got out of the truck, and yelled, "Hello?" The pit bull came down the steps and stopped. The breeze was moving my scent in his direction, and he looked more curious than antagonistic. I took another step, and he growled a warning. I jumped back in the truck.

Two middle-aged women were talking outside a trailer just down the road. I asked if they knew where B was. With a slight hint of disapproval, one of them said, "Mmm-hmm, he be up in the club mos prawly." She gave me directions and said to have a blessed day. Sometimes, when people in the South tell you to have a blessed day, it means fuck you and I hope you have a nice time in hell. But she didn't say it that way. It was genuinely warm and friendly.

The club was a ramshackle brick building with a group of men sitting on chairs outside the entrance. I felt very white and conspicuous as they watched me walking toward them. Their faces were uninviting, but not hostile. I said I was looking for B, and the men looked at each other. One said, "Is he here?" And in the next moment, by pure coincidence, B came out of the door squinting at the sunlight, and was startled to see me there.

"Whoah man," he said. "I been drinking whiskey, lost track of time. I's just fittin to go home. Yo airbody, this my homeboy from England. The one who stay at Dr. Foo house."

A gleaming black SUV pulled up outside the shabby club. Out stepped a young man with cold eyes and crisp clean clothes. He raised one eyebrow at me, and said, "S'up ma nigga," as he sauntered past. Nicely played, I thought. Situation acknowledged, dominance established, a note of humor introduced.

Another man, revved up and bug-eyed, came over dipping and prancing, sticking his toothless grin right up in my face, babbling, singing, laughing, then asking for money, "This ain't your place. Gimme five dollar, man."

B said, "Don't worry about him. Come on, let's have a drink."

Inside there was a scarred pool table, some wounded tables and suffering chairs. A large television was playing a sci-fi disaster movie. Pieces of brown cardboard were pinned all around the walls, and someone had written on them, "No drugs in the club," "NO Drugs," "Absolutely NO drugs." There were two or three blunts going around, and the air was hazy with weed and tobacco smoke.

The bartender kept the money in a cigar box. He'd seen it all, by the looks of him, and none of it had impressed him much. The only drinks available were Budweiser, Bud Light, Straw-Ber-Ita, and cheap vodka from a big plastic bottle. There was no ice, and no glassware, just a sleeve of plastic cups.

B asked what I was drinking. He turned to the bartender and said, "Beer for my man, and another whiskey."

The bartender put down a twenty-ounce bottle of Budweiser and poured a slug of vodka into a plastic cup. I said, "How much?" The round was four dollars. When I left a dollar tip, the bartender thought I'd made a mistake and tried to give it back to me.

I asked B why vodka was called whiskey. "It's just something we say, maybe because it's clear like moonshine," he said. "Whiskey really just means liquor." He introduced me around. Some people were friendly and courteous, some were cold and hostile, some were disinterested, and some so wasted they could barely speak. The young man with the cold eyes had already conducted some business and left.

B's friend Neta was the only woman there, and she sat down with us. She had a big outgoing personality, orange bangs laid down across her forehead, and a beautiful smile. "Welcome to the Hospitality State," she said. "I like your accent. Say something else."

I summoned up my most proper BBC accent, and said, "Hullo Neta, can I buy you a Straw-Ber-Ita?"

She said "Ooh chile! Are you married?"

"Good as."

"I don't see no ring on your finger."

"We're not technically married, but we live together like husband and wife."

"Why dontchawl get married then?"

"I don't like the law being involved in my love life."

"I bet she don't look at it that way."

"You're probably right. Okay, one Straw-Ber-Ita, one whiskey that's vodka, another beer for me."

I came back with the drinks. Neta said, "Mi-sippi, baby. I love it here, but I want to leave."

"And go where?" I said.

"Anywhere. Everywhere. But I'll come back. These are my people."

We had more drinks. Neta left, and B's conscience started tugging at him. His wife would be coming from work soon. "I'm fittin to leave and get my ass home," he said. "Those kids are depending on me, and I can't let em down."

We parted ways in separate trucks, and as I left Thornton behind, and reentered the orderly fields and genteel houses of Pluto, it felt I was crossing from one country to another. I used to live on a remote ranch in southern Arizona, eight miles from the Mexican border. Those two cultures, existing in such close proximity, understood each other fairly well, had familial and economic ties, but like here, they remained separate and unequal. One was in the first world, and the other lay just outside.

TWO WEEKS LATER, I was sitting in B's trailer, wishing I hadn't hit the joint a third time. How did they manage to get such potent weed out here? One wall was patched up with a piece of cardboard, the ashtray was overflowing, and the children knew to go into the far bedroom when the grown-ups started smoking weed. B had a couple of friends there, and the conversation turned to gun violence.

Bereaved white mothers were weeping on the television in the corner of the trailer. There had been yet another school shooting. B's friends started listing off all the African-American men they had known who had been shot to death in Holmes and Yazoo counties, and down in Jackson. Black males were the main victims of gun violence in America, they said, and most of them were killed with handguns, not military-style assault rifles.

B did not like where this conversation was going. He pulled out his .45 semiautomatic pistol and slammed it down on the table. "Ain't nobody taking my guns away," he said.

"Ain't nobody taking nothing," said his friend. "We just saying who's doing the dying."

B dug around in his wallet, pulled out an NRA membership card, and passed it around for inspection. "Damn right, I'm card-carrying," he said. "Check the date. I pay my dues every year. I'm serious about my right to bear arms. Motherfuckers want to infringe, and who else got my back? I love the NRA, man."

"You all the way with the NRA?" said his friend. "No background checks for crazy people?"

"Nope. That just leads to more gun control."

The friends left, and we went down to the club to straighten out our heads with a beer. When we got there, B said, "Wait, I forgot my .45. We got to go back." Then he felt around in his jacket pockets and found a .380 pistol. "I forgot I had this, we cool," he said, checking to see if it was loaded.

I was already feeling a little paranoid from the weed, and the slamming sound the .45 had made on the table, and it must have showed on my face. "Relax, man," he said. "It ain't no Wild West scene up in here, but I gots to be strapped. It's my constitutional right, and I don't want nobody to fuck with you, because you my friend. So don't be stressing like that. I see you stressing."

The club was half-deserted, and a cold beer calmed my nerves. B said he used to work on the plantations, driving tractors and harvesters, but something went wrong that he didn't want to talk about, because everything was going so well now. He was making good money with his scrap metal, his kids were doing fine in school, his wife was managing a restaurant, and he had two pickup trucks to his name. They were both old and struggling, but still, having two vehicles was a big deal in Thornton.

"The biggest problem I got is envy," he said. "My trucks may not look like much to you, but a lot of folks around here ain't got no wheels. I got a nice hunting rifle, and that look good too. They know I'm making money, and they be wanting some."

As the club started to fill up, people came over to us, one after another, asking for a drink, a cigarette, a joint, money to buy weed that they promised to share, or just money, which I guessed meant money for crack or meth or pills. B was keeping some complicated accounts in his head: who he owed for past favors, who had been asking too often lately, who would cause trouble if refused, who would return the favor down the line, and who wouldn't. I had a more straightforward approach. If I liked the look of somebody's face, and they were willing to talk to me, I would include them in the next round of drinks that I bought.

"You see how it is?" B said during a lull. "They see you, and they know you got money. They see how much scrap I be hauling, and they know I got money too. Women want what I got, even though it ain't hardly much. I would never do that with any of these women, but I have a hard time making their men understand that. I'm telling you, man, envy and jealousy. It's for real. Somebody always want what I got. I can't leave nothing laying around. Because if you take what I got, I got to shoot you. That's just how it is."

I STARTED GOING to the club every couple of weeks. It was the only place nearby to drink and socialize, and it was such a foreign environment to me that it satisfied my urge to travel. Mariah worried that it was too dangerous. So did the Thompsons. There was always racial tension when I was in the club, hanging in the air with the weed and tobacco smoke, but the fact that I was a foreign white person, and therefore a novelty, seemed to make a difference. Nevertheless, the possibility of being robbed, challenged, or caught up in mayhem was always there, at least in my mind. So I never stayed past eight thirty at night, never carried more than thirty dollars in cash, and never showed there alone.

Usually I went with B, or Monk, or Albert Johnson, who lived and worked on John Newcomb's plantation. In his younger days he had traveled all over the country playing guitar for a gospel group, and for Koko Taylor, the female blues star. He still played from time to time with a local gospel group called the Spiritual Kings, but his fingers hurt when he played the guitar these days. "It's arthur-itis and too much heavy farm work," he said. "At least I think it is."

When Albert drove himself to the club, he had a tendency to come home too late for his own good, or the good of his marriage. So it seemed like good strategy to ride there with me, since I always left early and could drop him off on the way home. Albert and his wife lived in a nicely furnished, spotlessly clean, two-bedroom wooden house with two big flat-screen TVs, an aquarium, and a rose garden in the front yard. The house was owned and maintained by John Newcomb, and they lived there rent-free and paid the utilities out of Albert's wages.

I picked up Albert at his front door one evening, and we drove along the shore of the oxbow lake toward Thornton, with the sun setting behind the cypress trees that grew out of the water, and the water turning pink, and long-necked birds flying across the sky.

Albert was in a somber, reflective mood. His nephew had just been killed in a motorcycle accident. "He was thirty-five years old with a wife and kids and a good job in the school system, a man in the prime of life, and the Good Lord pulled the road right out from under him," he said. When we got to the club, it was full of relatives that had come down from Chicago for the funeral.

"There'll be some carrying-on at the funeral for real," he said, setting our beers down on a scarred table. "People are gone hurt themselves, he was so young. We've already had a couple of ladies in the hospital with seizures."

I told Albert that I'd just lost a close friend to cancer. He was an Irish screenwriter in his forties, and the ending he wrote for himself was a deathbed marriage to his girlfriend. "You got to be strong," said Albert. "They don't want you to feel bad because of them. They understand that you're bound to feel bad for a while. But not too long. They don't want that. They want you to get on and live. They want you to enjoy every moment of life that you have."

A woman named Redbone came over, wondering who I was. She was one of Albert's relatives from up north, which you could tell at a glance from her big-city clothes. She had dyed, upswept hair and carried herself with a haughty pride. She quizzed me for a while, and then the conversation turned to travel. Albert said, "In the whole round world, the place I want to go most is the Serengeti. I watch Animal Planet all the time, and to see that place for real, that would be it for me. But folks like me never get to see the world."

"I refuse to accept that," said Redbone. "Don't be a prisoner of your own mind. You can do whatever you want to do, and go wherever you want to go. Look at me. I wanted to go to Paris, France, and I made it happen."

"Did you enjoy it?" I asked.

"I did not, because I was there with someone who no longer loved me. But I saw the sights. I'm glad I went."

Albert said that he'd won a Caribbean cruise in a contest some years ago, and the prize came with $2,500 in cash to spend on the boat. "All I had to do was get to Florida, but I didn't have the money for gas, or bus fare. Ain't that something?" He started laughing and shaking his head.

Redbone said, "You could have got to Florida if you'd set your mind to it. That's exactly what I'm talking about."

I said, "Nobody could give you a ride?"

Albert said, "I tried to get a ride. But I didn't have no gas money to give nobody. You see what I mean? Folks like me don't get to see the world."

The club was getting packed and noisy. People were gambling on card and dice games, and there was a loan shark on hand who would charge a dollar in interest for every dollar borrowed. It felt like time to go, and Albert was happy to leave with me. On the way back, he started reminiscing fondly about his childhood in a tenant shack. He called them the good old days, but they didn't sound that good to me. He was one of eleven children. His father was a gambler and a womanizer who was in and out of their lives. Albert started chopping cotton at the age of seven. He went to school until the eighth grade and then worked full-time in the fields.

"I can honestly say I had a happy childhood. Everybody knew each other, it was a real community, and I had a good mama. A real good one. She could turn a handful of flour and a few scraps into a meal for the whole family. You don't see women like that anymore. These young women nowadays, most of them are lazy. They just want to get high."

"But you must have been so poor," I said.

"So poor we stuffed cardboard in our shoes just to keep our feet off the ground."

"What was the worst thing about being that poor?"

He thought about that for a while. Then he said, "Not having it when you really needed it. When your children really needed it."

When we reached his house, he invited me in for a nightcap. His wife heard us talking, came out of the back bedroom, raised a quizzical eyebrow at me. "Don't worry," she said. "You're welcome here." Then she went back to watching TV in the bedroom.

Albert poured out two shots of moonshine from a Patrón tequila bottle. He took an electric guitar out of its case, and played and sang a couple of gospel songs. His voice was strong and soulful, but his fingers hurt and the guitar wouldn't stay in tune. The telephone rang, his wife answered, and he guessed correctly that it was the relatives in Indiana they were about to visit.

"They go to church five nights a week, and all day Sunday," he said. "You don't need to try that hard to get saved. Just be a good person, buy a man a beer if you got money in your pocket, give him a hit of your weed, you know what I mean?"

His wife called out, "Honey!"

He called back, "What?"

"They say don't pack your green suit."

He creased up laughing, and so did I.

"I look fly in my green suit," he said. "But they don't want Grandpa looking all fly up in they church. C'mon man, let's have another drink. You play something on the guitar. I'm enjoying this."

I said, "Albert, I've enjoyed it too, but I've got to get back. Mariah is waiting for me."

"Okay, okay, I know how it go," he said. He went over to the fridge and handed me a cold beer. "Here," he said. "I can't let you leave without something to carry you home."

AFTER A FEW months of going to the club, I had a small circle of friends there. One of them was Evander, who had traveled to Europe and Asia with the military, and stood apart slightly in the crowd. He was in his early forties now, tall and slim, with glasses and a Rasta hat. When he was talking, I didn't have to listen so carefully, because he spoke with a mainstream African-American accent, and used as many consonants as I did. He was kind, smart, often very insightful, but sometimes, and usually after a certain number of beers, he would start making connections that were too cosmic for me to follow, or he would talk around the edges of a conspiracy that I could never quite get a handle on. Still, we enjoyed each other's company, talked on the phone regularly, and visited each other's houses.

He was sitting on my front porch one day, telling me about the trials of his childhood. Other kids picked on him because he was tall and skinny, and because his family had more money and independence than most of the black people in the area. They owned and farmed a good-sized spread of land that backed up against the hills. "I was always different," he said. "I didn't grow up on a plantation like everybody else, and I don't have that plantation mentality," he said.

I asked him what he meant by "plantation mentality."

"My mother was a schoolteacher," he said. "I wasn't raised to be loyal to some white plantation owner. These other kids would fight each other on the school bus over whose plantation owner had the most money. I'm serious! The Pluto kids would fight with the Stonewall kids, and the Bonanza kids, and it would all be about, 'My bossman got more than your bossman! No he don't! Your bossman ain't shit! *Whack!*' I could tell you some stories. I could tell you some *stories*."

He stretched out his long legs, leaned back in his chair, smiled, and lit another cigarette. "Okay, let me ask you something," he said. "Since you've been living here, how many black folks have sat up on this porch with you? Monk, maybe. Who else?"

"No one. I've given up trying."

"They come around the back, right? That's what I'm talking

about, and I don't play that. I'm friends with a white plantation owner over thataway."

He extended his arm to the east and dipped the fingers, to indicate the other side of the lake. "He invited me over to have a drink, and I went in the front door, like I always do, and the black man working for him nearly dropped dead on the floor. He said to me, 'Git around the back, nigga. Don't you know no better?' This was in 2012, not 1965, or 1860. The plantation mentality. It's why the Delta doesn't progress. It's not having anything, and not really wanting anything, because that would mean change. That would mean taking on more responsibility. Too many of our people are not interested in progress and change."

"What about white racism? What's the effect of that?"

"Whites don't even need to be racist anymore. They can just sit back on their plantations, and send their kids to the academy, and hang out at the country club, and watch us keep each other down. I mean, it's wild, it's insane. The whites now, especially the younger ones, they don't want us to use the back door, or say, 'Yassuh boss,' or any of that. They don't care. They're waiting for us to change. But we don't, because change is what we're afraid of. We hold on to what we know, no matter how messed up it is. And when I talk like this in Thornton, everyone calls me crazy."

The next time I saw Evander, at his brick house at the end of a dirt road on his family's land, he was wearing a neck brace, and a cast on one foot. He had gone off the road driving a friend's car at one hundred miles an hour. The car was a write-off. He'd woken up in hospital with no memory of the accident. Now he was on a regimen of pain pills and Bud Light, with a lot of empties in the trash can.

"Apparently, the Lord wants me alive," he said. "I think I know why, too, because I've been talking with my minister, and there are so many dark things going on around here, with cousins marrying cousins, and voodoo stuff that I can't even get into, and the whole situation with my ex and what she was up to, and now you arriving here, and me with this incredible story, knowing everything I do, and it's all connected. It's *all* connected. Nothing happens without a purpose."

"Evander," I said. "You're getting too cosmic for me. But it's a miracle that you aren't dead. Please don't do that again. There's way too much tragedy around here as it is."

He said, "You got that right, my brother. How's Helen doing?"

"You know, under the circumstances, and with the Lord's help, she seems to be doing remarkably well."

HELEN MALONE, WHO cleaned our house, and Cathy's house, and Bobby T's house, and took Aunt Mary shopping and cleaned her house, had always been a strong person. Physically, she was a tall, broad-shouldered, good-looking woman at sixty, and she must have really been something in her youth. Now she had some arthritis setting in, but she was determined to stay active, because it was the best thing you could do.

She lifted weights, ate a lot of vegetables, and one reason she kept working was because it kept her moving. She needed the money too, of course, because she was always thinking about her five children, and fifteen grandchildren—fourteen now that the Lord had taken one back home.

Evander had been sitting there at Helen's son's house with a group of people, when the three-year-old boy toddled out into the backyard to feed the family pit bull. The dog attacked and killed him. We heard about it right after it happened. Cathy Thompson, setting aside her fears of black crime, went directly to the house in Thornton to help Helen, who was trying to comfort the boy's hysterical mother, make the funeral arrangements, and organize the household for the incoming flood of relatives. Cathy gave her a long heartfelt hug, assessed the situation, and went off to buy bread, cold cuts, chips, snacks, sodas—food that Helen wouldn't have to cook. Mariah asked what we could do, and Cathy said, "Paper plates, plastic cups, napkins, plastic silverware, garbage bags. That poor woman is going to have to feed everybody, and we don't want her doing the dishes as well."

When the news media got hold of the story, bloggers called for the family to be prosecuted for negligent homicide. Politicians called for pit bulls to be banned in Holmes County, as they had been banned in some other counties. Dogfighting was still a big underground sport in Mississippi, but the pit bull that killed Helen's grandson wasn't a fighting dog, as many commentators had assumed. It was the family pet, so no charges were filed, and the dog was euthanized by a vet.

"That boy loved that dog," said Helen. "And the dog loved him. I don't know what happened. All I can think is that somebody must have whupped that dog, and when he went over there to pet it, the dog felt pain and turned on him. He was such a sweet boy, and he sure loved that dog."

For Helen, there was no question that her grandson was now in heaven. God had taken him home early, and spared him all the trials and tribulations of adult life. "But the boy's mama can't sleep," she said. "And she won't take her pills unless I'm there to give her the pills. I'd like to get back home to my bed, but I reckon I'll be staying with them for a while longer."

HELEN'S GRANDSON WAS the most heartbreaking in a long series of local tragedies. James Jefferson died suddenly of a heart attack, leaving behind a young wife and son in very uncertain circumstances. One of Monk's neighbors, a female guard at Parchman, "a real nice lady," as he described her, told her nephew at a family gathering that he needed to take his sick baby to the hospital. He got angry, and said she was always telling him what to do. They got into a furious argument. He stormed out, got his shotgun, came back, and shot her at close range in front of the family, killing her instantly.

There was a senseless murder in a nightclub called Mr. T's Midnight Bar and Grill, a drive-by shooting in Tchula, a fatal DUI accident, a crib death, two more traffic fatalities, a trailer fire that killed a child, and another nightclub murder, all in west Holmes County in the space of a few months. Police were called to an African-American church in Lexington, the county seat, during Sunday services, because congregants were yelling and threatening each other. The deacons were trying to fire the pastor, and the pastor was trying to get the congregation to vote on whether to retain him or not.

Police were already there when the deacon's son Cacedrick White, twenty-six, arrived with his shotgun. He fired once in the parking lot, perhaps announcing his intentions, and was then shot three times by a police officer. He died later in hospital. The newspapers ran a photograph of him the next day, scowling at the camera and flashing a gang sign.

The grim tide of news was eventually pushed back by a miracle that made headlines all over the world. Walter "Snowball" Williams, a seventy-eight-year-old African-American farmer, was dying in hospice care at his home in Lexington. The hospice nurse called the Holmes County coroner, Dexter Howard, to say that Williams had passed away. Howard arrived with Byron Porter, from Porter and Sons Funeral Home. The coroner found no pulse and signed the death certificate. They put him in a body bag, and Porter took him to the funeral parlor.

Two hours later, the grieving family got a phone call. As the mortician was getting ready to embalm the body, he saw a leg move. Then

Williams started breathing again. The mortician called the paramedics, who found a heartbeat, and took him straight to hospital.

The coroner told reporters and the sheriff that the only possible explanation was a miracle from God. The family said the same thing. Rejoicing outside the hospital, they sang Snowball's favorite song, "I'll Fly Away," with soaring gospel harmonies. Snowball's nephew Eddie Hester, a big man wearing a Christian T-shirt, and a white sweatband around his head, said, "It's a miracle. It's just God. And we thank Him for it." Another relative said, "We know it's the Lord who brought him back. Praise Him, hallelujah!"

A Jackson TV station reported the story in the same holy fervor. "It *is* a miracle, I'm speechless," said the anchorwoman, Melanie Christopher. Cooler heads pointed out that county coroners are elected in Mississippi and are not required to have any medical training. When questioned again, Coroner Howard said he was absolutely certain that Williams was dead when he examined him but wondered if a defibrillator, implanted under the skin on his chest, might have jump-started his heart once he was in the body bag. "It could've kicked in, started his heart back," he said. "The bottom line is it's a miracle."

Williams died in hospital a week later, and it became yet another improbable, outlandish story that people told back and forth across the Delta. "I heard of being born again," said Monk, who thought a mistake by the coroner was the most likely explanation. "But around here, you can die again too."

Chapter 15

Morgan Freeman and
the Meaning of Life

WHEN I FELT like a more uptown drinking experience, I went for cocktails at the bar of the Alluvian Hotel in Greenwood, and that's where I met Jerry "Tank" Tankersley. He wore expensive designer clothes, always drank champagne, and as I confirmed with an email to Superintendent Lee's office, he had been the dentist for the maximum security unit and death row at Parchman. Tank had extracted wisdom teeth from serial killers, drilled into the rotten molars of some truly evil psychopaths, and by prison regulations, all he was allowed to give them for the pain was ibuprofen.

He quit Parchman a few years ago, and now he was producing movies, practicing dentistry in nursing homes, and playing a lot of golf with Morgan Freeman—yes, that Morgan Freeman—who was living in the Delta near Clarksdale. Tank lived in a luxury apartment opposite the Alluvian Hotel. He was a lean, strong, compact man in his early fifties, with cropped ginger hair and a slightly manic edge to his laughter, which wasn't surprising in the least when you learned what he'd been through.

"I would start work at four thirty in the morning, because I wanted them sleepy," he said. "Their criminal history was right there on their medical chart, so I would read about these grisly murders they had committed, in graphic, sickening detail. Then the guards would bring them in, and I would see them in the flesh, and start working on their teeth, trying to be gentle as I could, because I couldn't give them effective painkillers."

He took another sip of champagne and grinned at the insanity of it. He was wearing a slim-fit midnight-blue patterned shirt, with the cuffs turned up to reveal a paler blue pattern underneath. "Sometimes they were in restraints, sometimes there'd be a guard with a shotgun pointed at my patient's head," he said. "I'd see the end of that shotgun barrel start to droop and wobble around, as the guard got bored, or lost concentration. Sometimes I'd look up from what I was doing, and that shotgun would pointing right at my fucking head!"

Out poured a giddy burst of can-you-believe-that-shit laughter, and in walked Tank's girlfriend Suzy Bergner, a Houston socialite with a glossy mane of dark hair, a wardrobe that walked the line between glamorous and racy, and a personality that relished being fabulously over the top. She handed me her business card, which read as follows:

> *Here's to us in our high-heeled shoes,*
> *we smoke men's cigars*
> *and drink men's booze*

and when we kiss, we kiss so sweet
we make things stand that have no feet!

Cheers dears! xoxosuzyb

On the other side of the card was a drawing of a cocktail, her contact details, and these words in red letters:

fun-friends, cocktails and lunch . . . a "Drunch!"

Join me sometime
dahlin', that s what i do! [*sic*]

"She's got five ex-husbands, I've got four ex-wives, we're made for each other!" said Tank.

"So true!" she said. "But first I had to get rid of every piece of clothing in his closet, and give him a complete makeover. Tank didn't know a thing about clothes. He didn't even drink champagne, told me he didn't like it! So I turned him on to good French champagne, and good Russian caviar, and I got him into some Hugo Boss, as you see. Then he dragged me off to the Mississippi Delta, of all places, where there's absolutely nothing to do, and everything they eat makes you fat. I mean, my ass is reaching crisis point, I've *got* to spend more time at the gym."

"Isn't she something?" said Tank, beaming from ear to ear. "We have a blast together."

"Tank," I said. "Not to spoil the festive mood, but I've got to ask. Of all the dentistry jobs you could have picked, why death row at Parchman?"

"Sin and redemption, basically," he said. "I'm not big on organized religion, I think it's the greatest scam ever invented, but I had done bad things, and I needed to atone. I had gambled away all my money, and a lot of other people's money too. I had gone through four divorces, and way too many strippers. I was out of control. I sent myself to Parchman because I needed to be there."

"It's a crazy story," said Suzy B. "I mean, talk about Southern Gothic. I mean, *please*. You may as well start at the beginning, dahlin'. And we're going to need more bubbles."

TANK GREW UP in Greenwood as the son of a pulpit-pounding Nazarene preacher who had taken a vow of poverty and was a secret alcoholic. "Have you seen *The Apostle* with Robert Duvall?" he said. "That was my dad. He wasn't a bad guy, and we knew he loved us, but it's an abusive religion, or it was in those days. I had three sisters, and we had very few toys. He wouldn't allow a television in the house for a long time. We weren't allowed to go to the swimming pool on a hot summer day, because bathing suits showed too much flesh. I never learned how to swim properly.

"The worst part was looking in the refrigerator and seeing no food. We'd go hungry until Sundays when we got the leftovers from the parish dinner. Plus I got molested a few times by a guy across the street. I don't like to make too big a deal about that, but it definitely affects you later in life."

Tank immersed himself in martial arts and went off to study dentistry. He came home one weekend to find his father sprawled unconscious on the floor. There was a .357 magnum in his hand, and an empty fifth of Smirnoff on the floor next to him. His father had passed out while trying to get drunk enough to commit suicide. When he regained consciousness, his father confessed that demons in the bottle had been fighting with him for years.

"When you're raised in that hellfire tradition, with no middle ground between God and the devil, it brings out extreme behavior in people. It brought it out in me, but some of it was just my nature. I'm driven, obsessive, extremely competitive. When I got into martial arts, I went straight to black belt. When I started gambling, I became compulsive."

I was already taking notes, and at this point I pulled out a recording device. "Do you mind?" I said.

"I don't care," he said.

Suzy B said, "You really should."

Tank graduated in the top five of his dental class. He started practicing as a dentist, and teaching dentistry. James Meredith was one of his patients, "a good guy, tough as they come," and so was Byron De La Beckwith, the Greenwood white supremacist who murdered civil rights leader Medgar Evers. "When they finally put him away, he would send me all these letters," said Tank. "I burned them all. I wish I hadn't now for the historical value."

"What were the letters about?"

"White supremacy. I hate that shit. My dad hated it too, I'm proud to say. He stood up to the Klan."

While his dental career advanced steadily, Tank's personal life careened out of control. He had already lost his religion, and after his first divorce, he threw his conscience away. Having grown up with poverty and denial, he gorged himself on pleasure, sin, indulgence, excess. He cheated on his wives and girlfriends. He screwed his friend's wife with the friend passed out drunk in the same room. He drove flashy cars and lived for the action in the casinos and strip clubs.

He never got into cocaine, or pills, or weed, because gambling was his drug. When he was winning he would stay up for three days and three nights without sleep, "just getting laid and playing dice." When he lost, meaning that he had no money left with which to gamble, he plunged into the blackest despair. The only way out of that hole was to get money and start gambling again.

"I bet on football games, craps, blackjack. I was good at it. I won a lot. The most I ever gambled in a night was fifty thousand dollars and I won. Once I flew to Vegas with a hundred grand in cash, and I won another thirteen thousand dollars, then I lost it all in the last hour while I was waiting for the limousine to take me to the airport. I felt utterly sick, but if you can get another five hundred dollars and start winning, you're back on cloud nine."

He spent fifteen years as a gambling addict. In the last seven years, he said, he lost $4 million, most of it borrowed. He decided he had to quit, so he got in his Porsche with $60,000 in chips and drove to Tunica, where ten casinos were built in the Delta's poorest county and floated on big artificial ponds to satisfy the state's requirement that gambling be confined to riverboats.

"I gambled until it was all gone. After that, every time I got the urge to gamble, I'd go and hit golf balls, even if it was the middle of the night. You had to be careful of water moccasins, but it worked. Golf was how I quit gambling. Then I got hooked on golf, and that's when I saw an ad saying 'Dentist Wanted' at the Mississippi State Penitentiary. That word 'penitentiary' caught my eye, because penance was what I needed to do. So I put on my best clothes and went to Parchman, and they hired me on the spot. I was the only applicant. I could have showed up in overalls, and they would have hired me."

I said, "From gambling, to golf, to maximum security dentistry, to the movie business."

"And now to me!" said Suzy B. "It's too crazy! And I just found out his wives were like, low key, and I'm so out there! Alright, honey, tell him about your first day at Parchman."

"Well, before I started, I had to take a course called How to Work in Corrections and Not Get Arrested. You have to understand who you're dealing with. Prisoners are expert conmen, and they will do absolutely anything to get a leg up in their world. Give them a cheap plastic ink pen, and they can use it to kill. I can make you a shank right now out of a toothbrush, some chewing gum, a razor blade, some floss, and some tape. If they cut someone's throat with a shank like that, and you gave them the toothbrush, guess who's getting arrested."

On his first day at Parchman, he was shown to his dental office in the medical clinic. It was a small cinder-block room with a chair and some cabinets in the medical office. The previous dentist had quit some time ago, because of the prison violence, and there was a huge backlog of exams to catch up on.

"A female guard escorted me over to Unit C, which is where death row is. She had this Plexiglas shield in case they threw blood or urine, and all these comments were being hurled at us, like, 'I'm gonna fuck you in the ass,' and 'Come over here and suck my dick.' I finally looked at her and said, 'How do you stand this?' She looked at me and never blinked. She said, 'They're not talking to me.'"

Tank and Suzy then roared with laughter for a good thirty seconds, started to recover, and convulsed with laughter all over again. Tank ordered a hamburger. In the old *Cool Hand Luke* days, he said, it was the guards who inflicted the brutality on the prisoners. Now the guards were monitored by security cameras, as the result of an ACLU lawsuit, and the prisoners inflicted brutality on each other and bribed the guards to look the other way.

The gangs ran everything on the inside, and now they were recruiting their homegirls on the outside to get jobs as prison guards, to smuggle in contraband, and provide them with sex. There were a few different black gangs, who fought and schemed against each other, and the Aryan Brotherhood, the sole white gang in Parchman.

"If you're white, you've got to join them for your own protection.

I can only remember one white prisoner who refused to affiliate with them: Jesse Wilson, we called him Superman. He was about six-four and looked like Matthew McConaughey. He came in for larceny, and then had to start killing people to stay alive. He was an escape artist too, so they put him in a special Plexiglas cell, monitored by cameras 24/7. Somehow he managed to saw his way out of there and stab a child molester twenty-seven times. The medic took his pulse just a few moments later. It was normal. Jesse yelled, 'What's wrong with y'all! I just saved the state money.' He went off to the supermax in Colorado."

When Tank arrived at Parchman, he had compassion for the prisoners. That lasted for about a month. After reading about the rapes and murders his patients had committed, and then finding them to be utterly without morals or remorse, his compassion disappeared. "That messes with your head, because you're born with compassion toward others. When you can't feel compassion, you feel guilty. But they are incorrigible. In the first six months, I saw two murders, and so many stabbings and rapes. Some of the biggest, baddest sonsabitches you ever saw would come into the medical clinic with a blank thousand-yard stare and a blood-soaked behind."

He had to extract a wisdom tooth and give two fillings to Thomas Loden, an ex–US Marine, Gulf War veteran, and serial killer of women. "He would pick out his victims, drive around in a van, puncture their tire, pretend to help them change their tire in his Marine uniform, then take them in his van, and videotape rapes, sodomy, and murder. The prison psychiatrist, who had thirty-five years' experience, told me that Thomas Loden was the only man who made him cry, and vomit. He's still in there. His lawyers keep getting stays of execution."

The creepiest patient of all was Gary Simmons, who has since been executed. He shot a drug dealer and kept the dealer's girlfriend in a metal footlocker, letting her out only to feed her, let her go to the bathroom, and rape her. He was a butcher by trade, and he dismembered her boyfriend, carried him in pieces down to the bayou behind the house, and fed him to the alligators.

"I had to drain an abscess the size of a golf ball in his palate. He had cut the roof of his mouth deliberately with a paper clip, just to create an infection so he could get out of his cell and come to see me. I went in there with a scalpel and drained the pus out of that thing. His teeth were relatively good."

He had to count his instruments many times a day, because they were such deadly weapons. But nothing was deadlier in Parchman than a cell phone, Tank said. An inmate with a phone could call in a hit on the family members of a rival inmate or a guard.

"I was working on a gang leader, and I heard a distinct buzzing, undeniably the sound of a vibrating cell phone. I asked him if he had a cell phone. He denied it. The buzzing started again. I called the head of security, and the warden. They searched him, didn't find anything. Then they stripped him down, made him squat and cough, and out came a cell phone. I said, 'I told you somebody was calling his ass!'"

When Tank and Suzy B had recovered from laughing at that one, I asked him what made him finally quit the job. That's when he told me he wasn't just working eight hours a day at Parchman. He was also putting in another eight hours a day at the private prison in Tutwiler, and sleeping only three hours a night in a small room at the Parchman chapel.

"I did that for two and a half years," he said. "The last straw was a credible death threat against me from an inmate I'd worked on in Parchman. I'd had to surgically remove a wisdom tooth. He wanted something more than ibuprofen, understandably, but I couldn't give it to him. He told his cell mate that he was going to kill me, because I had hurt him. The cell mate told a guard. I'd had enough anyway. I'd been through a full-blown gang riot on the rec yard, doing triage on prisoners who'd been slicing each other up. I was ready to move on with my life."

Tank had now finished his hamburger. We'd all had a pleasant quantity of champagne. He paid the check and asked if I played golf. I said it had been a very long time, but I had been good at the game as a teenager. "Well, great," he said. "You'll have to come and play with me and Morgan and the guys."

"I don't have any clubs. I don't have any shoes."

"Just wear sneakers, and I'll lend you my spare clubs. The only thing you need to bring is a bottle of wine. It's an eccentric little country club, and that's the way we like it. They've got a bar, but you have to bring your own booze, and pour your own drinks. Morgan loves it there. He's there every Sunday when he's not on a movie."

"I'd love to come," I said.

"Alright, we'll see you Sunday. And don't forget the wine."

TO GET TO the Bayou Bend Golf and Country Club, I drove eighty-five miles to Webb, turned right through its decaying downtown, then turned left on a road that ran out into the country past a scarecrow in a white dress and wig and red lipstick. I saw golf fairways to the right, but no golfers, and then an old two-storey country house with a few vehicles parked outside it. There was no sign, the door was locked, but this had to be the place.

Tank arrived with Suzy in a black Hummer, handed me a set of clubs and some golf balls, and walked me across the road, where Morgan Freeman was waiting at the first tee with a few other people. He was taller than I had imagined, and he stood very straight and strong for a man in his mid-seventies. He was wearing jeans, a white golf shirt, a white cap, and sunglasses.

Tank introduced me, saying, "Morgan, this is our good friend Richard Grant."

I put out my hand, and Morgan Freeman looked off to the side. Tank said, "Morgan, you're terrible."

Then Morgan relented and smiled and shook my hand. "Do you know how many times I get that?" he said, in that unmistakable voice. " 'Morgan, *this a good friend of ours . . .'* You should try it sometime. Well shoot, let's play some golf. I'm ready to play some golf."

Tank introduced me to the other golfers. Morgan's girlfriend was a professor of sociology at the University of Mississippi, an attractive blonde woman in sporty golf clothes. Bill Luckett, Morgan's best friend and business partner in Mississippi, was a big, tall man with swept-back white hair and a take-charge personality. He was a lawyer, pilot, business entrepreneur, and aspiring politician. He had run for governor of Mississippi a few years ago and lost the Democratic primary. Now he was running for mayor of Clarksdale, where he and Morgan owned Ground Zero Blues Club. "You can ride with me," said Luckett, putting my borrowed clubs in his golf cart.

The others included a hungover film producer from LA, a local hunting guide named Catfish, and Sykes Sturdivant, the past president of the Bayou Bend. He was a jovial, self-assured character, half preppy, half jock, with a small to medium build and a rich, grainy voice. He owned a vast spread of prime Delta farmland and belonged to one of the few old moneyed families in the Delta that were still Democrats. Sykes was an avid golfer who hated playing out of sand traps, so he'd used his influence at the Bayou Bend to have all the sand traps filled in and turfed over. It was a nine-hole course built in the 1930s, and it ran alongside the murky stagnant waters of Cassidy Bayou, the longest bayou in the world.

Sykes was proud of the Bayou Bend's eccentricities. He preferred dove hunting to tennis, so he'd let the tennis courts get completely

overgrown in the hopes of shooting doves there. "It's not every country club in Mississippi that turns its tennis courts into a dove field,"
he said. "And our vice president is a black man who's married to a
white woman. Most country clubs around here won't even allow
black members."

Bill Luckett said, "When Morgan came back to Mississippi, he
was going to join a different country club. They wanted him, but they
had turned down another black man who was perfectly well quali-
fied to get in. I didn't like that, and neither did Morgan, so we started
coming here. It's a country-ass country club, and we're not big on
rules and regulations. I like to carry a chainsaw in my golf bag, which
they don't let you do at most places. If I get stuck behind a tree, or
a tree limb, hell, I'll just fire up the chainsaw and cut that bad boy
down."

There were twelve people in all, and we played a big casual
scramble with two teams. Morgan played off a forward tee and swung
the club with one arm. He'd been in a bad car wreck a few years ago,
and he had permanent injuries to his left hand and arm. He wore a
compression bandage on the wrist and forearm, and every twenty
minutes or so, the arm would give him a jolt of pain that would make
him grimace, and sometimes double over.

Balance, rhythm, and restraint were the keys to swinging a golf
club with the right arm only. If he tried to hit it too hard, the ball
would usually scuttle along the ground. If he kept his swing poised,
smooth, and easy, like his speaking voice, the ball would fly a hundred yards or more, and he was very good around the greens, holing
a number of putts in the fifteen feet range. It was obvious that he
loved the game of golf, and the fun, relaxed, gently competitive atmosphere in which it was played at the Bayou Bend. Morgan Freeman
was just one of the gang here, subject to a little teasing and ribbing
like any other golf buddy.

"Morgan's played God twice in the movies, and it's rubbed off on him some," said Bill Luckett, trying and failing to make Morgan miss a putt.

"I can call up a little supernatural intervention when I need it," said Morgan, as my putt lipped out of the hole and put his team in the lead.

Sykes won the match for Morgan's team by chipping in, and as he danced and whooped and crowed, Bill Luckett put on a big show pretending to be the devastated loser. Then it was time for drinks. It was not the kind of bar where one pictures A-list Hollywood actors, gubernatorial candidates, or movie producers having a drink after a round of golf. It had plastic laminate tables and taupe-colored chairs on wheels that looked like they'd been salvaged from the cafeteria of an old folks' home.

The toilet door was broken. There was stained carpet leading up the stairs into total disrepair. People poured their own drinks into mismatched glassware and lined up their bottles on the bar. Morgan's girlfriend made him a large vodka on the rocks with an olive. A mentally handicapped black man with a palsied arm brought in some skillet-cooked popcorn from the kitchen, and the cramped, dimly lit room turned into a hubbub of loud conversation and laughter.

Tank was talking about pulling down a patient's lip at Parchman and finding the words FUCK YOU tattooed on the underside, and Bill Luckett was talking about Dr. Weiner, his opponent in the up-coming mayor's election. Following his arrest for soliciting women on sugardaddyforme.com, Weiner was now known as Dr. Sugar-daddy on the black side of Clarksdale.

Someone had told Morgan Freeman that I'd done a lot of travel-ing, and he wanted to know why. We were sitting on opposite sides of a small round table, with people squeezing past. "Curiosity," I said.

"Just to get an idea of how the world works, and how different cultures deal with life, and think about life."

"And what conclusions have you drawn?"

"None, really. The more you learn, the more complicated it gets."

"And what if, somewhere on your travels, you could meet a man who could cut through all that complexity, and give you a few simple answers to your questions."

"I'd be interested to meet that man."

"You're sitting right across the table from him," he said in that marvelous voice, flashing a big smile.

"The first thing you need to understand is that death is a step forward," he said. "It can only be a step forward."

I said, "Wait a minute. A step forward into what, or where?"

He said, "Do I need to tell you the meaning of life?"

"Please."

"It's really very simple. The meaning of life, for every organism on this planet, including us, is to procreate and die. That's it. And you may as well enjoy the rest of it, because it really doesn't matter a damn."

"Procreate and die."

"Yup."

Then Bill Luckett sat down, and I said, "Bill, I've never thought of myself as a country club guy, but this is a country club I could join."

Bill said, "Great. We'd love to have you."

"What's the procedure?" I said.

"Hey Sykes," he called. "Richard here wants to join. I'll propose him."

"Sure," said Sykes.

"I'll second him," said Morgan.

"Okay, you're in," said Bill.

•   •   •   •   •

DINNER WAS A buffet line of fried chicken and fried catfish, with potatoes, salad, overboiled vegetables, lemon squares in little plastic dessert bowls. We all sat down at a long table in a big room with fixtures and furnishings that would have looked contemporary in 1968.

Bill Luckett had a politician's gift for working a room. During the golf game, and over drinks, he had extracted a lot of information from people, remembered it all, and he now wove it together into a speech, introducing everyone and welcoming them to the Bayou Bend. In the usual Mississippi way, he pronounced "bayou" as "bayo." He gave an impeccably memorized summary of my life and career, with all dates accurate, and asked that I be welcomed as the newest member of the Bayou Bend Golf and Country Club.

Then we raised our glasses and called out in unison, "To the Bayo Bend!"

"YOU DID WHAT?" said Mariah, when I got home.

"You're a member too," I said. "It's less than a dollar a day for both of us."

"But I don't play golf, and you can't make me wear those clothes."

"It's not about the golf. Or the food. And the place is kind of a dump. But you'll like it, I promise."

And so it was that we started driving ninety miles to the Bayou Bend a couple of Sundays a month, and then ninety miles back again. Despite her initial skepticism, Mariah enjoyed the eccentric bonhomie of the place as much as I did. Sometimes I played golf with Bill Luckett's clubs, and Mariah rode around in a golf cart watching us all play. But usually we arrived at the bar at 6:00 p.m. for the drinks, the conversation, the joviality, whatever entertainment might break out, and dinner.

Morgan Freeman was usually there, and one Sunday after golf

I asked him a stupid question: "Are a lot of people in your industry puzzled by the fact you live in Mississippi?"

"Of course," he said.

He still had a place in New York, and he went to California on movie business quite frequently, but for the last twenty years, his home had been in the Delta, on a 120-acre horse ranch near where he grew up. People often asked him why he chose to live in Mississippi, when he was rich and famous and could live anywhere in the world. "Because I can live anywhere I want, and this is where I want to live," he would answer.

The real reason was that Mississippi felt like home in a very basic sensory way. He liked the heat, the humidity, the lushness, the smell of the bayou, the sound of the blues, the taste of collard greens. He liked the people on the whole, and he understood the evolving racial complexity of the place. He appreciated the fact that racists here didn't bother to disguise it. But Mississippi bothered him too.

"It seems like we're determined to be at the bottom of every list, or the top of every list that you want to be bottom of," he said. "Teenage pregnancy, education, poverty, you name it. We've got one last abortion clinic fighting to survive. People vote against their own best interests, because they're culturally so conservative. Sometimes when I see how the electorate votes, I ask myself, 'What am I doing here?' And the next question is, 'Well, where else would I go?' And I don't have a good answer for that."

He took a sip of vodka and leaned back in one of those taupe-colored chairs on wheels. He looked around the room at Sykes and his wife Cindy, Bill and his wife Francine, Catfish, Tank, and the other regulars. "Journalists often ask me if I have friends in quote 'the real world,'" he said. "I say yes, in Mississippi. These are my friends. This is my golf club. I'm home."

Chapter 16

Election Day

THE THIRD TIME I played golf with Bill Luckett, I asked him if I
could observe some of his campaign for mayor. In true Delta style,
he invited me to stay at his house for the run-up to election night,
ride with him to all his campaign events, sit in on all his meetings,
and come to what he hoped would be a big victory party at Ground
Zero Blues Club.

He'd already cleared the biggest hurdle by winning the Democratic primary, as a white man in a town that's 79 percent African-
American. Now his strongest challenger was Dr. "Sugardaddy"
Weiner, the county supervisor and a wealthy cardiologist who was
spending a lot of money on television ads, billboards, and campaign
signs. The Weiner, as Bill and Francine called him, was running as an
independent. So was Brad Fair, a young black politician with a strong
network of support. There was a white Republican too, but in a town
as black as Clarksdale, she was almost a token candidate.

I met Bill for breakfast at McDonald's a few days before the election. He was wearing a suit and tie, his white hair was combed back and gelled into position, with an unruly little ducktail at the back, and he looked every inch the patrician lawyer-politician.

"There are only two ways to run for office," he said. "Unopposed or worried. My campaign manager says I'm in good shape, but there's been a lot of mudslinging, and you can't help wondering what might stick. If you include the primary, I've been called a racist, a convicted criminal, a member of the KKK, even though Francine and I have been lifetime members of the NAACP since 1985. I'm a slave driver. I'm a crook. I've covered up sexual harassment charges. I'm a failed businessman. Oh, I'm a bad guy! Sixty-five years I've lived in this skin, and never knew how bad I really was."

Crime was the biggest issue in the election. In the last seven weeks, there had been more than forty violent gun crimes in Clarksdale, a town of seventeen thousand people, including ten drive-by shootings, a mass shooting in a nightclub, and six armed robberies. Three people had died, with many more wounded, and the town was still in shock from a pair of brutal attacks on elderly women. Eighty-year-old Ethel Lewis was robbed, murdered, and set on fire by a seventeen-year-old; when the police arrested him, he was watching the Disney movie *Dumbo* on TV. Shirley Gordon, seventy-seven, was robbed outside her home and beaten repeatedly in the face and head with a chunk of concrete; a fourteen-year-old was charged with that crime.

"The fact that both those women were white and both perpetrators were young black males shouldn't make a difference, but it does," said Bill. "The perception among whites is that they're being overrun by black crime, even though it's the black community that suffers most from crime. The bottom line is that crime and gangs are a real problem. People are living in fear, longtime residents are moving away, tourists are getting scared to come here. I got a three-page letter the other day from a hippie lady who lives on West Second Street, and she said, 'I can't even sit on my front porch anymore.' She's terrified because of all the gunfire and armed robberies in her neighborhood. The question is: what are we going to do about it?"

Bill had just paid for an ad in the *Clarksdale Press Register*, outlining his position on crime. As a fairly liberal Democrat, he wanted to get out ahead on the issue. The ad acknowledged that crime was the most pressing issue facing Clarksdale, and called for increased police patrols, after-school youth programs, strict enforcement of existing laws, including curfews, and liaising with state and federal police agencies for major crime sweeps.

"We're going to reactivate the anonymous calls and rewards program," he said. "We need more community involvement. On Friday night, a church minister got word that there was going to be a gang fight, and he called the police, and they cordoned off the area. That's the kind of thing I want to see a lot more of."

Bill talked fast, ate fast, moved fast, made decisions quickly. He had a first-rate mind, and big reserves of stamina and energy. He had been going at it for fourteen, fifteen, sometimes eighteen hours a day if you included the rooms he worked in the evenings and the nighttime strategy sessions. But today was Sunday, and the only events on his calendar were two black church services, followed by some meetings. "There's no way to get elected without some black ministers on your side," he said, driving across town to the first church. "Black voters here really listen to their ministers. They came out for me in the primary, and I need for them to do it again on Tuesday."

He pulled into the parking lot of the Union Grove Missionary Baptist Church and spotted Francine pulling in at the same time. He checked his hair in the mirror, and squirted some Visine in his eyes, because he had been up very late the night before at Red's juke joint with some out-of-town visitors.

"Have you ever been to a black church?" he asked me.

"Once a long time ago."

"Well, it's lively and it lasts a good while. You'll enjoy it. The music is great here. L. C. Tyler is the preacher, and he can really carry on. You might see a woman get inhabited by what she believes is the Holy Spirit. She'll do a heebie-jeebie dance, in which case get out of the way. Alright, are you ready?"

We greeted Francine, a smallish blonde in a white suit who loved going to black church, and walked through the front doors. We were greeted by an old black man with gold-framed glasses and a wonderful smile. This was Amos Harper, who had worked for Bill for more than forty years, and was still working for him at the age of eighty-nine, having no interest in retirement. They had one of those quasi-familial biracial Mississippi relationships that were hard to classify. When I asked Bill to describe it, he said, "Hmmm. Love, loyalty, deep friendship, mutual dependence."

Mr. A, as Bill called him, went off to his usual pew, and the Reverend Dr. L. C. Tyler came forward to greet us. He was in his early sixties with a beard and spectacles, wearing a sharp brown suit and a big gold watch. "We're so glad you and Miss Francine could be here with us today," he said. "If you want to say a few words to the congregation, I'm happy to invite you up there."

"I appreciate that, and I'll keep it brief," said Bill. "Folks are here to worship, not talk politics, and I respect that."

The ushers showed us to a pew near the front, and glancing around, I saw that many of the congregation were looking at the Bible on their iPads. There was a band with drums, keyboards, saxophone, electric guitar, and a bass guitar with green strings. They struck up a gospel-tinged R&B groove, took turns with the vocals, and then the twenty-strong white-robed choir joined in, and it was such a power-ful, gorgeous, soulful sound that the hairs lifted off my arms, and tears welled up in my eyes. The congregation was clapping and danc-ing, Francine was grooving away, Bill and I were doing our best. Then a middle-aged woman in a green dress, green shoes, and white gloves went skittering down the aisle in a trance, overcome by the spirit.

A zoot-suited deacon stepped up to the microphone, rasping and roaring as he sang his praises. Then he signaled the band to quiet down, and he sang the Lord's Prayer as a moaning, improvisational blues, repeating the same phrases with different rhythms and melo-dies, bending and stretching them, kneeling down as he poured them full of yearning, then jumping up, with the band playing louder and faster, until he was shouting and wailing, and then the choir came in again, and it felt like the roof was about to lift off the building.

It was religion, it was worship, it was masterful musicianship and electrifying performance art, all rolled into one. It was a tradi-tion honed and perfected over many generations. It was a survival mechanism, an escape hatch, a way to feel exalted, sanctified, joined together in glory. It was a way to beat mortality and live forever in the perfect sky. These were some of the thoughts that ran through my envious brain, alongside memories of the Church of England as a yawning child, the droning hymns and reedy vicars, sermons about cups of tea, and how there was sound advice in the Bible that we could still use today in our fast modern world.

The music died down, the dancing stopped, women sat down and fanned themselves with small cardboard fans, with the names and numbers of funeral homes printed on the back. L. C. Tyler stepped up to the microphone. He asked the congregation to welcome Bill and Francine Luckett, and invited Bill to say a few words. Bill walked up there, and said, "Thank you for letting me worship with you. I'm not a preacher, but I'm on God's side. I really feel at home here, and I really thank you for your support and generosity. All we need now is to push it past the finish line on Tuesday."

He got a polite clapping ovation. L. C. Tyler shook his hand and said into the microphone, "It's so very important to have saved people looking over us. And let's not anyone forget to vote on Tuesday." That was the endorsement, right in the bag.

The service went on for another two and a half hours. There were many beautifully sung hymns and songs, and testimonials about miracle healings. One woman had been written off by the doctors, because there was only one pint of blood left in her body. When they cut into her, she smelled like something dead. But she had kept on praying, and never lost faith, and the Lord had made her good as new. The grand finale was Reverend Dr. L. C. Tyler's sermon, or "preachment," as he called it, with the band filling in organ notes and guitar bursts to amplify the emotions and emphasize the drama.

"At some point, you gone NEED somebody," he sang-preached.

The congregation said, "Ah-hah. That's right."

"At some point, you gone reach your midnight situation."

"Mmm-hmm. Yes sir!"

"Neighbor, how do you handle . . . your midnight situation?"

"Yeah!"

"Mr. Trouble might be waiting at your home to jump you."

"Uh-huh."

"Darkness is all around. Uh-huh. All Satan does is present to you. And all God does is present to you. YOU make the choice."

"Yes sir!"

"Don't you LIE to me and pretend you holy all day and all night long. Because all of us sometimes get LOW DOWN! So, how . . . do you handle . . . your midnight situation?"

"Yeah! Yeah, yeah!"

"The problem with Clarksdale is everybody is in love with they-self. And we play the blame game. If it wasn't for you, I wouldn't be in this predicament. And some people are so EVIL, that if they come up this aisle, I'm a go straight down the other one."

"Tell it, preacher!"

"We got to WAKE UP! We done learned how to die! We got to learn how to live! Clarksdale is in . . . a midnight situation."

Organ blast, drum roll.

"Midnight is deep darkness, and some of you don't come out till midnight cause you love darkness. Today could be tomorrow, but midnight stepped in between. Hmmm?"

Now he told us what we needed to do about Clarksdale's midnight situation. The first thing was to bring back prayer into the schools: "When they took God out of our schools, they opened the door for Satan." Secondly, parents needed to beat their children more: "It says right here in Proverbs 13, that whoever spares the rod of discipline hates their children, and whoever chastises them diligently is the loving parent." Thirdly, women needed to dress more modestly, and young men needed to quit wearing sagging pants. Fourthly, and most importantly of all, everyone needed to get down on their knees, and pray like they'd never prayed before.

"PRAYER! It'll bring a wounded son back home. It'll make you whole, it'll make you cry, it'll make you glad. PRAYER! It'll heal you when you're sick. I done had two heart attacks already, and the doctors say I got to quit preaching as hard as I preach, but I got PRAYER POWER! I got JESUS POWER! I got GOD POWER!"

The band was getting louder and louder, and the choir was starting to sway, and then it all broke loose into wild stomping song, with the bass player's fingers flying over those green strings, the saxophone wailing, the choir raising the roof, women skittering in the aisles, collapsing, and being helped away by the ushers, and L. C. Tyler was screeching and screaming, dancing like a jack-in-the-box, mopping the sweat from his brow with a white towel.

Afterward I felt utterly wrung out and exhausted, but it was straight on to the next black church. "Oh yeah, it's a workout," said Bill. "I've been doing three churches every Sunday. That was the twenty-eighth church I've done in this campaign, if you include the primary."

"How many churches are there in Clarksdale?"

"A hundred and twenty. We've got the most churches per capita of anywhere in the country."

POLITICS IN THE Delta, like so many aspects of life, was dominated by race, but Bill Luckett's victory in the Democratic primary, with 70 percent of the vote, proved that plenty of black voters in Clarksdale were willing to put race loyalty aside, depending on the circumstances and the individual. Bill's main opponent in the primary was Chuck Espy, a state representative and the son of Henry Espy, who became the first African-American mayor of Clarksdale in 1989 and went on to serve five terms. Henry's brother was Mike Espy, the US Secretary for Agriculture during the Clinton presidency.

The Espy years had not gone well for Clarksdale, although as Bill Luckett often pointed out, they were difficult years all over the Delta, with powerful social and economic forces at work, and there was only so much that a mayor and his administration could do. Nonetheless, he benefited from the fact that the Espy name was tarnished for a lot of black voters, associated with neglect and decline. Several people told me, in a bleak half-joking way, that the Espy family didn't mind the gang violence because they owned two funeral homes.

Bill also benefited from the fact that he was a well-known, high-profile figure in Clarksdale. Everyone knew about his friendship and partnership with Morgan Freeman. The older generation remembered his work for the NAACP in the 1980s and his friendship with the civil rights icon Aaron Henry. People knew that he hired a diverse workforce in his law office, blues club, restaurant, property developments, and other businesses.

When anonymous leaflets started circulating, saying that Bill was a slave master and a KKK member, and when Chuck Espy played the race card, most black voters weren't buying it, and most black ministers weren't selling it. The town was in such a violent shambles that black voters were more interested in Bill's reputation as a man who could get things done.

Bill's victory in the primary had broken some new political ground in Clarksdale and offered some hope to people who thought the Delta was crippled by its racial obsessions, that black and white expended far too much energy trying to thwart each other. But it was a primary that would be remembered, above all else, for a horrific act of violence that occurred early on.

Marco McMillian was running against Chuck Espy and Bill Luckett for the Democratic nomination. He was thirty-three years old, black, handsome, ambitious, and gay. Some said he was the first openly gay candidate to run for public office in Mississippi. When his murdered body was found dumped on a Mississippi River levee, the national media descended on Clarksdale, and the blogosphere erupted.

One news report compared the crime to the Emmett Till murder, and nearly all the coverage hewed to the same obvious conclusion: a gay black man had tried to run for mayor in a small town in Mississippi, and look what had happened to him. McMillian's family, and the firebrand lawyer they hired, announced that the body had been beaten, dragged, and burned, which surely, in Mississippi, could only mean one thing.

As Bill Luckett put it, "There was a clear inference that some redneck type of person must have done it."

Black activists said it was a racial hate crime. LGBT activists thought he'd been murdered for being gay. But the Clarksdale police department said there was nothing to suggest a hate crime. A twenty-two-year-old black man called Lawrence Reed had wrecked McMillian's Chevy Tahoe in a head-on collision on Highway 49. When they questioned him, he confessed to murdering McMillian and told them to go to the Mississippi levee twenty miles west of Clarksdale, which is how they found the body. Reed was arrested and charged with murder.

Doubters said the police were lying and quoted the old Nina Simone song as proof, "Everybody knows about Mississippi." McMillian's family and their lawyer, Daryl Parks, said that he'd been murdered for what he'd uncovered about corruption and the white power structure. The NAACP held a meeting, where people wore "Justice For Marco" T-shirts, and Parks demanded a new investigation into the murder. "Somebody will explain the burn marks on his body. Somebody has to explain the torture he went through."

LGBT activists, like Ravi Perry, a gay black professor at Mississippi State University and a friend of McMillian's, called for changes to Mississippi's hate crime laws, which do not apply to sexual orientation. "It is hard not to imagine the mysterious events had something to do with him being an agent for change," Perry told *The Atlantic*. "It's disturbing that it's not charged as a hate crime."

When Lawrence Reed's lawyers said that he'd murdered McMillian after an unwanted sexual advance, LGBT activists executed a pivot and directed their ire toward the "gay rage" defense strategy. It wasn't until the preliminary hearing, months after the murder, that the state presented any of its evidence. Then it came out that McMillian had cocaine, marijuana, caffeine, nicotine, alcohol, and duloxetine, an antidepressant, in his system. Phone records showed that Reed and McMillian had spoken many times, and on the night of the murder, Reed testified that McMillian had invited him to a party in Marks, over in Quitman County.

When they got to Marks, McMillian bought beers and cigarillos at a convenience store, then drove to a back road, started watching porn on his phone, and masturbating—or so Reed told the police. McMillian then made sexual advances toward him, Reed said, and he grabbed a chain from McMillian's belt and strangled him with it.

Reed drove back toward Clarksdale, where he dumped McMillian's clothes, cell phone, and wallet. He filled a bottle with two dollars' worth of gasoline, and drove out of town to the levee. He told police that he dragged the naked body through a barbed wire fence, poured gasoline over it, and set it on fire. He called a woman and told her what he'd done. She called 911. Reed then got back into the black Chevy Tahoe, turned onto Highway 49, and slammed deliberately into the first car he found, presumably trying to kill himself.

Reed's attorney tried to get the charges reduced to manslaughter, claiming there had been no premeditation. The judge pointed out that premeditation could exist for mere seconds under the law. Then Reed's attorney tried for murder in the second degree. That too was rejected.

Hundreds of media outlets carried the story of McMillian's murder when it appeared to be a classic Mississippi hate crime. At the preliminary hearing, when it began to look like one black man had freaked out and killed another on a weird, addled night, only one journalist was there covering the story, and he worked for the *Clarksdale Press Register*.

BILL AND FRANCINE lived in a spectacular Mid-century Modern house by the country club. The architect was E. Fay Jones, a disciple of Frank Lloyd Wright, and it was all red bricks, rich-toned wood, long spreading eaves, with a sunken living room and bar that Bill kept well-stocked with fine bourbons. I was in one bedroom. A Democratic Party campaign strategist from Jackson was in another. Bill had taken to keeping a loaded shotgun in the master bedroom, just in case Dr. Weiner flipped out and tried to do a Dr. Smith. "We know how it went bad between a doctor and a lawyer in Greenwood," he said. "I don't trust The Weiner not to do something crazy."

Dr. Weiner's campaign attacks were definitely starting to sound a little unhinged. When Bill, acting as the lawyer for a property owner, got Brad Fair to move his rally from one location to another, Dr. Weiner had this to say about it on his Facebook page. "Yesterday a travesty occurred when one candidate made a decision that to win at all costs trumps humanity. The victims were young children, the disenfranchised and a young up coming [*sic*] politician who wanted nothing more than to have a 'peace rally.' My thoughts and facts later. Remember this morning. In the Bible God said in Jerusalem there shall be peace and then prosperity will flow on the rivers. Thousands of years later in Clarksdale nothing is different."

Then there was the full-page campaign ad that Weiner had paid for in the *Clarksdale Press Register* headlined "Mississippi Cardiologist Won't Go to Prison for Online Dating." Not every candidate running for office would want to remind voters, right before an election, that he was arrested for soliciting prostitutes and Mann Act violations, even if the charges were all dismissed by a judge outraged that they had even been brought.

Big chunks of his correspondence on sugardaddyforme.com were on the public record. Anyone who was curious could read heartdocc's graphic messages to hotblondemama, DomesticAngel, and uppity1, a "23-year-old SugarBaby," to whom heartdocc wrote, one Sunday afternoon in February, "I want to fuck ur ass soooooooooooooo bad," and uppity1 wrote back, "you will get to pound it . . . PROMISE. If this works out you will get it as often as you like."

There were requests for other men to watch, and monetary incentives broadly hinted at, as one might expect from such a website: "I am willing to provide significant financial assistance," "the more adventuresome you are, the higher the fee," "We can do much better than make ends meet. How would you like to proceed?" I couldn't help wondering what a New York or a British tabloid would do with this stuff, which went on and sleazily on for about eighty pages.

Bill, and about half the people he knew in Clarksdale, had also been reading the online monthly installments of *SuggaDaddy and Me*, the autobiography of Tanya Keen, a former TV news anchor who had been in a five-year relationship with Dr. Weiner, who was thirty years older than her. He was portrayed in the book as generous, controlling, power-crazed, and sexually obsessed. Keen died of a drug overdose while she was writing it, aged thirty-three, and her mother's comments, theories, and recollections fill out the narrative.

As a source of information, the book is wholly unreliable, unsubstantiated with corroborating evidence, and shot through with bitterness and regret, both from the daughter while living and the mother after her death. Aside from lots and lots of perfectly legal, adult consensual kinky sex, it alleges anal rape, writing illegal prescriptions, soliciting prostitutes, and claims that Dr. Weiner first got Keen hooked on drugs. Were any of the criminal allegations true? It was impossible to say. The claims that Weiner was involved with the Jewish mafia certainly didn't boost the book's credibility, and no law enforcement agency had taken it seriously enough to launch another investigation.

Nevertheless, it was hard to believe that Dr. Weiner was still a viable candidate for mayor.

•　　•　　•

LUCKETT SIGNS WERE disappearing from the roadsides and street corners, and WEINER signs were sprouting up in their place. A rumor was going through the black community that Bill and Morgan were no longer friends because Bill was a racist who hated Obama. Dr. Weiner had bought up all the available airtime for television and radio advertising. One of his ads said Bill Luckett's approach to crime was to "give criminals jobs and hope they don't hurt us."

Bill held a strategy meeting in his downtown law office. He was not going to answer any attacks or give any credibility to false rumors by denying them. He was ahead in the polls, and the vital thing now was to get his voters out. "We've really got to beat the bushes, because a lot of our people think it's already in the bag," he told his team of canvassers. "Knock on their doors, ask them what time they vote, where they vote, and how are they going to get there? If they don't have a good way to get there, we'll get them there."

With the canvassers dispatched, Bill sat in his office, signing thank-you notes to campaign contributors, knocking down emails, working the phone, and getting more rumor updates. "Morgan and I have had a lover's quarrel, that's the latest," he said. "Oh, and I'm supporting hospital layoffs now. I tell you, when you're running for office, you need to grow thick skin."

I asked him why he went into politics. "Hmmm," he said. "Well, the main reason is really generational guilt. I saw how my parents' generation treated black people around here, and their parents were even worse. I want to help make things better on that front, and a lot of other fronts too. There's so much we need to do, and I'm known as a guy who can get things done."

"How is the racial situation here these days, if you had to sum it up?"

"You've got five to ten percent on either side who hate. Most folks get along now, treat each other with politeness, courtesy, and respect, and that's really all you can ask for. We don't all have to be best friends. In your life you're only going to have five best friends, and they're going to change over time, but still, most people will have five."

The biggest problem in Clarksdale, and the rest of the Delta, as he saw it, was the cycle of poverty and the nation's highest teenage pregnancy rate: "Get pregnant, drop out of school. Get pregnant, drop out of school. One generation after another. The way out is early education, we've got to get them young, but our Republican governor in his great wisdom refuses to adequately fund pre-K in Mississippi. So we have to come up with other ideas, like mentorship. At my age, I don't have the time, the energy, or frankly the desire to adopt a homeless black teenager, but I'm inspired by a woman who did."

Then it was off to a long series of meetings and conferences about ways to improve the schools, revitalize downtown, and engage the county and state Democratic parties, interspersed with telephone calls to black ministers and deacons. One deacon expressed his support by saying, "Evildoers shall lose."

Bill said. "Isn't that Job? Let's hope it's right."

"Oh, it's right, alright," said the deacon. "It's the word of God."

He spent the evening working the crowd at Ground Zero Blues Club, welcoming the tourists to Clarksdale, asking the locals for their vote, memorizing everyone's names with that uncanny ability of his, and stoking up the energy and enthusiasm. The Democratic party strategist from Jackson wanted Bill to run for governor again, because he had the rare ability to inspire people, and he could get both white country-club Republicans and black Democrats to vote for him. He had lost the Democratic primary in a runoff last time, and the strategist thought he could have run a stronger, smarter campaign. Bill was thinking about it. People asked him about it all the time. He didn't mind the hard work, or the mudslinging, but the money raising had got to him.

"You sit in a windowless room for eight hours with a list of names and a telephone," he said. "You don't leave until you've called every one of them and basically begged them to give you money. I spent so many days doing that. I wouldn't rule out doing it again, but let's see if I can get elected mayor first."

EARLY IN THE morning on Election Day, there was a weird call from the manager of an apartment complex that Luckett owns. The mother of Dr. Weiner's campaign manager lived there, and she had a snake in her apartment. Now the story was going around that Bill was evicting her from the apartment and he'd put the snake in there to hurry things up.

"Good Lord, so there's actually a snake in there?" he said to the apartment manager. "Can this son of hers get it out of there?"

"He's afraid of snakes."

"Hah! Well okay, send a man to get rid of it, and please tell her that we're glad to have her there, and we have absolutely no intention of kicking her out."

Later that morning, driving his grey Land Cruiser to the polling station to vote for himself, Bill was still shaking his head in disbelief. "I've been accused of a lot of things, but that one tops it all, I believe. Using serpents to scare old ladies out of apartments."

"How did the snake get in there?" I said.

"How the hell should I know? Maybe she left her door open. If her son really is afraid of snakes, we can be reasonably sure he didn't put it in there to frame me."

Outside the polling station a crew of Dr. Weiner's campaign workers were holding up signs. One of them, a teenage black girl, came up to Bill and Francine and told them to vote for Roger Weiner, the next mayor of Clarksdale. Francine pointed to Bill, and said,

"That's the next mayor of Clarksdale right there. Bill Luckett." The girl said, "Nope. Weiner got it."

The Lucketts cast their ballots in a basketball arena decked out with electronic polling booths and made plans to meet up later. Bill and I cruised around the town, visiting polling stations. He praised the neatly kept houses and tutted over the houses that needed repairs or tearing down, piles of trash on the sidewalks, cars parked on lawns, overgrown yards and alleys.

"We are going to have a *major* cleanup campaign in this city," he said. "Stuff like this is terrible for property values, it contravenes the existing city codes, and it's easy to fix. We'll give people some time to get their repairs and cleanup done, and if they don't do it, we'll come down hard with fines. It'll be unpopular with a few people, and that doesn't even matter, because it's going to get done. We're also going to have a major efficiency campaign. I'm going to ride all the garbage trucks and street cleaners, everything the city has, looking for efficiencies."

He pulled up alongside two women holding Weiner signs by the polling station, and lowered his window. "Hi, ladies, I'm Bill Luckett," he said. "Be sure to vote for me, and collect plenty of money from that other guy." The women cracked up laughing.

Bill drove on to the First Baptist Church, where Superintendent Lee from Parchman was giving exactly the same statistics-filled presentation about the penitentiary that he had given me and Martha. Afterward, Bill shook a lot of hands, and introduced me to the police chief, who was a bald, thoughtful, and slightly hangdog man named "Whit" Read. I asked him about the crime situation.

"Some of our citizens are extremely concerned about it, rightfully so, but it's nothing new," he said. "It was real bad in the early nineties, but it used to be contained across the tracks. The gunshots were faint. Now they're next door. The geography of the city has changed."

When I asked how it had changed, he said delicately, "More housing is now available in areas where it didn't used to be."

"What can you do about it?" I said.

He gave a long sigh. "A lot of it is the Constitution," he said. "We'd love to go in there like an arrow from a bow. We could lock up all the criminals tomorrow, but the Constitution won't let us. So we have to do it right and make absolutely sure we get convictions. Nothing embrazens them more than winning a court case."

Then Bill reappeared and whisked me away to his law office, where his campaign staff were reporting a fairly good turnout, promising exit polls, and the optimists were getting jubilant.

DR. WEINER WAS also confident of victory. I spotted him in the street opposite a polling station and introduced myself. He was wearing expensive-looking jeans, sunglasses, and a slim-fitting purple shirt with the cuffs turned back to display a fat gold bracelet on one wrist and a chunky Rolex on the other.

"It's an extremely important election," he said. "We've lost control of the city. We're outgunned, outmanned, juries are afraid to prosecute, we need a federal task force. I'm the only candidate with a realistic plan to tackle these problems, and get serious about crime, and the voters are getting the message. My campaign staff and I are feeling very positive."

He was originally from Philadelphia, Pennsylvania, and I asked him what had brought him to Clarksdale, Mississippi. "This is the highest ranked county in the country for heart disease," he said. "So as a cardiologist I was needed here, and it was a great economic opportunity. For me, it was a perfect fit."

At the mention of Bill Luckett, his skin flushed, and he bared his teeth slightly. "He has run the most distasteful campaign I have ever been involved in," he said. "The mudslinging has been horrendous. He has made misstatements about a court case I was involved in, which was ridiculous to begin with, because who gets prosecuted under the Mann Act anymore anyway? They've got me right there in the affidavit, saying I don't want a hooker, but they tried to prosecute me for soliciting a prostitute and bringing her across state lines! Unbelievable! There's no question in my mind that the whole thing was politically motivated. Some people down here are not too thrilled about having an East Coast Jew as their county supervisor."

BILL WAS IN his house, halfway up a ladder replacing a burned-out lightbulb, when the text came through saying that he'd won, and probably by a large margin. We got in the Land Cruiser and drove toward Ground Zero Blues Club. He passed me his phone, and I called out the numbers coming in by text from the different wards. He was particularly pleased with the outcome from Ward 4, where nearly all the voters were black. In a low turnout, he got 356 votes, compared to 153 for Brad Fair, and 97 for Weiner.

He had been inviting people all week to Ground Zero for the election night party, and the place was starting to fill up when we arrived. He got himself a tall gin and tonic at the bar and allowed himself to relax just slightly. "I'm feeling good," he said. "I'm also feeling daunted by how much we need to do, and how difficult it's going to be to do it. The only vote I get as mayor is to break ties between the city commissioners. I've got two black commissioners and two white ones, and they vote along racial lines almost every time. If I keep voting with the white ones, guess how that's going to look?"

Hiring workers for the city was a constant bone of contention. The two black city commissioners invariably wanted black applicants to fill the positions, arguing that the racial makeup of the city staff should reflect the racial makeup of the city. The two white city commissioners argued in favor of the best-qualified applicants, which went fine when that applicant was black, and produced angry scenes when the applicant was white. One of the black city commissioners, Buster Moton, fancied himself a firebrand, and was famous for his long disruptive rants.

The Clarksdale that Bill Luckett hoped for was already visible in one of the town's Catholic churches. It had a majority black, minority white congregation who enjoyed worshipping together, and had been doing it long enough that it seemed normal to them. When Bill and Morgan started Ground Zero, they hoped it would turn into something similar, in a secular setting, but only a few local African Americans frequented the place. That changed on election night, and Bill was delighted to see so many black faces in the room. While he was working the crowd, I talked to a professor, a musician, a street hustler, a teacher, a minister's wife, a paralegal, and a journalist, all of whom were black and had voted for Bill. They were all glad that he'd won and relieved that the Espy reign was over, although some felt a little bittersweet. Even though they thought Bill was the best candidate, even though they liked him personally, having a white mayor again was disappointing, when the city was so black.

The final results were in now, and it was a landslide: Luckett 2,398, Fair 603, Weiner 523. When Clarksdale's new mayor got up on stage to deliver his victory speech, he was not in a triumphant mood, but about equal parts happy and somber, reflecting his state of mind at the bar earlier, "What we face is daunting . . . there's only one way we can do what we need to do, and that's by coming together, and working together as one city."

There was a big party at Ground Zero that night, with live music and dancing, but we left fairly early. Bill had designated himself as the driver. On the way home, I told him it was encouraging to see black and white voting together and having fun together at the club. "We know how to get along with each other, I'd say better than most places, but most of the time we don't."

"Why is that?" I asked. "History? Lack of trust? Racism?"

"It's like smoking," he said. "People are hooked on it, even though they know it's bad for them. It's hard to quit smoking. It takes effort and willpower and perseverance, but millions of people have done it, and it's becoming a thing of the past."

Chapter 17

Grabbing Smoke

WE WERE FINDING the word *racist* to be increasingly unhelpful, because racism came in so many different forms and degrees. There were mild racists, who talked about "they" in ways that were not unkind, but didn't allow for much individual variation, and told racist jokes that weren't mean, but gently patronizing. There were hateful racists, who seemed to have a visceral loathing for black skin and blackness, and they put as much sneering contempt into the n-word as it would hold. That kind of racism was considered a sign of low, trashy breeding by the Delta gentry, and there was far more of it in the hills.

A kind of affectionate racism prevailed among the Delta gentry. They had kind, paternalistic feelings toward black people and a genuine appreciation for black culture, but they didn't want a black man dating their daughters or sitting down to eat dinner at their table, because that wasn't the way things were done, or meant to be. These were just a few rough starter categories, and within them there were innumerable variations, nuances, spillovers, and contradictions.

One Sunday morning I was at a milk punch party in Greenwood with a group of older moneyed white people. There are different recipes for milk punch, but the basic idea is a big slug of bourbon on ice, with a dash of milk, and a sprinkle of nutmeg. It was all tremendous fun, with the usual drawled repartee and hilarious telling of improbable tales. Then race found its way into the conversation, and I realized that some of these people were so racist they didn't even know they were racist.

"The Ns call each other the n-word all the time, but we're not allowed to say it anymore," a tipsy woman of a certain age protested in a honeyed drawl. "It's so ridiculous. It's just a word. And God forbid you get caught saying it on television these days. They practically string you up."

"Oh it's insane," another woman said. "It's a word we all grew up with. What are those nuts called that look like . . . ? Brazil nuts, that's it. Everybody called them 'nigger toes' and didn't think a thing about it."

At a different party, in a different county, I met a property developer and store owner who started throwing around the full, unabbreviated n-word. He talked about "nigger geese," which were cormorants, and "nigger sardines," which were the cheap ones, and good to use in animal traps. He told me that when a black customer came into his store, he would alert his floor staff by making an announcement on the intercom, "Dan's on aisle three," or, "Please help Dawn on aisle five."

Dan was an acronym for "dumb-ass nigger." Dawn was "dumb-ass woman nigger." "There's no harm in it," he insisted. "It's just a way to make sure they get prompt service, and we treat them just like we would any white customer. Sometimes they'll say their name isn't

Dan or Dawn, and we'll get their real name, and that's great. Next time they come in, we can call them by their name."

He denied up and down that he was a racist, with the following argument: "A black guy who's working hard and raising a family? That man's not a nigger. I've got respect for that man. If you call that man a nigger, you've got a problem with me, because he might be my friend. It's the same with poor white people. They're not all trash. You've got to act like a redneck before I call you a redneck. You see? Just because I call a nigger a nigger doesn't mean that I'm racist, because I'm not." The fact that he had a Jewish last name and ancestry was just another wrinkle.

Almost every night at the dinner table, Mariah and I would end up talking about race and racism in the Delta, comparing and contrasting it to the rest of the country, trying to pin it down and arrive at clear definitive statements. Mariah put something useful in a nutshell when she said, "If a white person is lazy around here, it's because they've got a poor work ethic. If a black person is lazy, it's because they're black." There were many different types of white racist, as I've outlined, but this belief, as far as we could tell, was common to all of them.

Then there was the whole charged question of black racism. Some academics and commentators maintain that black people can't be racist, because racism is an institutional arrangement of power relations and African Americans don't have the power to inflict their prejudices on whites in the same way. Be that as it may, there was no mistaking the hatred, contempt, and suspicion in some of the eyes looking at us. For Mariah, this was her first experience of being hated because she was white.

"I get it," she said. "At least I think I do. They see white people and assume they're all racist, that they trod on the backs of African Americans to get what they have, that our people enslaved their people, that we can't be trusted, that no matter what they do, we'll always look down on them."

"I get it too," I said. "But it doesn't help anything, and probably makes things worse. It seems about like Bill Luckett said. Five to ten percent on either side have real hatred."

Nathan Duff, a Clarksdale journalist, thought it was impossible to pin down racism in Mississippi. He wrote me a long, thoughtful email on the subject, and the core of it was this: "There are generalities that can be drawn, trends that can be measured, evidence and anecdotes of every stripe, but even when causes and effects are understood as clearly as possible, wrestling with racism in Mississippi is like grabbing smoke."

Institutional racism could be quantified, and the most glaring injustice was that black children didn't have equal educational opportunities. The academies, like the country clubs, were just starting to let in a few African Americans who could comfortably afford it. As far as job hiring, housing, and access to credit, I hadn't found any reliable statistics, but there were laws against discrimination in those areas, and Delta lawyers who specialized in those cases. Delta juries, being overwhelmingly black, tended to be sympathetic to black plaintiffs and black lawyers, and, conversely, hostile to white ones.

It was when you started trying to measure and quantify prejudice itself that it all turned to smoke. I had heard at least fifty different opinions on the subject. It was normal for members of the same family to have different perceptions of racism, and different attitudes toward race. To further complicate matters, individual levels of prejudice were not necessarily constant. People were becoming less racist, on the whole, but sometimes it went the other way. If a black person experienced an incident of racial discrimination or abuse, if a white person was victimized by a black criminal, for example, they might easily extrapolate their resentment to all members of the other race.

I found myself stereotyping more than I used to, and more than Mariah did. I thought it was funny that a man named Kunta Kinte Blissett had been arrested in Greenwood for contempt, and she thought I was chuckling in an oh-those-comical-negroes way. I was keeping count of the public officials who had been arrested for embezzlement and corruption in the Delta since we arrived, and so far, all of them without exception had been African-American. So was it a black thing? It was easy to think so until you considered that the great majority of public officials in the Delta were black, and that white public officials were embezzling away in other whiter parts of the state. Mississippi, in fact, had just been deemed the most corrupt state in the nation.

Having seen many black mothers hit and snatch their children in public, and having heard the Reverend L. C. Tyler's fire-breathing sermon about the dangers of sparing the rod, I assumed that all black parents were beating the hell out of their children, and I wondered if that was feeding into black-on-black violence. Mariah pointed out that many white Mississippians believed in beating their children too, and corporal punishment was legal in the schools.

In a place where the face of poverty is overwhelmingly black, it's easy to fall into mistaken assumptions about what's driving social problems. White people often thought black culture was to blame, and blacks would often say the same thing. Evander would go on long dire monologues about "my people, my people" and extrapolate outwards from his experiences in poverty-stricken Holmes County, Mississippi, to include all African Americans. "We've got a problem with love," he said one day. "Our women are so focused on what they can get out of a man that they're unable to love."

I said, "Come on, man, you can't sit here and tell me black women don't know how to love."

"Okay, maybe I went too far. But there's a problem with it in my community, and definitely with the women I've been involved with."

"Do you think poverty makes love hard to do?"

"Love is hard to do, period. I'm talking about deep, true, long-lasting love. Women in my community aren't focused on that. They're more materialistic-minded, and yeah, a man who's got material resources is a way out of poverty. What's love got to do with it? Love is off to the side, not front and center."

American poverty produces similar social problems wherever it occurs, whether it's on Indian reservations, in urban ghettos and barrios, in poor white trailer parks and back-holler Eastern Kentucky and West Virginia. The poorest places in America have the highest rates of drug and alcohol abuse, crime, broken families, and all the rest of it. But in poor black America, and perhaps nowhere more so than in poor black Mississippi, the debilitating, corrosive influence of racism is also at work, although again, the precise effects of that influence are very hard to measure and pin down.

"Why can't they get their act together? When are they going to get it together? When are they going to quit hollering racism and get on with it?" We heard these sentiments often from Delta whites. It was a denial of the idea that the past affects the present, that systematic oppression can damage a people. After 250 years of slavery, 90 years of plantation sharecropping and Jim Crow, and 50 years more of unequal opportunity, deep poverty, and very slowly diminishing racism, black folks were expected to shake all that off like it was nothing and be grateful for their civil rights.

MONK AND I would spend hours and hours talking about race and racism. It was a relief for both of us to be able to talk freely about such a charged subject, and it deepened our friendship. It was important for me to recognize that this was Monk talking, one individual man with his own individual views. He was not the voice of the black Delta, because no such thing existed. And his views were unusual in his community, even offensive to some.

"They say I like white people too much," he said. Through his mother, Lucy Neal, he had ties that felt like kinship to both the Thompson and the Foose family. Now he was working for Dr. Foose, helping him build a house on some land that he'd bought, and people accused him of cozying up to the white man to gain an unfair advantage.

Monk was always arguing with his best friend Calvin Head, who ran a small, struggling farmers' cooperative up the road in Mileston. They would argue about anything and everything—the weather if they had to—but one recurring argument was about Monk's attitude toward his own community. Calvin thought he should have a bigger heart for his people and help out the ones in need with some of that money he was getting from Dr. Foose. Monk, who was hardworking and dependable, wanted to know why they couldn't help themselves, as he was doing.

Monk and Calvin had tried to help an aspiring rapper who was living nearby with his girlfriend and kids in abject poverty. "They got nothing, and I mean nothing," said Monk. "I'm talking about no food for those kids. So, Beth Foose gave them a turkey for Christmas, I helped them out with some money, Calvin got a job interview for the girlfriend, but she didn't show up. Said she was too high. So, they got money for weed, but no food for the kids? Mmm-mmm-mm. Now, that man made two hundred dollars rapping at a show Saturday night, and he *still* didn't buy nothing for those kids. He bought weed and liquor and clothes. And he want my help? Man, I'm telling you. And some of these women out here be having mo kids, and mo kids, just so they check get bigger. I tell you, some people are so low-down my eyesight ain't got no business resting on them."

One afternoon, I saw Monk's burgundy truck coming along the levee toward the house. He was wearing his work clothes with a yellow bandanna tied over his head, and it was clear from his facial expression that he had something to say. Once he started saying it, I knew it was serious, because he wasn't stuttering. When Monk was completely relaxed, or when he needed to say something important, his stutter mysteriously went away.

"Listen, I'm not trying to tell you what to do, but you my friend, so the very last thing I want to do is to bring you trouble," he began. "I'm talking about the club. If you want to go there, that's your business. But I can't go there no more, not with you."

We had gone there a few days ago. Someone had challenged Monk and asked him what he was doing bringing a white man into the club. Monk said, "He ain't white. He from England." I thought that had cleverly and wittily defused the situation, and I'd told it to the Thompsons as a funny story, but Monk had been catching some ugly fallout. People were saying that he was a race traitor, who would rather be around white folks than his own people.

"How can I look at my skin, and the skin of my brother and sister, and my own son, and hate black people?" he said. "That don't make no kinda sense no way, but that's what they saying, that I hate black people. Man, I get so tired of it. So tired. You know why I like coming here to your house? I'll tell you. No arguments. We talk, it's relaxed, we have a good time, no one gets up in my face. It ain't like that when I'm in Thornton, or Mileston, or Tchula. Somebody always got to be arguing."

There were two more reasons, equally important, why he didn't want to go to the club with me anymore. He hated the way people swarmed us for free drinks. I didn't mind buying the occasional beer for people who had less money than I did, but Monk did mind, because he worked hard almost every day, while they sat around cadging drinks and getting high. The other reason was my safety.

"Sooner or later, somebody gone try you. They see a white man, they want your money. What you gone do? Pull your gun?"

"Monk," I said. "I don't take a gun in there."

"WHAT?"

"No gun."

"Sheeyit, don't tell nobody but me. Who else you go there with?"

"B, Albert, Evander."

"Okay. Everybody know B be strapped, and that muh-fucker can't wait to shoot somebody. And Albert, when he get to drinking, he a go-rilla. He wild. But listen, I ain't telling you where to go. I ain't telling you what to do. But sooner or later, trouble is gone find you in that place."

So Monk would come over to the house instead, and we would cook him Mediterranean or Mexican food, or he would take over the grill, bringing out a blowtorch from his truck to heat up the charcoal, working with rubs, marinades, butter, and slow-smoking techniques to transform cheap cuts of meat into something memorable. After dinner, Mariah would usually go to bed with a book and leave me and Monk to stay up drinking whiskey, which led inevitably to Howlin' Wolf on the turntable—Monk was a huge fan, and knew all the lyrics—and frank talk about race.

"It'd be the easiest thing in the world for me to hate white people," he said one night. "You know why I don't? Because that hatred will poison your mind. I don't want that poison in me."

Monk was against all forms of prejudice, and it upset him that some black people were racist toward the Mexicans who had come into the area to do farm labor. "As a black person, you experience prejudice every day, *every day*, and you know exactly how it feel," he said. "How you gone turn around and put that on somebody else? Because he's Mexican and working hard and sending money to his family? You gone hate him for that? Maaaaan . . . and some of these

Mexicans got prejudice for black folks too. I get so tired of it, I get so *tired* of it."

Something about these conversations led me further into the whiskey bottle than normal. Normally there was so much unsaid about race. To be able to ask anything, say anything, with no fear of offense, felt like a holiday. And as Monk said one night, "We making history right now, you and me, just by sitting in your front room and drinking whiskey together. I'm fittin to get ready to have me another. You?" That was a hard drink to refuse, and so was the one after it.

One night we were talking about his relationship with the Thompson family, and I asked him how he felt about the Confederate flag flying from Bobby T's carport. "Bobby T was the reason I left Pluto," he said. "He's the oldest and he was raised in that time when prejudice was bad around here, and I mean real bad, so he got more of it than the others. Plus he was just naturally arrogant, and wild, and he could get real ornery.

"So, one day I was working for Bobby T, doing just exactly what he'd told me to do, and he yelled and cussed at me, and said I was doing it wrong. He didn't call me a nigga or nothing like that, but he was yelling and cussing, and for me that was just the last straw. It was hot, I wasn't making hardly any money, I was tired of it all, so I told him I quit, and went on home. Now Bobby T, he came straight over to my house and apologized, and asked me real nice to come back. I appreciated that, but I was done with Pluto. I went off and got a job working construction, and it was the best thing I ever done did."

"What about Bobby T now?" I asked.

"We got no problem with each other. He's changed a lot."

"And Louie?"

"He grew up with some of that prejudice. How could he not, right? But he's changed too. You know, when I see Louie it's like seeing my cousin, because my momma was a part of his family when I was growing up. Now Dr. Foose, he never really had no prejudice, or maybe just a little bit way back in the day. Now he's all the way over to the other side. He won't let a black man call another black man 'nigga' if they working for him. And you know we do that all the time, right?" He boomed out his big laugh, "Hah-hah! I mean, *all* the time. Nigga dis, nigga dat, nigga please. But not if Dr. Foose is around. No sir."

"And Martha?"

"No, uh-uh, she don't have a racist bone in her body."

So you see the difficulty in trying to generalize about racism even in one tiny pocket of the Mississippi Delta. It's a shifting target, a grouping of perceptions about other people's perceptions. There's a huge social chasm between the races, a deep history of prejudice, and bonds so close they feel like kinship.

MONK'S MOTHER, LUCY NEAL, had been finding it harder and harder to draw breath. Dr. Foose had been visiting her almost every day, and it seemed she was slowly improving, right before she died of a heart attack at home. She was five days short of her seventy-first birthday. Donald couldn't make the funeral, so I accompanied Martha to the little whitewashed church next to the old rusting cotton gin in Thornton. At the front entrance was a small stone statue of an angel with a missing wing.

I was wearing a black suit, white shirt, and black tie. Martha said I looked like an undertaker and had dressed completely wrong. When I saw the colorful finery of the other mourners—a fawn-striped zoot suit, a scarlet zoot suit with matching hat, jewel-toned dresses, leopard-print blouses—I understood what she meant. And these mourners weren't talking about a funeral, but a "homegoing celebration."

I stood outside the church with various Fooses and Thompsons, as Lucy's friends and relatives came over to greet them. There was a lot of talk between black and white about each other's relatives and family trees. They had lived side-by-side for so long that they remembered each other's grandparents, and the names of each other's children, although the white people had difficulty with the new-style names like Lataijahla, Joshawun, and Tydarrion, who were three of Lucy's six great-grandchildren. A woman with a gold front tooth, blue eyeshadow, and a gold dress came up to Mike, and said, "Dr. Foose! Do you remember me?"

He said, "I'm sorry, I don't."

"I'm the one who drove into the lake. You saved my life."

"Oh my, how wonderful to see you again," he said. She had been driving down Highway 49 on the anniversary of her son's death, she said. Preoccupied by her grief, she had gone off the road in her brand-new car into Parker Bayou. She tried to get out of the sunroof, but the opening was too small, and when she opened the door, the water came rushing in. She struggled out and managed to get up on the roof, where she stood waving and shouting for help. "So many cars streaked past," she said.

"I just caught something out of the corner of my eye, and did a double-take," he said.

"I'm so thankful," she said.

Then it was time to go into the church. A sign on the front left section of the pews said, IMMEDIATE FAMILY ONLY, and this is where the ushers put the Foose and Thompson families. A relative down from Chicago didn't like it, but Monk told him that's what Lucy had asked for, and that's how it was going to be. Mike and Beth Foose, and their children Mary Margaret and Hannah, were seated at the front with the closest blood relatives.

Everyone was given a sheaf of stapled-together pages entitled "Homegoing Celebration of Mrs. Chrisper (Lucy) Neal." Many were surprised to learn that her real name was Chrisper, because she'd always been Lucy. There was a photograph of her on the front page, wearing a white dress with the Thompsons standing around her, and on the next page was a dedication:

> Family is not always blood. It's the people in your life who want you in theirs, the ones who accept you for who you are. The ones who would do anything to see you smile, and who love you no matter what. No words could ever express our appreciation for the love and support your family gave to "Lucy" during her time here with us. You will forever be a part of our lives. We love and thank you!
>
> Dedication to Dr. Michael & Beth Foose, Mary Margaret and Hannah Saulters. Robert and Martha Foose, and the Thompson Family.

There were poems and remembrances from her children and grandchildren, and photographic collages of them all, interspersed with photographs of Mike and Beth's wedding and various Foose and Thompson children at different ages. In the pews around me, those grown children were already starting to well up with tears, and no one had even started singing yet.

The open casket was at the front of the church. It was surrounded by a gorgeous, extravagant display of her favorite flowers. The choir filed in, took their positions at the back of church, and started singing her favorite gospel songs. At the sound of those soaring, aching, beautiful voices, the white women around me started crying and sobbing, and I leaked a few myself. There were readings from scripture, then a tall elderly man stepped up to the microphone. He did not look in good health, but out of him poured an a cappella song in a voice so rich and pure that I thought of Sam Cooke.

Then came the Expressions. One after another, Lucy's friends and relatives stepped up to the microphone and offered their thoughts, feelings, remembrances. Many commented on the coming together of black and white in Lucy's life, and here at her homegoing.

"She lived through a time when whites learned—some whites learned—to appreciate blacks. And blacks learned to appreciate whites," said one man. "We are all gathered here today in love to send her home, and that's alright."

The next speaker said, "We heard Lucy talk for many years about Dr. Foose. If someone was sick, if there was a problem, she'd always say, 'Call Dr. Foose.' I'm glad to finally see the man in person, and glad that he could be here today."

The relative from Chicago had a different slant. He got up there and said, "She lived on a plantation, and we all know what that was like back in the day in Mississippi. She wasn't blind to it, but she always said these white families were fair and generous and good people, and that's what she believed."

Cathy Thompson did not like that one bit. It was proof of how little that man from Chicago knew about Lucy, she said later. After another round of gospel songs, the eulogy was delivered by the Reverend Leroy Gibson. It was both a rousing farewell from this world and a welcome to the next one, "The vessel has shattered. She ain't using it no more. Sister Lucy is living in a brand-new home."

"Say it, brother!"

"God doesn't care about what you have, or don't have, or the color of your skin. He cares about how you treat people. He wants you to treat all people with love, like Sister Lucy did."

"Amen."

"A Cadillac can't carry you to the other side. Only love and Jesus can. Sister Lucy has left her vessel and gone on to her brand-new home, where she don't need to call Dr. Foose."

"That's right."

"She don't need to take her medicines."

"Mmm-hmm."

"And she got all the breath she needs."

"Amen."

Monk got up there, and I wondered how his stutter would be-have, but as so often, when it really counted, he spoke fluently and confidently. It was a short speech, thanking everyone for being there, acknowledging that we were all hurting, and reminding us that hurt doesn't last forever.

Then came the procession past the open casket, a glance at the undertaker's work. One woman screamed and wailed and fell to her knees sobbing and clutching at the coffin. She was helped away, and we all filed out of the church, and got in our vehicles, and drove a quarter mile to a small cemetery on the shores of the oxbow lake. They put Lucy in the ground next to Joseph Newton Sr., who had given his name to Martha's son and Joseph Brake. He had a fine engraved tombstone depicting him with a rifle and a hunting dog, going after a squirrel in a tree. As they were putting Lucy in the ground, it started to rain hard, and the wind came gusting off the lake, and the women fled for the vehicles before their hair and clothes were ruined.

You might take that funeral as evidence that black and white were coming together remarkably well in this little corner of Mississippi. Or you might look past that cemetery to the scruffy fishing trailers just up the road. "You don't go there if you're black, unless you've got a specific job of work to do," said Evander. "Those people are bad news."

Last time Helen went to the cemetery to visit Lucy and clean her grandson's grave, some people from those trailers drove up and started shooting birds out of the trees all around her. They told her she couldn't fish there by the cemetery anymore, where she had been fishing for years. They said that none of "her people" were allowed to fish there.

When it comes to racism in Mississippi, complexity and contradiction are the most solid, reliable things to hang on to. Southerners love black people more than Northerners do, said Barry Hannah, and hate them worse than anyone in the world. He was illustrating the difficulty of making generalizations. Having been run out of the cemetery in a rain of dead birds, for no reason except the color of her skin, Helen went to see the white landowner. He was just as nice as he could be, she said, and invited her to fish there whenever she wanted, and call him if she ran into any trouble.

Chapter 18

You Send Me

THEN T-MODEL FORD died. Somebody tracked down his date of birth in the county records, and it was confirmed that James Lewis Carter Ford had made it just past his ninety-second birthday, on a staple diet of fried chicken and Jack Daniel's. The cause of death was having lived a long, full life. I went up to Greenville for the viewing and the wake, which was another yard party with Lightnin Malcolm playing, and a lot of the same guests. The funeral was held the following afternoon. It wasn't as moving as Lucy Neal's funeral, because it took place in a big convention center that was barely half-full, and the great singing preacher Reverend John Wilkins, whose record T-Model had mistaken for his own, couldn't be there as promised to send him home.

The choir sang a light, clean, syrupy gospel music, and the pastor's eulogy got too weighed down with "amens" to achieve liftoff. "He has lived a life, amen. He was a great man, amen amen. A joking

man, amen. God bless him, amen. God is a good God, amen amen."
He noted that there weren't many blues singers in heaven, and he
knew that many people here today were concerned about T-Model
Ford's immortal soul. But he was able to remove all doubts, because
he had been there with two witnesses at T-Model's bedside when the
bluesman accepted Jesus Christ as his savior. "So I'm happy standing
here today, amen," he said. "Because I know he made it home."

T-Model was almost unrecognizable in the coffin, like a shrunken
waxwork of his younger self. His jowls were gone, his eyebrows had
been dyed black and trimmed. His skin looked thirty years younger.
He was wearing a soft black corduroy hat with a small bottle of Jack
Daniel's discreetly tucked under a fold of white sheet. Stella, as she
was almost required to do, hurled herself at the coffin, collapsing,
clutching, wailing, and then we all drove out to the burying ground.

It wasn't until they lowered him down that it really hit me, that
hollowed-out aching somber feeling, and it was for T-Model, and
Lucy Neal, and James Jefferson, and friends of my own age who had
died long before their time.

MARIAH AND I had been in the Delta for nearly a year, and we still
didn't feel like we understood the place well. It spread out so wide and
sank down so deep through the tangled generations and fossilized
family trees. It was a feudal relic. It was a showcase for modern industrial agriculture. It was a foretaste of a dystopian social future, when
machines free capital from the burden of labor. Sometimes it made us
want to weep and scream, and return to the familiar. Sometimes we
felt ruined—*rurnt*, as they say—for anywhere else.

We were never bored here, and our minds had broadened. We
looked back at our former selves as narrow, picky, and judgmen-
tal. The shared adventure of tackling a new life in a new place had

deepened our relationship. Food had always been a vital pleasure and a staple conversation, and now that we were eating closer to the land, we felt closer to each other.

In addition to the deer meat, there were ducks, geese, rabbits, and pieces of wild hog in our freezer now. We'd developed a taste for the bullfrogs you could grab out of the swamp at night or spear with a trident-like gig. And with one of us taking over when the other lost heart, and vice versa, we had managed to fight off the bugs, weeds, birds, deer, armadillos, fungi, and diseases and raise a thriving summer vegetable garden.

To eat a roasted pepper salad, with yellow and red peppers, tomatoes, cucumbers, and basil all picked from the garden, and mixed with olives, capers, sea salt, and olive oil, tasted like victory after a long gardening ordeal. We had eggplants for ratatouille, and beautiful glossy zucchini—until the squash bugs murdered them. All summer long, we had a steady supply of spicy shishito peppers, which we flash fried with salt and pepper, and snacked on with cold beer.

It was our first experience growing okra, and we had raised six plants from seed. They were dauntingly prolific, especially after Monk whacked them with a stick to increase productivity. Mariah made jar after jar of pickled okra. I ate okra for lunch almost every day and cooked it according to Lucy Neal's simple, perfect recipe. You picked the okra small, which meant you picked okra every morning, because the pods could double or triple in size overnight. You fried them in a little olive oil with salt and pepper, added a splash of water, and put a lid on the pan. When they started to get tender, you gave them a good squirt of lemon juice, which dissolved the sliminess.

We gorged ourselves on ripe figs, and sometimes ate them with yogurt, mint, and honey, or roasted them in the oven with a dollop of goat cheese. Mariah made spicy chutney from the pears, pickled the jalapeños *escabeche*-style with carrots and onions, and canned enough tomatoes to keep us in red sauce all winter. The muscadine grapes were another problem of overabundance. Southerners made muscadine jelly out of them, but we didn't like it that much. I ate them straight off the vines, not minding the thick bitter skins and fat seed clumps, but we had hundreds of them all ripening at the same time. Helen's brother Jerry came up with an excellent solution and turned them into muscadine wine, which I found pleasant, earthy, and heady, and Mariah thought was too rough.

Visiting urbanites often asked why we didn't have chickens, and I would list off the reasons: egg-stealing skunks, chicken snakes, raccoons, bobcats, foxes, weasels, quite busy enough with chores already, don't want to build a Fort Knox chicken house, and who looks after them if we want to make a run down to New Orleans or up to Memphis? My wanderlust was reduced, but I still needed regular road trips to keep from going stir-crazy.

In cities, we harvested French and Spanish wine, good olive oil, real Parmesan cheese, prosciutto, and whatever else we'd been missing. We got excellent coffee via Turnrow Books, who ordered it from a roaster in New Albany, Mississippi, and we kept ourselves supplied with lemons, black beans, pinto beans, bacon, rice, pasta, and other staples from the Delta supermarkets and Walmart. Our little fantasy of self-sufficiency in the backwoods was exactly that, but still, most of our meals contained something we'd grown or shot. One of my curses in life is an allergy to fish (it makes me nauseous), and here, with catfish and bream in the pond by the front porch, and a lake and a river teeming with fish, it was particularly irksome. I tried to get Mariah interested in fishing, but she didn't have the time.

She was finishing up her degree and had already found herself a job. After graduating, she would be the new librarian and archivist at Mississippi Valley State University in Itta Bena, a historically black university with a dismally low graduation rate and a reputation for chronic dysfunction. Most of its students were coming out of the Delta public schools, and she was warned at the interview that many of them had trouble with basic reading and comprehension.

She was going to be the only white woman in a library staffed almost entirely by African-American women, at a university with an overwhelmingly black student body and staff. Some of our Delta friends thought she might be in for a rough ride, but she was looking forward to it. It was a good new library, she was eager to start organizing the archive, and she thought the experience couldn't fail to be interesting. By national standards, the pay was on the low side. By Delta standards, it was fairly good, and it put us on a firmer footing at the house, especially if you exercised plenty of denial about all the student loans she had to pay back.

We had stopped correcting people when they referred to us as husband and wife. It was so much easier that way. We even started referring to "my husband" and "my wife" when making arrangements with handymen, exterminators, and the vet. At first it choked in my throat, but in time I got used to it.

I was driving back from Oxford, having addressed a class of Bill Luckett's law students, when the voice of my dead Irish screenwriter friend started whispering in my head, "Go on man. Do it." He'd got married on his deathbed, and I'd missed the wedding and funeral both. Before he died, he'd been after me to marry Mariah, and now, from beyond the grave, he came after me again. I could hear his voice so clearly, because I knew it so well, and because I'd absorbed his way of thinking and seeing things into my own.

Nothing would make Mariah happier, it would be a grand excuse for another big party, and it might even improve our life together. I came down out of the hills on to the broad alluvial plain that was starting to feel more like home and less like a foreign planet. I would drive her out to a high bluff behind Tchula that Cadi Thompson had shown me, and propose on one knee with the sun setting over the Delta.

When I got home, I couldn't contain myself. I asked her to marry me while holding on to her in the doorway of the bedroom. "I'd given up hoping," she said through her tears.

WHAT I HAD in mind for the wedding was something like the spring party, with a brief, fun marriage ceremony as the centerpiece. To make it work, we would need the right mix of people, a great live band, and Tom Vaught as the best man. Most weddings were too stilted, scripted, formal, boring and predictable. I wanted minimal expenditure, minimal fuss, maximum spontaneity and fun. With the right people, and the right band, we could make it work with a keg of beer in the Pluto tractor shed, if we had to, and spend the money we'd save on a honeymoon in New Orleans.

Cathy Thompson was ecstatic that we were getting married, and she saw it as a kind of training event for the three big Delta weddings she intended to throw for her daughters. She had been planning and budgeting for these weddings since her daughters were born. Even by Southern standards, Delta weddings were famously lavish and overblown, and the main way in which the landowning families measured each other's social status.

"You're going to spend a minimum of fifty thousand dollars, and that is absolute bare bones, if you know a florist, and someone like Martha to bake the cake, and someone else to give you a deal on the catering," Cathy told me. "It's not just the wedding. You're going to have nine months of parties leading up to the wedding, and every one of them needs to have food, printed invitations, and an open bar. I'm talking about announcement parties, multiple bridal showers, pottery showers, engagement parties."

A proper Delta wedding also required a themed bachelorette trip to New Orleans or the beach, with matching outfits, transportation and accommodation. It required a stock-the-bar party, where everyone brought more alcohol than they could drink, and the surplus went to the all-important open bar at the wedding.

Cadi Thompson was one of fifteen bridesmaids in a Delta wedding that was now up to thirteen bridal showers, each of them extravagantly catered, laden with party favors and swag, and thoroughly sodden with booze. The bride's family had bought all the bridesmaids matching dresses, shoes, and jewelry for the ceremony. The Thompson fridge was perennially covered in save-the-day magnets, featuring photographs of young Delta squires with flicked bowl haircuts and their brides-to-be. Wedding fridge magnets were a fairly recent development, so no one could use the excuse of forgetting, and of course there were wedding websites and hashtags too.

When you asked Louie Thompson about his daughters' weddings, his head would hang down slightly and he would hold up three fingers like a man destined for the gallows. Three weddings meant $150,000, at what Cathy called the bare-bones minimum. I asked her how it had got so out of hand. Were people trying to outdo each other?

"Not really," she said. "It's just the bar has been set so high, and we're all trying to reach it."

"How did the bar get so high?"

"Nobody knows. It's just the way it is. If your daughter needs to spend ten grand to get the right dress, or ten grand getting her mother's dress remade, because that means more to her than buying a new dress for half the money, then that's what she needs to do. To get a really great band will cost another ten grand. Then you're looking at the flowers, the décor, the lighting, the catering, the outfits for the bridesmaids and groomsmen, transportation and accommodation depending where you have the wedding, and open bar for three hundred people. You wouldn't believe how much booze three hundred people can get through at a Delta wedding."

One way to save money was to throw the reception at your house, rather than hire out a country club, and Cathy envisioned her daughters' wedding receptions on the grounds of their house in Pluto. Behind the house was a beautiful setting, with majestic trees and a gentle slope leading down to the cypress-studded lake. So she offered to stage our wedding reception there as a kind of trial run, to see how the logistics would work.

Mariah was being pulled in two opposite directions. She had to explain to Cathy that we would be paying for our own wedding on a very limited budget. Our families might help out a little, but they didn't place the same social importance on weddings. Mariah's parents had got married in the desert wearing sandals and hiking boots.

While scaling back Cathy's hopes for a big Delta wedding on Pluto, Mariah was also battling me to get what she wanted in terms of invitations, flowers, food, tablecloths, napkins, stemware. It didn't make any sense to me to spend three hundred dollars on pretty little paper invitations with stamped RSVP envelopes when you could do it for free by email. So we had a fight about that, and just about everything else. When she started buying bridal magazines, I wanted to call the whole thing off, and we nearly did.

I couldn't believe she wanted to squander so much of our meager financial resources on such silly shit. She couldn't believe I was being such an asshole about the whole thing, when she was scrimping, scavenging, spending the absolute minimum that could be spent on things that any normal woman would want at her wedding. In the end it was Louie Thompson who took me aside and explained that the only thing to do here was abandon any illusion of control and let the womenfolk take over. Cathy had him stringing up lights all over the backyard, fetching tents and tables, and he was doing it all with a calm good grace that I tried and failed to mimic.

The only thing that Mariah trusted me with was the music. Martha's cousin Daniel was in a great Brooklyn-based band called the Gold Magnolias. They were scheduled to play Pigfest in Tallulah, Louisiana, on the Saturday we had picked out for our wedding day. So we shunted the wedding to Sunday, and I got the band that I wanted. Then, like so many bridegrooms before me, I spent weeks yearning for the day when it would all be over and we could talk about something else.

WHEN THE GUESTS started arriving, and the house filled up with people, all of them excited to be here, excited about the wedding and eager to help, I started getting excited too. Some early drama was supplied by an actor-stuntman friend from Tucson. He was bitten on the boot as he jumped away from a cottonmouth. The next day he sprained his ankle in an armadillo hole. Both these incidents happened on the front lawn, where the wedding guests would be lining up as we got married on the front porch.

My friend Raj Modak, an Indian-American doctor living in Tucson, had sworn as a young man never to set foot in the state of Mississippi, because he was so horrified by the racism and violence in its history. He was willing to forgo that vow to be at our wedding, but he was concerned about being brown in Mississippi with his white girlfriend Wendy. I told him I didn't think it would be a problem, and definitely not on Pluto. Our house was full, so we put them up with Martha's aunt Mary, who laid on the full Southern charm and hospitality, just like everyone else they encountered in Mississippi. Raj said later said that as a mixed-race couple, they didn't catch a single sidelong glance. "That's good to hear," I said. "But don't leave here thinking racism is over in Mississippi."

Tom Vaught arranged the bachelor party with John Newcomb. Two Cadillac Escalades arrived at the house at sunset, with Albert Johnson driving one, and another of John's farmworkers driving the other. I rode with Tom and John, and as we pulled away from Pluto, I asked Albert why he married his wife. "Something about her wouldn't let me let her go," he said. "She got down on her knee. She proposed to me."

Albert was always coming out with sentences that sounded like song lyrics, and Tom pounced straight on that one and started singing it in his big gruff voice,

> *"Something about her*
> *Wouldn't let me let her go*
> *She got down on her knee*
> *She proposed to me*
> *Something about her*
> *Wouldn't let me let her go."*

We stopped off in Yazoo City for steaks and gargantuan whiskey drinks, and convoyed on to the Blue Front Café in Bentonia to hear Jimmy "Duck" Holmes perform in his own juke joint. It was a shabby little place with a weathered concrete floor, barstools hammered together from raw lumber and painted blue, graffiti on the walls, and a few beaten-up chairs and tables. Tom got behind the bar and sold the beer while Duck played the spine-tingling Bentonia blues.

The Reverend Timmy James asked him a question about his finger technique, and that turned into a guitar lesson, and then Duck handed him a guitar and told him to play along—a big thrill for blues fanatic Tim. Then Duck found a third guitar, and Albert joined in too. That was my bachelor night, with the freight trains rumbling past, the lonesome whistle blowing, the moon and the stars visible through the open door.

ON THE DAY of the wedding, the forecast said it was going to rain, but Cathy refused to believe it, on the grounds that it was going to look too beautiful for the rain to ruin it. Mariah thought it might rain, but she was too busy getting ready to worry about it, so the bridesmaids and other volunteers busied themselves ironing tablecloths, driving up to Greenwood to rent more aesthetically pleasing chairs than the ones Louie had borrowed, making the flower arrangements and place settings, all of it under the open sky. Once again, Louie had to take me aside and tell me not to question any of this. If it rained, we'd just move people inside and make the best of it.

Tom was always good for morale. When he saw me getting tense, he gave me a brief, well-aimed pep talk, and he picked just the right moment to shake up a brace of martinis, which was right after we'd gotten into our suits and ties, and fastened on the cotton boll boutonnieres that the bridesmaids had woven for us. When the guests started arriving, I was feeling nicely lifted and expansive.

It was Bill and Francine Luckett's first visit to the house, and they couldn't get over how remote and isolated it was. Neither could Bill's first cousin Semmes, who I knew from Oxford. He was a tall, aristocratic figure with horn-rimmed glasses and a crinkle in his combed-back white hair. He had sisters named Lucretia and Money. His father, Semmes Luckett Sr., was a staunch segregationist who led the legal battle against integrating the schools in Clarksdale and a cultured Southern gentleman who invited the opposing Yankee lawyers over to his house for cocktails in the evening. Semmes Jr. had the same courtly manners and bearing, but very different habits of mind. He had spent most of the 1970s in Aspen, Colorado, where he became Hunter S. Thompson's great friend and private secretary.

"Good Lawd, I was raised in the Delta, but I've never been anywhere close to here," he drawled, as he came up the back porch steps. "I feel like I've come upriver looking for Colonel Kurtz. I nearly didn't make it. I've been suffering most horribly from the after-effects of an ill-considered chicken enchilada. The body was unwilling, but the spirit was strong, so here I am, and I've brought you a token."

He handed me a wedding present, wrapped in tissue paper, and stuck together with a Band-Aid. I introduced him to Sam Olden, and they did what Mississippians always do when they don't know each other. They went back through each other's family trees. "Okay, I've got you now," said Sam, and then rattled off some Lucketts who had lived in Yazoo City a long time ago.

The Gold Magnolias arrived, fresh from Pigfest, and I introduced Semmes to Martha's cousin Daniel. It took Semmes a moment to piece together Daniel's lineage. "Foose, Foose, Foose . . ." he said, and then, "Hah-*hah!* I know your daddy. We found some pre–Civil War opium in a mansion down in Natchez one time. We snorted it up and your daddy spoke in rhyme for three days straight." In Semmes's accent, snorted was *snoahted*.

The aisle was the paved walkway bisecting the front lawn. We assembled some guests along it and trusted that the noise and hubbub would keep the snakes away, and the ominous-looking sky would hold back the rain, at least for a little while. The Gold Magnolias set up with acoustic instruments just below the porch, and we got the call that Mariah was on the way in a white Dodge Charger.

When she stepped out on her brother's arm in all her veiled white loveliness, Savanna trotted over to greet her. The Gold Magnolias started playing Sam Cooke's "You Send Me," with interlocking vocal harmonies, and Mariah came up the aisle with her brother on one side and Savanna on the other. She got about halfway when the rain came pouring down. She laughed and told everyone to get up on the porch.

The Reverend Timmy James was wearing a string tie and a double-breasted black suit that a New York tailor had copied from a photograph of Elvis in 1968. With everyone on the porch sheltering from the rain, there was barely enough room on the porch for him to marry us. He began the ceremony by saying he was "curiously empowered" to perform weddings. He derived this power from the Church of Spiritual Humanism, an Internet ministry that ordains anyone for a small fee and keeps an open mind about the existence of God. Nonetheless, its ministers have the power to perform legally binding marriages, and Reverend Timmy had performed several over the years.

We had all agreed that the ceremony would be brief. Our unconventional minister pointed out that we had a catfish farmer, a stunt man, and an ornithologist present, and surely this was a good omen for a Delta wedding. Then it was time for the vows, the rings, the ecstatic hug and kiss.

The rain stopped during the ceremony and now returned as a heavy slanting deluge. It drowned the flaming lanterns lining Louie and Cathy's driveway and swamped the tablecloths and table decorations. It nearly ruined the magnificent three-tiered lemon cake that Martha had made and decorated with edible magnolia blossoms that looked like they'd just been plucked off a tree. The cake was outside in a little gazebo with a chandelier, and people were rescuing it when we arrived at the reception.

The rain washed away the formality, dissolved inhibitions, encouraged improvisation and spontaneity. There were tents over the food, the bar, and the dancing area, and people huddled in closer than they would have done. The Gold Magnolias squeezed themselves into the sheltered back porch, nearly got electrocuted early on, and then let it rip. They call it "southern soul." Borrowed from funk, R&B, country, blues, and swamp rock, it's good-time party music to make you dance and shout. They're superb musicians—Daniel has another career as a virtuoso jazz bassist—but when they get together as the Goldmags the point is to generate as much rhythm and feeling as possible. They threw in a few covers with their own material, including an epic dirty-funked-out version of "Born on the Bayou" which sounded just right in the Delta rain and mud.

Both Mariah's bridesmaids are semiprofessional belly dancers, so when the band took a break, they got into their costumes and broke new cultural ground. "First-ever belly-dancing bridesmaids at a Delta wedding," as Martha observed. There was a lot of love and joy in the air, people coming together from Britain, New Zealand, South Africa, Arizona, New York, Mississippi, Louisiana.

During the band's second set, Bobby T quit dancing in his wheel-chair, took the old stained Confederate battle hat off his head, and put it on Monk's head. There were a few different ways that gesture could be interpreted, but Monk, who has known Bobby T all his life, took it as a warm gesture of inclusion, and put his black cowboy hat on Bobby T's head. Then Bobby T put his hat on my head for what I assumed was a similar reason: you're here now, and one of us.

When Monk asked my permission to dance with the bride, and double-checked, I wondered if he was feeling slightly cautious about the old taboo. There were still places in Mississippi where a black man might get himself into trouble for taking a white woman in his arms and dancing with her. He checked with Mariah too: "It's cool?" She didn't bother with a response, just grabbed him and started danc-ing. He was dressed in black with his black cowboy hat, and she was in her white wedding dress. The band just happened to be playing an X-rated country singalong number, and it was a memorable moment.

As Mariah put it afterward, "It's not every bride that gets to dance with Monk to 'Bear Trap Poon.'"

It was the wedding I had hoped for, in other words, and I like to think that all its memories are stored up in the stains and spatters and map-like patterns left by the Pluto mud on Mariah's wedding dress. There's only one thing I regret missing. Albert Johnson decided to assemble his gospel group without telling us and give us a heavenly serenade at the house the next morning. By the time they got here, we were already on the road to New Orleans.

Acknowledgments

IN CLOSING, A Delta-sized thank you to everyone on Pluto, Gum Grove, and Stonewall who welcomed us into their midst. I'm extremely grateful to all the people I've written about in the book, and hope that I've portrayed them accurately and fairly. I'd also like to thank Hank Burdine for showing me how to hunt ducks and stab hogs, for sharing his library, his whiskey, and his irrepressible love of life. Scott Barretta was generous with his encyclopedic knowledge of the blues and Delta history. Many other people contributed valuable insights and fine company, including Jane Rule Burdine, Yolande van Heerden, Sid "Bo Weevil" Law III, gator-hunting Guy Ray, Lisa Barker, the Kornegays, the Howorths, Jacob Carroll, Sarah Blackburn, Doug and Lyn Roberts, and Sonny and Jamie Peaster.

Index

About the Author

RICHARD GRANT is an author, journalist, and television host. He comes from a good English family and now lives in the backwoods of Mississippi. He has traveled extensively in Africa and Latin America, and made the first disastrous attempt at rafting the unexplored Malagarasi River in Tanzania. That journey is described in his book *Crazy River*, which won the Best Adventure Travel Book award at the Banff Mountain Festival in 2012. His best-known book is the adventure classic *God's Middle Finger*, about his travels in the lawless Sierra Madre mountains in Mexico. His first book, *American Nomads*, was about the lure of the open road and was made into a BBC documentary of the same name.